Concepts and Reality in the History of Philosophy

There are unacceptable metaphysical presuppositions at the heart of the epistemology of Locke, Berkeley, Nietzsche, and Kant. This controversial claim is laid out and explained in this book.

Transcending the division between 'continental' and 'analytical' philosophy, Fiona Ellis shows how Hegel offers a way out of this philosophical error. This rethinking of the history of modern philosophy is a breath of fresh air for the discipline.

An original and impressive volume, this is a book which will interest all scholars of the history of philosophy.

Fiona Ellis is a lecturer in Philosophy at Wadham College, Oxford University, UK.

Concepts and Reality in the History of Philosophy

Tracing a philosophical error from Locke to Bradley

Fiona Ellis

Routledge
Taylor & Francis Group

LONDON AND NEW YORK

First published 2005
by Routledge
2 Park Square, Milton Park,
Abingdon, Oxon OX14 4RN

Simultaneously published in the USA and Canada
by Routledge
270 Madison Ave, New York, NY 10016

Routledge is an imprint of the Taylor & Francis Group

© 2005 Fiona Ellis

Typeset in Times by GreenGate Publishing Services, Tonbridge, Kent
Printed and bound in Great Britain by MPG Books Ltd, Bodmin

British Library Cataloguing in Publication Data
A catalogue record for this book is available from the British Library

Library of Congress Cataloging in Publication Data
A catalog record for this book has been requested

ISBN 0-415-33478-0

To my parents and the memory of my late uncle,
Leslie Nicholson

Contents

Acknowledgements   viii

Introduction   1

1 A philosophical syndrome   9

2 Concepts and reality: Nietzsche   34

3 Concepts and reality: Kant   53

4 Concepts and reality: Hegel   77

5 Truth   102

6 Philosophy and dialectic   125

Conclusion   145

Notes   153
Bibliography   165
Index   169

Acknowledgements

There are many people I have to thank whose support, interest, and criticism helped me to write this book. The philosophers to whom I am most grateful, and whose influence is evident on every page, are Roger Scruton, Paul Snowdon, and David Wiggins. Their intellectual honesty, open-mindedness, and willingness to engage in serious metaphysics have been a source of inspiration to me for many years, and I can only begin to aspire to their greatness as thinkers and teachers. I have been helped enormously by friends and colleagues who have commented upon drafts of chapters and discussed the issues at hand. I am grateful in particular to Michael Ayers, Harvey Brown, Quassim Cassam, Gerry Hughes, Brian O'Shaughnessy, Julia Simon, Galen Strawson, Zita Zigan, and the two anonymous referees for Routledge. I am indebted also to The Queen's College, Oxford who provided me with a perfect environment in which to work on my book, and whose generous support gave me sufficient time to arrive at a penultimate draft.

My non-philosopher friends have played an equally important role in bringing this book to completion. Special thanks go to Sally Adams, May Allen, Mansour Badawi, Cathy Ellis, Rosemary Franklin-George, Christine Garbutt, Gohar Goddard, Jules Goddard, Harold McMullen, and Tania Tuft. Finally, I thank the Kenwood Ladies' Pond, Highgate, for providing me with enough icy water to renew my inspiration and to fend off momentary lapses of reason.

Some of the material of Chapter 6 appeared in the journal article 'On the Dismounting of Seesaws', *Philosophy*, volume 76, issue 1, January 2001, pp. 31–54. I am grateful to the editor for permission to make use of this material.

Introduction

There are two themes in this essay. The first is the epistemological theme of how we are to understand the relation in which we stand to things, and the implications that this understanding has for an account of the relation between concepts and reality. The second is the meta-philosophical theme of how we are to respond to a pattern of argument – henceforth referred to as 'the syndrome' – which has occurred repeatedly in the history of philosophy to confound the issues to which it has been applied. The syndrome has found expression in a range of positions which exceed my present concerns, and I will be drawing some more general conclusions about its nature and scope in the final chapter and the conclusion. For the most part, however, my focus will be its expression in accounts of the relation between concepts and reality.

The syndrome involves the separation of two concepts that belong together, the result being that one of them dwindles into empty indeterminacy, while the other is left to float adrift, cut loose from its moorings in the first. Applied to the problem of how we are to comprehend the relation between concepts and reality it assumes a variety of forms, all of which are shaped by its defining framework. According to this framework, things in themselves are to be dualistically opposed to the realm revealed in our concepts, the conceptual realm comprising the things which are available to experience – the things we see and feel, as Berkeley puts it. The point of referring to this distinction as dualistic is to capture the sense in which its terms resist intelligible connection. Thus, the idea is that there is no intelligible way of relating the things we conceptualize to things in themselves. Locke and Berkeley provide the initial illustration of the syndrome – significantly so, given that their arguments about substance are decisive in shaping the positions I go on to consider in subsequent chapters. Hume would have served equally well for my purposes, however, and I exclude him simply because his predecessors provide ample material by means of which to construct the required picture.

Both Locke and Berkeley are concerned with the problem of knowledge and, in particular, the capacity we have to acquire it. It is this concern which generates Locke's interest in the concept of substance, his aim being to give an account of how we perceive and think about a material world. He accepts with Berkeley that knowledge presupposes ideas, ideas being the immediate objects of perception. Hence, his interest in the problem of empirical knowledge is converted into the question of how we are to conceive of the relation between ideas and substance, or, more exactly, the immediate objects of perception and substance. Locke's thoughts about this distinction are not entirely consistent. However, much of his argument suggests that the things we perceive are really just groupings of sensible qualities which stand opposed to substances or things in themselves, these latter being inaccessible to us. The further implication is that these groupings are constructed by us, not with respect to the qualities they involve, but rather with respect to the way these qualities are grouped together. The position then is that substance is to be set apart from the things we perceive – the things we perceive being collections of sensible qualities, and it is an error to suppose that these qualities are substance-involving. I shall argue that this position is indicative of the syndrome.

There is, however, an alternative way of thinking to be found in Locke – one which evades the syndrome. According to this alternative, substance and quality cannot be prized apart in the manner that the first model demands. Rather, the claim is that the things we perceive already presuppose the substance from which they are set apart were the syndrome to be applicable. And precisely because it is denied that substance itself lies in some inaccessible realm, there is no longer any need to suppose that the things we perceive *qua* things are constructions of consciousness. On the contrary, the claim is that the things we perceive – qualitied things – are independent of mind.

How are we to explain the existence of these two conflicting frameworks in Locke's scheme of things? Put simply, the answer is that his acceptance of the first stems from a variety of metaphysical and grammatical muddles surrounding the concept of substance, and his concession to the second comes with an acknowledgement of the difficulties which arise when substance and quality are dualistically opposed in this manner. I shall argue that, notwithstanding Locke's awareness of these difficulties and his recognition of the framework which would put them to rest, his continued if not reluctant commitment to the first way of thinking prevents him from completing this diagnostic task.

There are commentators who will take issue with my interpretation, doing so on the ground that it is the second way of thinking which predominates in Locke's arguments. The evidence I cite should go some way towards quelling the force of this objection – evidence which suggests that there is at least a serious tension in his position. Furthermore, it is the first more problematic framework which is assumed and appropriated by Berkeley. Berkeley is anxious to avoid the scepticism he takes to be an inevitable by-product of the Lockean standpoint – a scepticism, which, he believes, forces us to conclude that our relation to things is indirect. He sums up this sceptical position as the view that things are distinct from ideas, things in this context being material substances and ideas being the things we perceive. The alternative he proposes to this brand of realism is idealism: an alternative which promises to guarantee that our relation to things is direct, which it achieves by forsaking any reference to the notion of material substance. We shall see, however, that Berkeley's use of the notion of *immaterial* substance brings with it a version of the sceptical framework he is so anxious to avoid. It follows therefore that his idealist 'solution' is equally problematic with respect to the question of whether we can be said to stand in a direct relation to things, and that it is afflicted likewise by the syndrome.

It is an important theme of my essay that the relation between idealism and realism is not as straightforward as some would have us believe. In particular, it is quite wrong to suppose that these positions must invariably be opposed. My reason for saying so is that idealism, as understood by the figures with which I shall be concerned, is intended to be equivalent to realism. However, the realism in question is to be distinguished from the brand of realism which affirms that things in themselves are inaccessible to us – a doctrine which can be read most obviously into Locke's scheme of things, but which also has its analogue in Berkeley.

In Chapter 2 I introduce a distinctly Kantian way of comprehending the relation between things in themselves and the things we perceive. On one interpretation of this position – the Nietzschean interpretation which is going to be my focus here – things in themselves are to be set apart from the realm revealed in our concepts, while concepts are viewed as instruments which structure the experiential data we receive from without, doing so in a manner which corresponds in no way to things in themselves. Once again, we have a restatement of the empiricist view that things in themselves are to be set apart from the realm of ideas, and that the things we perceive *qua* things are constructions of consciousness.

My discussion centres on Nietzsche's early position as it appears in his essay 'On Truth and Lies in a Nonmoral Sense'. Some will object that I am making a straw man of Nietzsche by focusing upon a text which arguably stands opposed to his later and more considered philosophical views. Furthermore, one could substantiate this accusation by pointing to the 'History of an Error' as adumbrated by Nietzsche in *Twilight of the Idols* – a 'history' which is concerned with the error of dividing our one world into two, the 'apparent world' and the 'real world', and, as such, seems indicative of just the syndrome I am concerned to criticize here. Conceding this point, so the objection goes, I should surely be giving due weight to Nietzsche's own diagnosis and treatment of the syndrome, if, indeed, it is really so different from my own approach.

I agree that the error referred to in Nietzsche's 'History of an Error' is the error to which I have referred as the syndrome, albeit one which finds expression in a different philosophical context. I agree also that his treatment of this error has something in common with my own – at least, it does so on the assumption that he is seeking to dispense with a dualistic framework so as to allow that the world to which we have access – the only world there is – involves a realm of mind-independent things. Certainly, Nietzsche's description of the sixth and final stage of the history lends itself to an interpretation of this kind. For he claims that:

> The true world we have abolished. What world remains? The apparent world perhaps? But no! *With the true world we have also abolished the apparent one!*[1]

However, this passage raises a difficulty. The difficulty is that although it makes sense to suppose that Nietzsche is making the rather obvious logical point that the empirical world can no longer be considered illusory once we have abandoned the idea that 'true being' belongs to a second inaccessible world, there is another interpretation which is easier to reconcile with what he says elsewhere and which better explains the prophetical language which accompanies his announcement here. According to this second interpretation, Nietzsche is telling us not merely that we must now be content to exist in the only world there is, but that this one remaining world is lost to us too – that it has been 'abolished' with the true world.[2]

I am not going to tackle this interpretative issue, and I mention it here simply to make a case for allowing that we cannot assume what is perhaps the most obvious reading of Nietzsche's remarks, and that if we do not make this assumption, there is a real question to be asked about whether Nietzsche succeeds in replacing the dualistic framework it is his purpose to disarm. Second, however, even if we allow that he has defined the form of a solution in stage six of his history, there still remains the question of whether he himself succeeded in taking on board this alternative. It is my belief that he does not succeed, and that the explicit and enduring love he has for incoherence-generating separations is testimony to his inability – or perhaps refusal – to reject the way of thinking which dominates his early work.[3]

In one sense, the question of whether or not Nietzsche succeeds in relinquishing his early way of thinking is unimportant. For regardless of where he stands, the conclusions he reaches at this early stage have been accepted by many figures whose work has had a profound influence in the current intellectual climate. In particular, it has become something of a commonplace in some circles to suppose that truth is an outmoded concept, that it makes little sense to suppose that there exist genuine things, and that interpreting the world is really just like interpreting a text. I shall argue that these claims are indicative of the syndrome and that they do not stand up to philosophical scrutiny. The implications of this conclusion for an assessment of Nietzsche's iconoclastic aspirations – and those of his more contemporary disciples – should be obvious.

Nietzsche, I shall claim, is stuck in the mire bequeathed to him by Locke, Berkeley, and Kant, and it will take Hegel to anticipate several of his problems and provide solutions to them that Nietzsche missed. It may strike some readers as odd that Nietzsche makes his appearance before Kant and Hegel in the sequence developed here. Perhaps the best response to such a worry is to point out that philosophy has no need to be chronological. However, in the present context there are additional reasons for respecting this order. First, the syndrome as it is exhibited in Nietzsche's argument is both focused and lucid whilst being structurally equivalent to its expression in Locke and Berkeley. Thus, the use of his essay offers me an easy stepping stone to the concerns of subsequent chapters. Second – and this provides a further sense in which Nietzsche's arguments serve as a stepping stone – these subsequent chapters involve a complex and detailed discussion of the ingredients of Kant's philosophy, ingredients to which we are introduced in accessible if not oversimplified terms in Nietzsche's arguments. Third, I find it both appropriate and amusing that Nietzsche should be rescued by a figure who not only precedes him in time, but whom he treats as the catastrophic spider par excellence – the figure whose philosophical web-making is thought to stand in the way of genuine philosophical progress.

Having provided a description of the syndrome as it is to be found in a distinctly Kantian context, I turn in Chapter 3 to the question of whether Kant himself can be criticized along similar lines. It would be misleading to suppose that the problem of external world scepticism is the only or even the principal concern of the first *Critique*. Kant's professed focus is the problem of the possibility of a priori knowledge of objects, and, to the extent that he is concerned with empirical knowledge, this interest is subservient to that of providing an account of the possibility of *synthetic* a priori knowledge. We shall see, however, that the position he endorses has crucial implications for an assessment of scepticism with regard to the external world. Thus, although we can agree that Kant's concerns outstrip those of his empiricist predecessors, the position he defends provides a continuation of the theme which had been set in motion by Locke.

My question will be whether Kant's contribution to this debate constitutes a significant shift with respect to the framework assumed by his predecessors and Nietzsche. Much of the contemporary literature suggests that the answer to this question is at least unclear, there being several commentators who would deny that the relevant dualistic way of thinking can be ascribed to Kant's position in the first *Critique*.[4] I shall argue that there is indeed evidence for this more favourable interpretation, but that there are further elements of his position that are more difficult to accommodate in this sympathetic way – elements which are indicative of the syndrome. My conclusion then will be that Kant has not succeeded in providing a satisfactory form of idealism with respect to the problem of external world scepticism, and that, in this respect at least, his position does not provide a significant advance upon that of Berkeley.

I introduce Hegel's approach in Chapter 4, concentrating upon those aspects of his position which are of relevance to my own epistemological concerns.[5] My aim here is to provide a model for diagnosing and treating the syndrome as it applies to the problems at hand. One might object that the process of extracting an aspect of Hegel's thinking from his overall system is bound to involve a distortion of his views, on the ground that the parts can be understood only by taking account of his more general philosophical outlook.[6] The further related difficulty, so the objection goes, is that this outlook is indefensible. Now as I see it, Hegel's outlook – and the absolute knowledge to which he aspires – is best understood in methodological terms. That is to say, it is to be found in the particular approach he adopts towards philosophical problems – an approach which, at the most general level, could be said to involve a repairing of the conceptual separations which render these problems insoluble. Understood in this sober light, it is an outlook which sidesteps Schopenhauer's rather spiteful complaint that it involves the 'serving up of sheer nonsense', the 'scrabbling together senseless and maddening webs of words' and is a 'lasting monument of German stupidity'.[7]

There will be those who remain sceptical about my appropriation of Hegel, doing so on the ground that his methodological stance cannot be accommodated in the terms I have suggested, or, alternatively, that his conception of the concept/reality relation is at odds with the realist interpretation I shall be assuming on his behalf. My conclusions should serve to deflate the force of these objections. However, to those who remain doubtful, I can only respond that it would not be fatal to my enterprise if I were to describe my interpretation of Hegel as belonging simply to the *spirit* of his intent.

My discussion of Hegel falls into two parts. To begin with, I examine his *Encyclopaedia Logic, Faith and Knowledge,* and *Lectures on the History of Philosophy.* Hegel's arguments in these works have a scope which exceeds the limits of my enquiry – a scope which incorporates the work of German Idealist figures such as Jacobi and Schleiermacher. My more narrow focus will be a consideration of the relevance they have to an assessment of Kant's epistemological position. As we shall see, Hegel believes that Kant is indeed committed to a dualistic conception of the relation between things in themselves and the things we conceptualize – that, to put it in my terms, he is in the grip of the syndrome.

The second part of the chapter provides a more thoroughgoing vindication of Hegel's positive position, and it involves a study of the opening three chapters of the *Phenomenology of Spirit.* These chapters have significance for my enquiry at several levels. First, they are focused exclusively upon the problem of how we are to view the relation between concepts and reality. Second, they offer a clear and concise account of the structure of Hegel's approach to this problem. Third, the negative and positive aspects of his approach can be mapped quite straightforwardly onto analogous aspects as they occur in my discussion of Locke, Berkeley, Nietzsche, and Kant. Finally, the position I reach on Hegel's behalf will allow me to touch upon the question of how, if at all, the concept of God can be said to be of relevance to an understanding of the concept/reality relation. This further question would seem to be at best tangential and at worst entirely irrelevant to such a problem. Given the centrality it assumes in Berkeley, and to a lesser but equally significant extent in Kant, it is important that we clarify the nature of this putative connection. The form of the solution I propose – again Hegelian in origin – promises to avoid a conflation of these two problems, whilst leaving open the possibility that the syndrome may well be operative in this theological context too.

By the end of Chapter 4 I shall be suggesting that we have the makings of a form of idealism which promises to allow that we are capable of exercising conceptions of mind-independent things. Chapter 5 involves a discussion of the implications which this position has for an understanding of the concept of truth. That there is a connection to be made between these issues should be clear from previous chapters. Thus, Berkeley complains that Locke's brand of realism implies that there can be no truth and knowledge with respect to things, and Nietzsche makes a distinction between two conceptions of truth – 'pure' truth and 'anthropomorphic' truth. The first of these 'truths' is inaccessible to us in much the way that Locke's substance and Kant's thing in itself are inaccessible on one interpretation of their positions. The second 'anthropomorphic' alternative, by contrast, is accessible to us. However, it is a conception which is concerned solely with 'the relations of things to men', and is said to be unable to capture the sense in which a true thought can correspond to the way things really are. Again, this second position has an obvious analogue in the problem of accounting for the status of the things we conceptualize, relating as it does to the position according to which the nature of these things is determined by us.

Nietzsche's paradigm of 'pure' truth provides the starting point for Chapter 5, and I compare it to a version of the correspondence theory which generates a similar set of difficulties. These difficulties are articulated with the help of F.H. Bradley. I introduce Bradley into the discussion because his positive conception of truth involves a peculiar and interesting hybrid of the positions with which I shall be concerned. According to this view, we are to endorse an identity theory of truth. Such a theory, in Bradley's hands at least, has similar implications to Nietzsche's paradigm of 'pure' truth, implying as it does that our thoughts cannot be true. To repeat his rather striking terminology, truth is said to require 'thought's suicide'. We shall see that this verdict gains support from Bradley's overall metaphysical stance – a stance which suggests that he, too, has fallen victim to the syndrome.

There is a further reason for devoting attention to Bradley's identity theory, namely, that there is a version of this theory which is compatible with the realist position I seek to defend. This version has found expression in the work of some contemporary philosophers – most notably, John McDowell[8] and Robert Brandom[9] – who have taken issue with the metaphysical commitments of the correspondence theory, at least, as that theory is given expression in a position like that of Nietzsche. One of my aims will be to make explicit the nature of the relation between these putatively distinct identity theories of truth, and it is in the context of examining this contemporary version of the theory that I shall consider whether the correspondence theory admits of a similar bifurcation.

The chapter as a whole involves a vindication of the idea that theories of truth can be metaphysically motivated. In particular, we shall see that a distorted metaphysics can give rise to a distorted conception of truth, and that a correction of the metaphysical distortion has corresponding implications for an understanding of truth. Although a positive conception of truth can be said to emerge from my argument, it would be wrong to exaggerate the nature of the constraint which has been imposed upon an adequate account. The point is simply that the relevant position must be metaphysically motivated to good effect, and in particular that it must avoid the distortions imposed by the syndrome. It remains open therefore that an adequate conception of truth can assume a variety of forms.

My next task will be to consider where Hegel's conception of truth is to be situated. Given the conclusions I have reached on his behalf it will come as no surprise that much of what he says is consistent with the conception upheld by McDowell and Brandom. However, we shall see that there are aspects of Hegel's position which are more difficult to accommodate in this manner – aspects reminiscent of the identity theory endorsed by Bradley. Assuming then that Hegel's conception of truth is consonant with the metaphysical position I have advanced, it may look as if we have a possible vindication of Bradley's version of the theory. I shall argue that no such vindication is possible, whilst conceding that there are insights to be found in his account of truth – insights which gain proper expression only when it has been prized apart from the offending metaphysical framework.

In the final chapter I discuss some of the meta-philosophical questions which are thrown up by my essay. Perhaps the most obvious question, given the shape of my inquiry, is that of how my argument's structure is to be related to Hegel's dialectical method. Much of what I say in the first five chapters assumes and, I hope, vindicates the suggestion that there is considerable common ground to be found between these two approaches, and one of my tasks will be to see how far this comparison can be pushed. To begin with, I offer a more detailed clarification of the negative and positive aspects of my line of thought, leaving it open that it may involve characteristics which set it apart from its Hegelian origins. To this end, I make contact with some more contemporary figures whose methodology invites a similar comparison, the most notable being McDowell in his *Mind and World*.

My discussion of the positive aspect of the approach will lead me into Wittgensteinian territory as I examine McDowell's appropriation of the later Wittgenstein's meta-philosophical stance. That Wittgenstein's position has relevance for an understanding of my approach should be obvious from the use he himself makes of the syndrome metaphor – a use which finds expression in his idea that philosophical problems are like illnesses which stand to be diagnosed and treated. I shall express reservations about some of the conclusions Wittgenstein draws in this context, in particular, the implications they carry that philosophy is a fundamentally distortive activity. It is at this point that I shall make contact again with Hegel in order to clarify where he would stand with respect to such a suggestion.

The positive position I reach on Hegel's behalf is testimony to his belief that philosophy can yield explanatory and informative claims about the issues to which it is applied, and it is with this point in mind that we can best appreciate his aim of attaining absolute knowledge and truth. This aim can be made to sound both pretentious and absurd. However, it becomes less obviously so when viewed from within the parameters which are set up by Hegel in response to the methods of his predecessors. It is the aim of philosophical truth which motivates the present essay. Furthermore, in so far as it is conducted from within the required Hegelian parameters, it is an aim which is intended to escape the accusations which so readily and justifiably apply to proclamations of this ilk. The extent to which I succeed in this regard remains to be seen, but it would be entirely in keeping with my Hegelian aspirations if there is a large measure of open-endedness in the results here attained. As Hegel himself has said, philosophy must beware of the wish to be edifying, and the philosopher must avoid the conceit of genius.

1 A philosophical syndrome

Locke on substance: some tensions

In the various disputes between Locke and Berkeley, the concept of substance plays a major part. Berkeley takes Locke to be identifying substance as a supporter of properties, where this latter notion is equated with 'being in general'. He claims that this identification is incomprehensible:

> If we enquire into what the most accurate philosophers declare themselves to mean by material substance, we shall find them acknowledge, they have no other meaning annexed to those sounds, but the idea of being in general, together with the relative notion of its supporting accidents. The general idea of being appeareth to me the most abstract and incomprehensible of all other; and as for its supporting accidents, this, as we have just now observed, cannot be understood in the common sense of those words; it must therefore be taken in some other sense, but what that is they do not explain. So that when I consider the two parts or branches which make the signification of the words *material substance,* I am convinced there is no distinct meaning annexed them.[1]

Locke himself argues against the charge that he is committed to this conception of substance, and much of what he says in the *Essay* – in particular, in the chapter on space – serves to echo Berkeley's disparaging remarks in this context. For example, in response to the question of whether a space 'void of body, be *substance* or *accident*' he claims that 'I shall readily answer I know not, nor shall be ashamed to own my ignorance, till they that ask show me a clear distinct *idea* of *substance*'.[2] And further on, having retold the story of the Indian philosopher who claims that the world is supported by an elephant, and the elephant by a tortoise, he remarks that the notion of substance would have done just as well as a support in this context. He then adds, somewhat sarcastically, that this latter response is no worse than that which is given by European philosophers when they claim 'That *Substance* without knowing what it is, is that which supports *Accidents*'[3], concluding in an equally sarcastic tone that:

> (w)ere the Latin words *Inhaerentia* and *Substantia,* put into the plain English ones that answer them, and were called *Sticking on,* and *Underpropping,* they would better discover to us the very great clearness there is in the Doctrine of *Substance and Accidents,* and shew of what use they are in deciding Questions in Philosophy.[4]

Edward Stillingfeet interprets Locke as being a sceptic about substance, claiming that he had 'almost discarded substance out of the reasonable part of the world'.[5] In his third letter to him, Locke makes reference to the above quoted passage about the elephant and tortoise, claiming that his remarks:

> were not intended to ridicule the notion of substance, or those who asserted it, whatever that 'it' signifies; but to show that though substance did support accidents, yet philosophers, who had found such a support necessary, had no more clear idea of what that support was, than the Indian had of that which supported his tortoise, though sure he was it was something.[6]

And in his first letter, he complains that:

> It is laid to my charge that I look at the *being* of substance to be doubtful; and rendered it so by the imperfect and ill-grounded idea I have of it. To which I beg leave to say, that I ground not the *being* but the *idea* of substance, on our accustoming ourselves to suppose some substratum: for it is of the idea alone that I speak there, and not of the *being* of substance. And having everywhere affirmed and built on it, that *man* is a substance, I cannot be supposed to question or doubt of the being of substance. Further, I say that sensation convinces us that there are *solid and extended substances,* and reflection that there are *thinking substances.*[7]

These extracts from Locke are not easy to interpret. At first it looks as if he is agreeing with Berkeley that there is 'no distinct meaning annexed to the notion of substance', and that he would be happy to dispense with it. Such is the most obvious implication of his remark that the notions of substance and accidents are of little use in deciding questions in philosophy. By contrast, if we turn to his responses to Stillingfeet, we find Locke insisting that he is not to be read as wishing to 'question or doubt of the being of substance' – a response which tells against a sceptical interpretation of his position. What is less clear is where he stands with respect to the questions of what the notion of substance signifies, whether it is meaningful, and whether it is of any use to philosophy.

In his first letter to Stillingfeet, Locke draws a contrast between the *being* of substance and the *idea* of substance. He tells us that the *being* of substance is involved when we are concerned with solid and extended substances and thinking substances, and it is something we can neither question nor doubt. The further claim – implicit in his remark that the being of things does not depend upon our ideas – is that the being of substance is mind-independent. The *idea* of substance, by contrast, is grounded on our 'accustoming ourselves to suppose some *substratum*'.

One way of taking these remarks is to suppose that Locke's sceptical worries are directed not at the idea of individual things such as cats and men, but rather at that of a substratum or supporter of properties. Certainly, there is evidence in the remarks I have quoted to suggest that Locke was concerned with the ambiguities surrounding the notion of substance. In his third letter to Stillingfleet, for example, after having insisted that he does not wish to ridicule the notion of substance, or those who assert it, he adds 'whatever that "it" signifies'. According to the present interpretation then, Locke is complaining that those who have wished to accept the notion of substance have been unclear whether they are talking about individual substances or substrata. The further claim is that if they are talking about substrata, their position is unjustified.

A difficulty with this interpretation is that it fails to explain why Locke continues to insist that our idea of substance is obscure and confused, doing so in a manner which suggests that he is not concerned with an idea it is his purpose to reject. This difficulty could be avoided by allowing that our ideas of individual things can be obscure and confused even if they do not involve the idea of a substratum. However, the problem with making this move on Locke's behalf is that there is evidence in his writings to suggest that he is, after all, committed to accepting the idea of a substratum, and that he takes it to be inextricably involved in our ideas of individual things.

Such evidence is to be found in the extracts I have cited already. For example, when explaining the true import of his tale about the elephant and the tortoise, Locke tells us that his aim was to show that:

> though substance did support accidents, yet philosophers, who had found such a support necessary, had no more clear idea of what that support was, than the Indian had of that which supported his tortoise, though sure he was it was something.

The implication here is that substance *is* to be understood as a supporter of properties, that it is an indispensable notion, and that our idea of it is unclear.

Further evidence of a commitment to the notion of a substratum and an acknowledgement of its importance is to be found if we look elsewhere in the *Essay*. Thus, when discussing our ideas of distinct sorts of substances – of men, cats, horses, and so forth – Locke claims that these ideas are to be understood as complexes in which the 'supposed or confused Idea of Substance, such as it is, is always the first and the chief'.[8] These complexes are composed of the various sensible qualities characteristic of the kind of thing in question, and it is made clear that it is the role of substance to lend support to the relevant qualities. Elsewhere, Locke identifies this supposed or confused idea of substance with 'substance in general', claiming that:

> Whatever therefore be the secret and abstract nature of substance in general, all the ideas we have of particular distinct sorts of substances, are nothing but

> several combinations of simple ideas, coexisting in such, though unknown, Cause of their Union, as makes the whole subsist of itself.[9]

The idea that substance in general is the unknown cause which makes the whole subsist of itself suggests a move away from the claim that it is a supporter of qualities to the claim that it is the causal ground of those qualities. To use Locke's more familiar terminology, it functions as the real essence of the thing to which the qualities belong. On this way of thinking, the idea of substance is of considerable importance. A substance is now claimed to sustain in existence the relevant complex of qualities, allowing this complex to exist as a self-subsisting, mind-independent thing which can undergo change. Yet Locke believes that this important idea is, at best, confused and unknown, and at worst, one we do not really possess. Pursuing this more sceptical line of thought, the obvious conclusion to draw is that our ideas of things do not really involve the idea of substance – that our ideas of the things we perceive are nothing but ideas of collections of sensible qualities. As Locke puts it in the *Abstract of the Essay:*

> substance … is but a supposed but unknown substratum of those qualities, something we know not what, that supports their existence; so that all the idea we have of the substance of anything, is an obscure idea of what it does, and not any idea of what it is.[10]

Finally, if we return to the opening sections of Chapter xxiii of Book II of the *Essay,* we find Locke giving expression to a rather different line of thought. For in addition to the sceptical worries he expresses about the idea of substance, he seems to be suggesting that, construed as the idea of a substratum, it is merely a human construction. The following extract gives expression to this way of thinking and serves also as a continuation of the theme according to which the things we perceive are really just collections of qualities:

> (w)hen we talk or think of any particular sort of corporeal substances, as *Horse, Stone,* etc. though the *Idea,* we have of either of them, be but the Complication, or Collection of those several simple *Ideas* of sensible Qualities, which we use to find united in the thing called *Horse* or *Stone,* yet because we cannot conceive, how they should subsist alone, nor one in another, we suppose them existing in, and supported by some common subject; *which support we denote by the name Substance,* though it be certain, we have no clear, or distinct *Idea* of that *thing* we suppose a support. [11]

Thus far, there have been a variety of potentially conflicting themes in Locke's arguments. One theme is that our idea of substance is to be called into question – a theme which compels philosophers like Stillingfeet to conclude that Locke is a sceptic about substance. However, even if we concede the presence of this scepticism in Locke's position, it is unclear how strongly it is to be interpreted and what its true target is intended to be.

Problems pertaining to the target of Locke's scepticism arise when we try to clarify his conception of the relation between 'substance', 'substratum', and 'substances'. Much of his scepticism is directed towards the idea of a substratum. His further remarks, however, suggest not merely that the idea of a substratum is of some philosophical significance, but that it is that without which there would be no individual things. If this *is* what Locke is claiming, then we are left with the problem of explaining why he feels compelled to call into question the idea of substance.

In fact, even when Locke expresses scepticism at the possibility of our having an idea of substance, he is adamant that his sceptical arguments are not intended to call into question the *being* of substance. However, his suggestion that the idea of substance is a construction of consciousness sits rather awkwardly with the claim that the *being* of substance is not affected by our inability to entertain ideas about it. At least, this is so on the assumption that the object of the relevant constructed idea converges upon the *being* of substance. However, and more in line with Locke's occasional insistence that we have no idea of substance, he may wish to deny that the constructed idea of substance corresponds to anything in the world. In this way he could continue to insist that the *being* of substance eludes us, whilst allowing nonetheless that our cognitive powers yield a surrogate idea by means of which the experience of things is secured. Yet on this interpretation it is difficult to see how Locke can continue to defend the claim that our idea of substance is obscure and confused. For this latter claim implies that we have some kind of grasp of substance, in which case there need be no implication that the *being* of substance eludes us, nor that the idea thereof is a construction of consciousness.

Real and nominal essence

Locke sometimes suggests that we treat the unknown substratum which supports the sensible properties of a thing as the causal ground of these properties, 'causal ground' in this context being a placeholder for real essence. We must consider then where he stands with respect to the question of whether real essence is knowable and how he views its relation to the idea of a substratum. The most helpful place to begin is with the distinction he makes between real and nominal essence. Real essence, he claims, is 'taken for the very being of any thing, whereby it is what it is', and constitutes the 'real internal, but generally in Substances, unknown Constitution of Things, whereon their discoverable Qualities depend'.[12] Nominal essence, by contrast, applies not to the 'real constitution of Things', but rather to the 'artificial Constitution of *Genus* and *Species*'.[13] Thus understood, the nominal essence of a thing comprises the various sensible qualities by means of which we recognize things of the relevant sort. These qualities figure in our complex abstract idea of the thing, and it is this complex abstract idea to which we refer when we talk about the substance kind in question. To use Locke's familiar example, the nominal essence of gold involves the qualities of being yellow, of a certain weight, malleable, fusible, and fixed, these qualities figure in the complex idea of gold, and it is this complex idea that the word 'gold' stands for.[14]

Locke claims that the nominal essence of any substance is to be distinguished from its real constitution, and that its real constitution serves as the 'foundation and cause'[15] for its nominal essence by virtue of being that upon which 'any collection of simple *Ideas* co-existing, must depend'.[16] He insists, however, that 'Things are ranked under Names into sorts or *Species,* only as they agree to certain abstract *Ideas,* to which we have annexed those Names', and that it is wrong to suppose that such ranking is based upon 'the supposition of Essences, that cannot be known'. He concludes that we should 'content ourselves with such *Essences* of the Sorts or Species of Things, as come within the reach of our knowledge',[17] claiming that in the case of substances, these respective essences are 'always quite different'.

The idea that a concern with real essence is a concern with the being of any thing calls to mind the contrast Locke makes elsewhere between the *being* of substance and our *idea* of substance. It will be remembered, however, that his use of this terminology is not entirely clear. At times he seems to be suggesting that the *being* of substance is a placeholder for the individual things which belong to mind-independent reality – things which are to be distinguished from our ideas of them, which latter involve the unwarranted notion of a substratum. Elsewhere, the implication is, rather, that the *being* of substance is to be identified with this substratum, and that our inability to form an idea of it in no way impugns its existence.

Certainly, if we look carefully at Chapter vi of Book III there is evidence to suggest that this ambivalence is replicated at the level of Locke's understanding of the notion of real essence. For much of what he says seems expressive of a wish to question the usefulness of this notion. We are told, for example, that real essences are such that we 'only suppose their Being, without precisely knowing what they are', that they are the 'supposed foundation and cause' of nominal essences,[18] and that it is the nominal essence alone which determines substances into sorts.[19] In support of this latter claim, Locke insists that 'our Faculties carry us no farther towards the knowledge and distinction of Substances, than a Collection of those sensible *Ideas,* which we observe in them'.[20] Thus, he compares the plight of one who seeks to sort things by reference to their real essences to that of a blind man who attempts to sort things by reference to their colours.[21] His conclusion is that the ranking of things under general names is regulated not by their real constitutions but by their 'obvious appearances',[22] that we have no idea of the real essence of substances,[23] and that nominal essences are '*made by the Mind,* and not by Nature'.[24] The implication here is that the groupings we impose upon the sensible qualities we perceive correspond to nothing in the world – that things *qua* things are constructions of consciousness and are to be set apart from things in themselves which latter are unknowable.

Finally, and unsurprisingly given that the real essence of a thing is to be identified with its causal ground, we find Locke expressing a similar scepticism towards the possibility of our gaining knowledge of the causal properties of things, in particular, those by virtue of which they interact with other things, those which bind them together as individual things, and those by virtue of which they impinge upon our minds. Thus, we are told that, with respect to the powers and operations of bodies, it is doubtful 'whether with those Faculties we have, we shall ever be able to carry our general Knowledge (I say not particular Experience) in this part much further';[25] that it is in vain that we shall

> endeavour to discover by our *Ideas,* (the only true way of certain and univer-
> sal knowledge,) what other *Ideas* are to be found constantly joined with that
> of our complex *Idea* of any Substance: since we neither know the real
> Constitution of the minute parts, on which their qualities do depend; nor, did
> we know them, could we discover any necessary *connexion* between them;[26]

and that it is 'inconceivable … how any Body should produce any Thought in the Mind'.[27] He concludes that it is 'lost labour' to seek after a 'perfect *Science* of nat-ural Bodies'.[28]

All of these remarks, and many others to the same effect, are reminiscent of Locke's attack on the idea of substance, implying as they do that the idea of real essence is at best obscure and confused, and at worst one we do not possess at all. The further implication – again to be found in his attack on the idea of substance – is that we should question the philosophical usefulness of the idea of real essence. The justification for this conclusion in the present context is that real essence is unnecessary to the task of classifying things into kinds. Second, we can note that the positive conception of things which arises in the light of these scep-tical arguments – namely, that they are collections of sensible ideas[29] which are not themselves substance-involving – echoes the viewpoint which finds expres-sion in Locke's remarks about substance.

It will be remembered, however, that Locke's attack on the idea of substance is set against a quite different line of thought – one which gives expression rather to its philosophical significance. According to this line of thought, substance is that which underlies and unifies the qualities which are available to experience – it is that which makes the whole – i.e. the individual thing – subsist of itself and which grants us the right to allow that it is genuinely independent of mind. To the extent that it performs this unifying role, Locke tells us that it is an idea which is the 'first and the chief' with respect to those which figure in our complex idea of a thing.

A similar theme can be discerned in some of the remarks Locke makes about real essence – remarks which appear to involve something of a retreat from the idea that the real essences of things are *in principle* inaccessible to us. He tells us, for example, that real essence is to be understood as the 'real Constitution of Substances, upon which depends this *nominal Essence,* and all the Properties of that Sort',[30] and that the nominal essences of things, although 'made by the mind' are not made arbitrarily. They are not made arbitrarily because:

> the Mind, in making its complex *Ideas* of Substances, only follows Nature,
> and puts none together, which are not supposed to have a union in Nature. [31]

And, in response to one who would question our ability to make judgements about mind-independent things on the ground that there is no intelligible account of how we could be affected by such things, and who would deny that their real essences can be made manifest to us, he tells us that:

> the certainty of Things existing in *rerum Natura,* when we have the testimony of the senses for it, is not only *as great* as our frame can attain to, but *as our condition needs.* [32]

> In fine then, when our Senses do actually convey into our Understandings any *Idea,* we cannot but be satisfied, that there doth something at that time really exist without us, which doth affect our senses, and by them give notice of it self to our apprehensive Faculties, and actually produce that *Idea,* which we then perceive: and we cannot so far distrust this Testimony, as to doubt, that such Collections of simple *Ideas,* as we have observed by our Senses to be united together, do really exist together.[33]

We can conclude that Locke's remarks on real essence oscillate between two seemingly incompatible positions – positions which have analogues in the remarks he makes about substance. According to the first position, real essence is to be identified with the internal constitution or the *being* of the kind of thing in question. However, it lies beyond the realm to which our faculties provide access, and is unnecessary to the task of distinguishing things into kinds. The implications here are that the *being* of things eludes us, that the realm to which our faculties provides access is a realm of appearance, and that the groupings we impose upon these appearances are constructions of consciousness. The further suggestion is that the notion of real essence, understood as the 'supposed' foundation and cause of our ideas of things, is insignificant from a scientific and philosophical point of view.

According to the second position, the real essence of a thing is to be identified with its internal constitution or structure, but there is no longer any implication that this internal constitution is in principle inaccessible to us. Rather, the claim is that it serves as the causal ground for the sensible qualities and powers possessed by the relevant thing which has this constitution, or as Locke puts it elsewhere, it is that upon which these qualities 'depend'.[34] Thus understood, the notion of real essence is of considerable importance from both a scientific and a philosophical perspective, and hence, an unlikely candidate to be rejected on sceptical grounds. It is important from a scientific perspective because it renders intelligible the idea that the things we investigate have natures which are there to be discovered – natures which are responsible for the appearances they exhibit. It is important from a philosophical perspective for it allows us to make sense of the claim that our ideas of things are answerable to the world for their correctness.[35]

Berkeley's objections

For the moment I want to postpone the question of why Locke is pulled in these two contrary directions, and to examine how Berkeley responds to his position. One cannot help but be struck by a sense of déjà vu when approaching Berkeley's remarks on substance. First, Berkeley wishes to attack the idea that substance is a supporter of qualities – 'being in general' as he refers to it – on the ground that it is an idea which is 'incomprehensible' and 'inconceivable'. In this respect, he would seem to be acquiescing with Locke's complaint that we have no idea of such a substratum, and that 'the doctrine of substance and accidents' is entirely useless in deciding questions in philosophy. Second, he can be read quite naturally as wishing to call into question the reality of things. Third, his response to this accusation is strikingly similar to that delivered by Locke in the face of a similar charge. Thus, just as Locke objected to Stillingfeet's complaint that he had 'almost discarded substance out of the reasonable part of the world', so too, we find Berkeley complaining that he 'ought not to be accused of discarding Substance out of the reasonable world'.[36]

Berkeley is not intending to ridicule the notion of substance *per se*. On the contrary, his aim is to give a more positive response to Locke's criticism that this notion has been inadequately understood in philosophical contexts, and to do so by providing an alternative framework in terms of which to comprehend its significance. Furthermore, he makes it quite clear that the alternative framework he proposes is intended to vindicate the reality of individual things. The following remarks of Philonous – who is speaking on behalf of Berkeley – serve to lend emphasis to this fact and to challenge the conception of substance against which his own position is defined. The similarities with the previously quoted extract from Locke's first letter to Stillingfeet should be obvious:

> (I)f by *material substance* is meant only sensible body, that which is seen and felt, (and the unphilosophical part of the world, I dare say, mean no more) then I am more certain of matter's existence than you, or any other philosopher pretend to be. If there be anything which makes the generality of mankind averse from the notions I espouse, it is a misapprehension that I deny the reality of sensible things … I do therefore assert that I am as certain as of my own being, that there are bodies or corporeal substances, (meaning the things I perceive by my senses) and that granting this, the bulk of mankind will take no thought about, nor think themselves at all concerned in the fate of those unknown natures, and philosophical quiddities, which some men are so fond of. [37]

However, there is a crucial departure from the Lockean conception of substance. For whereas Locke insists for the most part that substance is independent of mind, Berkeley argues that it can be no such thing. I shall return to the question of how we are to understand the force of Berkeley's objection here. First, let me consider the difficulties he finds in Locke's position. The main difficulty is encapsulated in the following extract from his *Philosophical Commentaries:*

> (t)he supposition that things are distinct from Ideas takes away all real Truth, and consequently brings in a Universal Scepticism, since all knowledge and contemplation is confin'd barely to our own Ideas.[38]

As Berkeley sees it then, it is an implication of Locke's position that things are to be distinguished from ideas, and hence, that we are 'confin'd barely to our own Ideas' when perceiving things. It is unclear from this extract how we are to comprehend this confinement imagery, but it is held to be a consequence of our being so confined that knowledge and truth with respect to things is impossible.

It is undeniable that there is some justification for supposing that Locke's position carries this sceptical implication. For there is a strand running through his argument which suggests that the *being* of things is inaccessible to us, and that 'our Faculties carry us no farther towards the knowledge and distinction of Substances, than a Collection of those sensible *Ideas,* which we observe in them'.[39] Assuming this interpretation then, we arrive at one sense in which Locke is committed to claiming that things are to be distinguished from ideas, namely, the sense in which substance is to be set apart from the groupings of qualities which are said to constitute sensible bodies. Obviously, if we accept this line of thought, then Berkeley's confinement imagery gains a point, as does his worry that knowledge and truth with respect to things is excluded.

However, we have seen that there are further features of Locke's position which tell against this interpretation – features which suggest, rather, that our experience of things already presupposes the *being* to which they are opposed on the sceptical line of thought. On this alternative way of taking his position then, the sensible qualities we perceive are substance-involving, and it makes no sense to suppose that *qua* things they are constructions of consciousness. It follows therefore that the confinement imagery loses its point, as does the claim that there can be no knowledge and truth with respect to things. The further suggestion in Locke is that we shall dispense with this second way of conceiving of the thing/idea relation only at the cost of losing our grip upon the idea of a thing.

I shall return to the question of whether Locke is right in his diagnosis of what follows if substance and quality are distinguished in the above-described way. For the moment though, let me continue with Berkeley's line of thought, and in particular, his denial that substance is independent of mind. Given his wish to avoid the sceptical difficulties he takes to be endemic to Locke's position, it seems plausible to suppose that, on one understanding of the claim that substance is independent of mind, the implication is that it is *inaccessible* to mind. That is to say that it lies beyond the realm revealed in our ideas.

Assuming that this interpretation captures what Berkeley is trying to say, we can see why it is so important for Berkeley to reject the claim that substance is independent of mind, and why he believes that its acceptance yields a universal scepticism. For according to the way of thinking under attack, substance is to be identified with the being of things, it lies beyond the realm to which our faculties provide access, and it is to be set apart from the things we perceive. The upshot is that these things are relegated to the status of mere appearance. By contrast, if it is denied that the being of things is independent of mind in this sense, then it becomes possible to allow that substance is, after all, accessible to experience, and hence that the things we perceive are genuine.

This first reading of the denial that substance is independent of mind fits well with the non-sceptical side of Locke's position, implying as it does that we are capable of exercising conceptions of mind-independent things. It seems to correspond also to the position Berkeley himself is wishing to endorse. So, for example, in the *Three Dialogues,* we have Hylas accusing Berkeley's representative, Philonous, of turning things into ideas and of succumbing to the very scepticism he is aiming to avoid. Philonous replies to this accusation as follows:

> You mistake me. I am not for changing things into ideas, but rather ideas into things; since those immediate objects of perception, which according to you, are only appearances of things, I take to be the real things themselves.[40]

Philonous's insistence that the immediate objects of perception are the real things themselves suggests that we are to take his claim that ideas are things as the claim that ideas are *of* things. That is to say, he is interpreting the term 'idea' from the point of view of its content as opposed to conceiving of it as a mental act, and he is claiming that the things revealed at the level of content are such that their objective status cannot be undermined by a further realm of things in themselves.

Nothing that I have said so far on Berkeley's behalf is incompatible with the idea that the things we perceive are independent of mind. Rather, the point is simply to guarantee that they are accessible to mind. We shall see, however, that Berkeley's denial of the claim that things are independent of mind is not captured by this epistemological interpretation, and that he is wishing, rather, to claim that things are dependent on mind in an ontological sense. This latter claim is clearly rather problematic for one who seeks to avoid the sceptical implications of the Lockean account. For although it need not imply that the things we perceive are mere appearances of a further inaccessible realm of things in themselves, it does suggest a commitment to a version of the claim that we are confined barely to our own ideas when perceiving things. We must consider then why Berkeley feels compelled to make this move, and whether he has a way of avoiding the sceptical implication it seems to carry.

We get a clue to his train of thought if we return to the discussion quoted above between Hylas and Philonous. For having made the point that the immediate objects of perception are the 'real things themselves', Philonous responds as follows to the charge that he has left us with 'nothing but the empty forms of things':

> What you call the empty forms and outside of things, seems to me the very things themselves. Nor are they empty or incomplete otherwise, than upon your supposition, that matter is an essential part of all corporeal things. We both therefore agree in this, that we perceive only sensible forms: but herein

we differ, you will have them to be empty appearances, I real beings. In short, you do not trust your senses, I do.[41]

Berkeley is making two points here. First, he is denying that the things we perceive are mere appearances which are to be set apart from things in themselves; second, he is complaining that they could only be taken to be such on the assumption that matter is an essential part of all corporeal things. The first point is familiar from what I have said already on Berkeley's behalf, implying as it does that we must resist the 'universal scepticism' which arises if things in themselves are held to be inaccessible to the realm revealed in our ideas. The second point, by contrast, is less familiar, and it purports to provide an explanation of why it should be thought that the realm revealed in our ideas is a realm of mere appearance. According to this explanation, it is the assumption that *matter* is an essential part of all corporeal things which generates this belief.

Why should it be thought that such an assumption carries this sceptical implication? Berkeley – who is focusing exclusively upon the sceptical strand in Locke's position – is moved to conclude that the mind-independence of a thing implies its inaccessibility, and hence, that we shall avoid a sceptical position only at the cost of denying that things really are independent of mind. However, if we focus upon the non-sceptical strand in Locke's position – the strand which implies that material things *do* impinge upon the mind, albeit in a manner which leaves room for the possibility of ignorance and error with respect to those things – then a very different picture emerges, one which is consistent with the claim that these things are independent of mind, and which no longer carries the implication that, in perceiving things, we are confined barely to our own ideas.

Berkeley's arguments against materialism[42] are spectacularly bad, and could have a semblance of success only to one who was already persuaded of the truth of the immaterialist position he is seeking to defend by their means. To one who is not so persuaded, they serve at best to undermine just one version of materialism, namely, that according to which material things are to be set apart from the things we perceive. It is unnecessary to provide an exhaustive account of these familiar arguments, and for present purposes I am going to focus upon those which are of most relevance to my concerns – to begin with, the one which occurs at sections 16 and 17 of *Principles*. The line of thought here provides a stark illustration of Berkeley's commitment to this problematic conception of materialism, and it involves a development of some of the issues which were bothering Locke in his attack on the 'doctrine of substance and accidents'.

Berkeley begins by repeating Locke's complaint that we do not have an idea of material substance – understood here as that of a substratum. It is important to see that, for Berkeley, the fact that we lack an idea of material substance does not present a serious difficulty. For his aim is to vindicate the reality of the things we perceive, and to do so by denying that there is a further realm of being – the realm in which material substance is to be located – which impugns their objective status. The further suggestion – crucial to the present line of thought – is that the things we perceive cannot be material. Hence, the idea of material substance not only becomes irrelevant to the task of accounting for the things we perceive, but is one the possession of which is rather difficult to defend. Thus, if the materialist is operating with this conception of material substance, we might be prepared to agree with Berkeley that we do not have an idea thereof, and that it is an idea we can do without when seeking to comprehend the nature of the things we perceive. It does not follow yet, however, that this conception of material substance is mandatory.

Having drawn this negative conclusion, Berkeley claims that it is possible to uphold the materialist position only by allowing that we have a *relative* idea of material substance. We have a relative idea thereof, he continues, only if we can explain what relation it bears to its accidents, and what is meant by its supporting them. He then argues that if one characterizes this relation in terms of the idea of a support, one will be unable to say what is meant by 'support' in this context. His reason for drawing this conclusion is that this term cannot be understood here in its ordinary sense, as when a pillar supports a building, and there is no alternative sense forthcoming in the materialist's argument. He concludes that the materialist framework is without meaning.

There are various ways in which the materialist could try to meet this challenge. At the most general level, however, he could object to the assumption that an analysis is required of what it is for something to have a quality, and that this analysis must proceed by way of the idea of a support. Berkeley himself provides an implicit justification for this second point, namely, that use of the term 'support' in this context encourages one to think that the relation between a substance and its qualities is like that which exists between a pillar and the building it supports. That is to say, it encourages one to think that these two terms – 'substance' and 'quality' – refer to separable entities, and hence that it is possible to isolate them from one another.

Berkeley has a further argument which is intended to call into question the possibility of allowing that we perceive material things, and which, if successful, implies that material substance has to be set apart from the things we perceive. The argument – which can be gleaned from sections 68–70 of *Principles* – has its origins in Locke's complaint that we cannot understand how material things affect us, and it purports to show not merely that we are epistemologically limited in this respect, but more seriously, that there is no way in which material things *could* affect us. Berkeley begins by pointing out that matter is unperceivable. This observation is important to him, for he believes that the only objects of perception are ideas, in which case it follows that material things have to be distinguished from ideas, and cannot therefore be objects of perception. Having made this assumption, his next move is to block the possibility of allowing that material things function as the unperceivable causes of our ideas. Berkeley is going to be happy to allow that there is more to reality than the realm of the perceivable – a move which offers considerable hope for one who seeks to defend a materialist standpoint by this means. He objects, however, that material things are 'inert' and 'passive' – in this respect they are comparable to our ideas, which, we are told at Section 25, have 'nothing of power or agency included in them' – and cannot therefore perform the required causal role. It follows that we require an alternative explanation for the origin of the things we perceive as well as for the causal properties they seem to exhibit.

There are various objections to be levelled at this argument. First, we might object to Berkeley's claim that material things are unperceivable. To be sure, he offers an argument for this claim – insisting that the objects of perception are ideas, and that ideas are to be set apart from material things. The difficulty, however, is that this argument depends for its cogency upon the prior acceptability of the immaterialist position he wishes to defend. Second, Berkeley assumes that material things are causally inactive. The version of this claim which is of interest to him is the one he reads into Locke's philosophy, namely, that material things are to be set apart from the things we perceive and function as their unknowable causes. Furthermore, we may be prepared to agree with him – as Locke does at times – that there are difficulties with such a position. At this point, however, it is open to the materialist to deny that material things are to be set apart from the things we perceive and to allow that they are causally responsible for our veridical perceptions. Again, there is nothing in Berkeley to rule out this possibility – nothing apart from the familiar immaterialist claims he is so eager to repeat and which could have a semblance of plausibility only to one who was already persuaded that a materialism of any form is bound to be unintelligible. It is to his immaterialist alternative that I now turn.

Berkeley on substance: some tensions

Berkeley's aim is to vindicate the reality of sensible bodies, where this task is at one with that of avoiding the 'universal scepticism' which, he believes, is implied by Locke's position. His reason for claiming that Locke's position yields this result is that 'all knowledge and contemplation is confin'd barely to our own ideas', where the ideas in question are the things we perceive, which latter are set apart from things in themselves. According to one interpretation then, the task of vindicating the reality of sensible bodies is that of showing that their objective status cannot be undermined by the existence of some further inaccessible realm – a realm which relegates their status to that of mere appearance.

It seems undeniable that the things we perceive must be 'real' in this first sense if we are to avoid universal scepticism. As noted, however, Berkeley wishes to claim further that they are ontologically dependent on mind, and although the details of this proposal have been left unspecified, it appears to involve a commitment to an alternative version of the claim that 'all knowledge and contemplation is confin'd barely to our own ideas'. As such, its acceptance seems inimical to Berkeley's anti-sceptical aim. Berkeley's gloss upon the claim that things are ontologically dependent on mind is that their being consists in their being perceived, or as he puts it, that their *esse* is *percipi*.[43] The further claim is that these things are collections of ideas. Now it seems central to the idea that the things we perceive are real that they are precisely *not* ontologically dependent on mind, if being so dependent is intended to imply that their existence is tied to particular acts of perceiving them. On the contrary, it is built into our understanding of these things that they are self-subsisting, and not dependent upon the existence of a perceiver.

Berkeley accepts the spirit of the claim that things are 'real' in this sense. He does not accept its letter, however, due to his rejection of materialism. It follows therefore that he is unable to express this realist intuition as the claim that things exist independently of particular acts of perception. His solution is to make a distinction between *finite* perceivers such as ourselves and the infinite perceiver which is God, so as to claim that things are held in existence by God's act of perceiving them. The further crucial claim is that these things are rendered accessible to us by virtue of His divine activity. Thus, Berkeley can allow that the things we perceive exist independently of finite acts of perceiving them, and in this way can sidestep the worry that the mind-dependence of things implies that, in perceiving them, we are 'confin'd barely to our own ideas'. He can deny, however, that they are self-subsisting in the manner demanded by the materialist.

When Locke talks of things being self-subsisting, he tells us that material substance is that which makes the whole subsist of itself, the whole in this context being the quality-bearing thing which is available to experience. He implies further that if we dispense with the idea of material substance, then we shall lose our grip upon the idea of a thing. There would appear to be several reasons why this should be so. First, things will be reduced to groupings of qualities with nothing to sustain them in existence; second, it will not be possible to account for the sense in which the things we perceive are unified individuals which can undergo change; third, we shall be forced to conclude that the existence of things is tied to particular acts of perceiving them, in which case we shall be unable to capture the sense in which things are responsible for their own existence as opposed to being dependent upon the existence of a perceiver. It is for these reasons that Locke stresses – although not entirely consistently – that the idea of material substance is of chief importance.

It is not easy to determine where Berkeley stands with respect to this Lockean line of thought. He seems prepared to accept that a rejection of the idea of material substance must give way to a position according to which things are collections or groupings of ideas – ideas in this context being placeholders for the sensible qualities of things.[44] However, he purports to sidestep the difficulty that there will be nothing to sustain these qualities in existence, for he tells us that these qualities are *'inert, fleeting, dependent beings'*[45] which are sustained in existence by God.[46] I have suggested already that this theological move grants Berkeley the right to allow that the things we perceive are not tied to finite acts of perceiving them. Perhaps we are to suppose also that it offers the resources for allowing that these things are unified individuals.

Berkeley prefers impressionistic gesture to detailed exposition when it comes to describing the relation which exists between the mind of God and the sensible qualities He perceives. The best we can do then is to consider whether and how his immaterialist framework might be exploited to the end of comprehending the nature of the things we perceive. There are two directions Berkeley could take. According to the first alternative, he denies Locke's claim that the idea of substance is required if we are to make sense of the idea of a thing. It would be a consequence of pursuing this line of thought that substance is not, after all, of chief importance with respect to our ideas of things, and hence, that the mind of God is not to be viewed as a philosophical substitute for material substance. The second alternative, by contrast, has Berkeley agreeing with Locke that the idea of substance is a central component in the idea of a thing. Given his objections to materialism, however, he must allow that an immaterialist framework can be exploited in this context – that it is the idea of *immaterial* substance which is of chief importance.

Berkeley's claim that things are just groupings of sensible qualities lends support to the first interpretation of his position. Furthermore, it is an interpretation which is implied by his advocacy at times of the idea that the concept of a thing is little more than a convenience which provides a useful way of ordering experience, but which corresponds to nothing fixed in the nature of things.[47] Nevertheless, it is a position which threatens to generate the very difficulties which led Locke to conclude that we need the idea of substance if we are not to lose our grip upon the idea of a thing. The further implication is that we shall have no way of making sense of the idea that the qualities we perceive belong to something which is independent of our minds, in which case we are in danger of returning to the conclusion that, in perceiving things, we are, after all, confined barely to our own ideas. At this point our intuitive conception of a thing has been very seriously undermined, and Berkeley's insistence that his position vindicates our ordinary ways of thinking begins to look rather dubious.[48]

We are returned then to the question of whether Berkeley's reference to God can solve the relevant difficulties – whether he can allow that the idea of *immaterial substance* is of chief importance with respect to the idea of a thing. If this *is* what Berkeley is wishing to say, then he faces a potential difficulty – a difficulty which arises before we even begin to clarify the details of this proposal. The difficulty in question is that he denies that we have an idea of God. The implication then is that any reference to God in an account of the nature of the things we perceive is going to be quite without meaning.

It will be remembered that Berkeley is happy to allow that we do not have an idea of material substance – unsurprisingly so, given his adherence to a framework which excludes the possibility of there being anything the idea could be of. At first sight then, his denial that we have an idea of God suggests that God and material substance are on the same level in this respect, in which case, we might wonder whether his position is going to constitute a significant advance upon that of the materialist. Certainly, some of his remarks lend justice to this comparison, for his warrant for the claim that we do not have an idea of God is that God is not a possible object of perception. Thus, to the extent that material substance is not a possible object of perception when taken to be distinct from the things we perceive, it seems plausible to suppose that Berkeley is treating the two cases alike. The further implication, of course, is that the idea of God will be of no more use in accounting for the unified-ness of things, than the idea of material substance is when taken to be distinct from the things we perceive.

When Berkeley claims that God is not a possible object of perception, he does so on the ground that He is an active Being, whose nature is to be distinguished from the passive phenomena which are the proper objects of perception and which He sustains in existence.[49] The idea that the limits of reality exceed the limits of the perceivable is familiar from my discussion of Berkeley's objection to the idea that matter could be viewed in these active terms. The further crucial claim here is that our cognitive powers can take us beyond these limits, and hence, that there is more to cognition than the perception of sensory ideas. Thus, we can be said to have an idea of God in a broader sense of the term 'idea'. Berkeley's way of expressing this point is to say that we have a *notion* of God.[50]

Perhaps the most obvious objection to this line of thought is that it introduces a framework which stands to be exploited by the materialist in the context of defending his own preferred position. That is to say, the materialist can embrace this broader conception of cognition and use it to arrive at the conclusion that we have a *notion* of material substance. Furthermore, he can vindicate this move on the ground that the sensible qualities we perceive must be conceived of as belonging to mind-independent things. Berkeley is aware of this potential objection and has Hylas complaining to Philonous that 'to act consistently, you must either admit matter or reject spirit'.[51] Now we have seen that Berkeley has a ready response to this complaint, for he believes that the nature of matter is incompatible with the possibility of its serving the required causal role. Arguing along these lines then, he could happily 'reject matter' on the ground that it is useless to the task of accounting for the things we perceive, whilst denying that such a move implies the rejection of spirit. The difficulty is that Berkeley's conception of matter – as inert and passive – is not adequately defended, and could have a semblance of plausibility only to one who was already persuaded of the truth of the immaterialist position he is seeking to advance. On the face of it then, the materialist is free to trade upon Berkeley's broader conception of cognition and to use it as a way of lending credence to the suggestion that we have a notion of material substance and that spirit should be rejected.

The significance of this objection will become evident in due course. For the moment though, let me continue with the question of whether Berkeley's conception of the God/world relation can be of any service in accounting for the nature of the things we perceive. As I have said, it is Berkeley's contention that there is no causal agency in the world, that the contents of the world are passive and inert. The further claims are that only spirits are active, the main source of activity coming from the infinite spirit which is God,[52] and that God holds things in existence by perceiving them.

It should be clear from all of this that there has to be a distinction between God's manner of perceiving things and ours. Berkeley's way of making this distinction is to say that whereas God causes what he perceives, we don't. This crucial difference is captured by distinguishing between ideas of imagination and ideas of sense. Ideas of imagination are caused by the mind that perceives them, and can be produced both by finite minds and by the mind of God. Ideas of sense, by contrast, are not caused by the mind that perceives them, and they are peculiar to finite minds. Thus, Berkeley holds that God's ideas of imagination are to be identified with our ideas of sense, and that ideas of sense are the things we perceive.[53]

Even if we concede that God *perceives* the things he causes, it is difficult to accept that perception is the fundamental relation in terms of which to explain the manner in which He stands to these things. On the contrary, it looks as if it is the relation of *being causally responsible for* which is doing the main philosophical work in this context, in which case, it seems more appropriate to say that the being of a thing consists not in its being perceived, but rather, in its being caused to exist by God – the causation in question requiring essential reference to an act of volition.[54] If this is right, then we are left with the following questions. First, has Berkeley succeeded in providing a genuine and viable alternative to the materialist standpoint? Second, does his position incorporate a version of Locke's claim that substance is of chief importance with respect to our ideas of things? Third, is it important that it does so?

Much of Berkeley's argument suggests that God is to be distinguished from the things which exist in his mind – and our minds – in just the way that a pillar is to be distinguished from the building it supports. For not only does he explicitly employ the 'support' metaphor when characterizing the relation between spirits and ideas,[55] but he tells us that the knowledge we have of spirits is not immediate, and that we can know of their existence only by means of their operations or of the ideas they excite in us.[56] He claims also that the causes which produce things 'are not so much as aimed at' when we perceive things[57], and that, in our quest for knowledge of the things we perceive, we must 'proceed warily' and content ourselves with the regularities in nature which are accessible to us, and which allow us to 'make very probable conjectures' and 'to predict things to come'.[58] He adds that that it is the 'will of the *governing spirit,* who causes certain bodies to cleave together, or tend towards each other, according to various laws'.[59] Finally, we are told that all causal activity is to be understood in terms of the relation of a mark or sign with the thing signified,[60] the idea being that the things we perceive are 'marks or signs for our information' – signs which are instituted by God and our interpretation of which brings us closer to an understanding of His divine plan.

The implication in all of these claims is that God is to be set apart from the things we perceive in much the way that material substance is set apart from these things on the position Berkeley reads into Locke. Now such a position need have no implications for an understanding of the things we perceive provided that a distinction is upheld between the question of how we are to view the God/world relation and that of how we are to view the substance/quality relation. That is to say, it is perfectly consistent to suppose that God is to be dualistically opposed to the world whilst denying that the things we perceive are groupings of qualities or that He has some kind of causal role to play with respect to their nature as individuals. Berkeley, however, does not uphold this distinction. On the contrary, he makes it quite clear that the things which are to be set apart from God are groupings of sensible qualities, and that the only substance of which we can speak meaningfully is immaterial substance. On this way of thinking then, the question of how we are to comprehend the God/world relation is absolutely central to that of how we are to comprehend the substance/quality relation. And once it is insisted – as Berkeley seems to be insisting – that God is to be dualistically opposed to the world, then it follows that He can play a causal role with respect to the unified-ness of things only at the cost of introducing a position which has it that the sensible qualities we perceive are unified by reference to something which is to be dualistically opposed to them.

At this point it looks as if we have been returned to an immaterialist version of the claim that the causes which produce things are inaccessible to us – an idea which leads Locke to despair of allowing that the idea of substance can be a central component in the idea of a thing and to conclude that it is lost labour to seek after a perfect science of bodies. The further worry is that we are now landed with a conception of substance which is just as problematic as the one Berkeley finds in Locke. At this stage, of course, it is open to the materialist to reverse the tables with a charge of incomprehensibility with respect to the ingredients of Berkeley's position, and to use this charge as a way of vindicating the possibility that reference to material substance and the corporeal causes it involves may yet provide the best hope we have of understanding the nature of the things we perceive. It would be crucial to the defence of such a position, of course, that these corporeal causes be ascribable to the things we perceive as opposed to being dualistically opposed to them.

Does Berkeley have room for manoeuvre here? Presumably if his position is to succeed in accounting for the unified-ness of the things we perceive, it will be necessary for him to deny that God is to be dualistically opposed to them. Certainly, there are elements of his position which tell in favour of such a denial. For he tells us that it is the will of God that 'causes certain bodies to cleave together or tend towards each other', that we know God 'certainly and immediately',[61] and that 'we need only open our eyes to see the sovereign lord of all things with a more full and clear view, than we do any of our fellow creatures'.[62] For the moment we can ignore the fact that these claims could have a semblance of plausibility only to one who was already persuaded of the truth of Berkeley's immaterialist position, the current point at issue being whether his God can be brought back down to earth so as to perform the required unificatory role with respect to the things we perceive. The most obvious way of effecting such a feat is to take seriously the claim that God 'causes certain bodies to cleave together' so as to allow that the qualities we perceive belong to Him. Certainly, this position promises to avoid any appeal to the notion of a transcendent God, and in this respect is in no danger of re-introducing an immaterialist version of the thing/idea distinction as this distinction is understood by Berkeley's Locke. Nevertheless, it is problematic for several reasons. First, the claim that God just *is* the things we perceive takes us some distance from the more traditional conception of God to which Berkeley seems committed for the most part, and suggests a version of pantheism which renders the theological vocabulary superfluous. This difficulty is not fatal, for one might argue that Berkeley's version of immaterialism stands in need of revision in this respect, or alternatively, that it is possible to retain a more traditional conception of God whilst also dispersing him, so to speak, across the things we perceive. Second, however, if one is compelled to make either of these moves, it will be necessary to clarify the sense in which the resultant position is to be distinguished from the materialist standpoint against which it is defined.

Presumably Berkeley would insist that he is analysing the substance/quality relation in terms of the mind/idea relation, and explicating the latter by reference to the idea of perception. As we have seen, however, the mind in question is the mind of God, and although it makes sense to suppose that He *perceives* the relevant groupings of ideas, it seems clear that this relation is not itself philosophically fundamental. Rather, it is the fact that God *causes* the things he perceives that is fundamental. The claim then is that the mind of God is causally responsible for the ideas he perceives, the ideas in question being the sensible qualities of things. If we assume further that God is to be identified with the things we perceive, then the position we end up with is that the things we perceive are ontologically responsible for the qualities they exhibit – a position which sounds rather similar to the materialist standpoint it was intended to replace.

The immaterialist would insist that there is a crucial difference to be acknowledged, namely, that the things in question are to be understood in immaterialist terms. But what does this amount to? Given that we have rejected any reference to the idea of a transcendent God on the present interpretation, the claim has to be that the things we perceive have minds and that the activity they exhibit is to be understood in volitional terms. All of this sounds fanciful to say the least. From the immaterialist's point of view, however, it offers the only way of making sense of the idea that the things we perceive are active beings – the only way, that is to say, of lending substance to Locke's claim that the things we perceive are self-subsisting beings who are responsible for their own existence as opposed to being dependent upon the existence of a finite perceiver. Nevertheless, once we acknowledge that there have been no good arguments against the possibility of there being a form of materialism which can guarantee that material things are the things we perceive, and that Berkeley's conception of substance can be made plausible only to the extent that it is articulated in non-dualistic terms, it begins to look as if the position we have reached on his behalf is really just a terminological variant for one which can satisfy the required constraints. That is to say that the things we perceive have minds only in the innocuous sense that they have a genuine mode of activity and, thus understood, are guaranteed to be accessible to us.

Locke, Berkeley, and the syndrome

I want now to provide a more focused diagnosis of the tensions and difficulties identified in the positions of Locke and Berkeley and make a case for concluding that they are in the grip of the syndrome. The starting point of their arguments is the question of how we are to comprehend the concept of substance. It is not made entirely clear what 'substance' denotes, but it is a shared presupposition of their positions that the answer one gives to this question has important implications for an understanding of the things we perceive – things like cats, dogs, and men, for example. From this point on, it becomes rather more difficult to comprehend the direction of their arguments. At a certain stage, however – and it is here that the syndrome begins to take a hold – substance, understood here as material substance, is distinguished from the things we perceive in such a way that it cannot be intelligibly related to them. Locke's way of making this distinction is to oppose the idea of a substratum to that of individual things like cats, dogs, and men. Berkeley talks of 'philosophical quiddities', and sets them apart from the things we perceive.

Why is this separation effected? One reason is that both Locke and Berkeley give weight to the idea that substance is a *supporter* of qualities – an idea which encourages the thought that it is a separable entity, and further, that it supports the qualities of the things which are available to experience. It is an implication of this latter claim, however, that substance is to be set apart not merely from the sensible qualities of the thing, but also from the thing we experience as having those qualities. The obvious conclusion to draw, pursuing this line of thought, is that substance is to be treated as a substratum, that it lies beyond the realm which is revealed in experience, and that the things we perceive are nothing but collections of qualities.

Even if we resist the metaphor of support, there is still a temptation to be misled by the claim that a substance has qualities. For this way of talking suggests that in order to get at the substance itself it is necessary to remove all of its qualities, even the quality which serves to identify the kind of thing in question – the quality of being a man, for example. It is a natural corollary of this line of thought also that the substance itself is to be distinguished from the things we perceive – in this case, the man, and further, that this thing is nothing but a collection of qualities.

It is undeniable that these grammatical confusions gain some kind of expression in the arguments of Locke and Berkeley, and further, that they are not unique to the case of *material* substance. With respect to this latter case, however, these confusions are sustained by an ideologically based reason our protagonists have for distinguishing between material substance and the things we perceive. Perhaps the most significant consideration – one for which Locke shows some sympathy and which is embraced wholeheartedly by Berkeley – is that the things we perceive cannot be material, the justification for this claim being that there is no intelligible account of how such things could causally effect us.

With this dualistic distinction in place, Locke and Berkeley proceed to reveal material substance in the manner this model demands. And given that it is an implication of this model that such a revelation demands the removal of the things we perceive, it is unsurprising that both Locke and Berkeley feel compelled to deny that substance can be a part of these things. Locke, as we have seen, is reluctant to draw this sceptical conclusion, believing as he does that the idea of material substance forms an essential component of the idea of a thing. Hence, there is a certain ambivalence in his attitude towards this concept – an ambivalence which finds expression in his desire both to dispense with it on the ground that it is unintelligible, and to retain it because it is of 'chief importance'.

Berkeley, by contrast, has no reservations on this score, for he is of the opinion that the materialist framework has to be rejected, and that, in any case, immaterialism is sufficient to make sense of our ideas of things.

Both Locke and Berkeley are under pressure to conclude on the basis of their sceptical arguments that the things we perceive are nothing but collections of sensible qualities, and that the idea of a thing to which those qualities belong is a constructed idea – something we invent to make sense of the way these qualities can hang together. Locke, however, wavers in his commitment to this conception of a thing – unsurprisingly so, given the reservations he has about dispensing with the idea of material substance – and in such moments implies, rather, that the real error occurs when this positive conception is accepted. His further suggestion in such contexts is that the relevant collections of qualities are irreducibly substance or thing-involving, where this is intended to imply that there are mind-independent things to which these qualities belong, namely, the things we perceive.

Berkeley, however, sticks resolutely to the claim that things are just collections of qualities, confident as he is that immaterialism provides a philosophically acceptable substitute to the materialist position which Locke is so loathe to reject. One possibility here is that he is simply failing to acknowledge the problems which Locke so rightly foresees in the claim that things are just collections of qualities, and hence, that his confidence in this context is misplaced. A further difficulty is that it looks as if he has ended up re-introducing a version of the dualistic distinction he claims to be surmounting, namely, that which exists between things and ideas. The alternative, I have suggested, is to suppose that he would be prepared to bestow a unifying role upon the mind of God with respect to the qualities we perceive. If this is so, however, then he has wavered in his commitment to the claim that things are just collections of qualities, and in this respect is advancing a position which is just as ambivalent as that of Locke. The further consequence is that he has introduced a new set of difficulties – difficulties which come to the surface when we press the question of how best to comprehend the nature of the relation which is said to exist between God and the things we perceive and look more carefully at the conception of causation to which he is committed hereby.

It appears then that Locke and Berkeley have much in common. First, they are tempted to impose an insurmountable distinction between material substance and the things we perceive. Second, they accept that no content can be given to the idea of material substance if it is distinguished in this manner. Third, and Locke is more hesitant in this respect, they conclude on the basis of this negative claim that the things we perceive are collections of sensible qualities. The implication here is that the idea of material substance has been rejected, and that it would be an error to re-introduce it. Finally, having reached this sceptical conclusion, they both advance claims which are suggestive of a rejection of this positive conception of a thing. Locke does so by allowing that the idea of material substance is of chief importance with respect to our ideas of things. Berkeley does so by implying that the things we perceive are unified individuals, and hence that they involve more than a set of free-floating qualities. In neither case, however, is this alternative position consistently maintained, and for some of the time – more so in the case of Berkeley – they are happy to allow that the relevant groupings of qualities do not belong to anything.

Why is it concluded that the things we perceive are groupings of qualities? On the face of it, this conclusion is a direct consequence of the claim that no content can be given to the idea of material substance if it is set apart from the things we perceive. Now I have noted that both Locke and Berkeley are prepared to accept that there is something highly problematic about this conception of material substance – hence the sceptical attitude they express towards it. According to the line of thought under current consideration, however, we are to conclude on the basis of these doubts that the things we perceive are groupings of sensible qualities – groupings which do not belong to anything. Yet this conclusion is itself just a further expression of the framework according to which material substance is to be set apart from the things we perceive – the framework expressive of the syndrome. It appears then that our protagonists – to the extent that they follow this line of thought – have responded to the claim that no content can be given to the idea of material substance when it is set apart from the things we perceive, by concluding that it has to be conceived of in this manner.

It is no good responding on Berkeley's behalf that his rejection of a materialism of any form rescues him from the charge of buying into the offending conception of substance. For as I have said, it is built into his immaterialist standpoint that the things we perceive are collections of sensible qualities. Given that this is so, and ignoring for the moment my suggested modification of his position, it seems undeniable that he has ended up with an immaterialist version of the very distinction it was his purpose to avoid. As my previous findings should testify, his mistake is to suppose that the proper object of attack is materialism *per se* as opposed to the problematic framework which accompanies a certain conception thereof.

We can conclude that the syndrome has some kind of hold on Locke and Berkeley in so far as there is evidence in their arguments for a framework according to which substance – material or immaterial – is to be set apart from the things we perceive. It is Locke's commitment to such a framework which makes sense of his reluctance at times to allow that the things we perceive are substance-involving, and of the corresponding attitude as it occurs in Berkeley's scheme of things. By contrast, it becomes more difficult to accommodate Locke's claim that substance is of chief importance with respect to our ideas of things, and to comprehend the criticisms our protagonists direct towards the possibility that it could be distinguished from the things we perceive. For according to the present framework, it is an error to suppose that the qualities we perceive belong to anything.

By contrast, if we dispense with this dualistic framework, it becomes possible to allow that the qualities we perceive belong to something – that we perceive things which *have* qualities as opposed to things which just *are* qualities. The further implication is that substance as presently conceived precisely does have relevance to an understanding of the things we perceive. For it is the thing to which the qualities we perceive belong. It is a consequence of accepting this alternative framework then that the idea of substance is, after all, of chief importance with respect to our ideas of things. Thus, to the extent that it makes sense to talk about erroneous conceptions of substance, the error occurs, according to the present line of thought, not when substance is held to be presupposed in the qualities we perceive, but rather when it is dualistically opposed to them.

It should be clear from what I have said that both of these frameworks are operative in the arguments of Locke and Berkeley, that the first one is indicative of the syndrome, and that it constitutes the problematic and ultimately unstable option. It is the residual presence of the syndrome which helps to explain certain features of their respective positions. We have seen, for example, that Locke expresses some dissatisfaction at what he takes to be the only alternative to the rejected conception of substance, namely, that things are just collections of qualities, and he does so on the ground that the idea of substance is of chief importance. At the same time, however, he is reluctant to grant this point – a reluctance which finds expression in his claim that things are just collections of qualities. The most obvious explanation for this reluctance is that he is assuming that any reference to substance must bring with it the dualistic picture he wishes to reject – that the claim that substance is of chief importance is to be read as the claim that substance as dualistically opposed to the things we perceive is of chief importance. By contrast, once the second framework is in place, it becomes possible to reject the offending conception of substance whilst resisting the consequence that substance *per se* must disappear from the picture. It is the idea of substance in this second sense which is of chief importance with respect to our ideas of things.

It is Locke's inability to relinquish fully the framework which should be the real object of his attack which explains why it is so difficult at times to work out what he is saying, and why he often seems to be arguing for two quite contrary positions. According to the present line of thought, this ambivalence is to be expected given that the framework for which he retains a residual commitment serves to vindicate the object of his attack. Thus, he is led to say things which are expressive of the position he is seeking to reject, even whilst seeking to defend an alternative which, if adequately articulated, would serve to undermine this position. An obvious case in point is his adherence to the claim that the things we perceive are just collections of qualities, and the suspicion he retains that they can be no such thing.

The interesting thing about Berkeley is that he expresses no dissatisfaction at the positive position it is his purpose to defend. On the contrary, he insists that it provides an adequate account of the things we perceive, and that it offers the only way of avoiding the errors of the Lockean standpoint. The expectation then is that the problematic framework has been transcended and the syndrome avoided. I have argued that this is not the case, and that, on the contrary, Berkeley retains an immaterialist version of the framework it was his original purpose to reject – a framework which finds expression in his claim that the things we perceive are collections of ideas. To be sure, this claim is set against others which suggest, rather, that he is courting an immaterialist version of the position which allows that the things we perceive are substance-involving. All that this shows, however, is that there is an ambivalence in his position which echoes that to be found in Locke.

How then are we to proceed? The first thing we must do is to acknowledge that the problem of comprehending the relation between thing and idea is not to be solved simply by embracing immaterialism, except in so far as immaterialism is defined as the position which breaks the offending dualism. Second, to the extent that we are prepared to embrace idealism in this context, we must show how it is that the relevant idealist option succeeds in breaking this dualism. It will be a condition of making good this aim that we clarify the various meanings of the term 'idea', leaving open the possibility that the relation between mind and idea may be distinct from that which exists between substance and quality.

In the following chapters I shall be looking at the way in which philosophers subsequent to Locke and Berkeley have taken up the challenge bequeathed to them by their predecessors. In particular, we shall see how it is that the tensions I have described seem compelled to re-emerge in their arguments, dogging their attempts to complete the 'idealist' task set in motion by Berkeley. It will be left to Hegel to expand upon the diagnosis towards which I have gestured in this final section, and to pave the way towards a solution which promises to provide a genuine corrective to the view that, in perceiving things, we are 'confin'd barely to our own ideas'.

2 Concepts and reality

Nietzsche

Some introductory remarks

I have been concerned to identify a syndrome which involves the separation of two concepts that belong together. This syndrome plagues the empiricists' dispute about substance, and it finds expression in the distinction they impose between the substance itself and the groupings of qualities which are said to constitute the things we perceive. I want to argue now that a structurally similar framework is to be found in Nietzsche's early conception of the relation between concepts and reality, my focus being his 1873 essay 'On Truth and Lies in a Nonmoral Sense'.

Nietzsche's arguments, like those of Berkeley, are premised upon two insights. The first insight is that our capacity for knowledge and truth is bound up essentially with the perspective by means of which the world is rendered accessible to us. The second is that this capacity is undermined if the world in question turns out to be a world of mere appearance. Berkeley's way of giving expression to these insights is to insist that we stay within the realm which is revealed in our ideas, and to warn of the sceptical and unnecessary difficulties we face if tempted to call into question the objective status of this realm. Nietzsche does not express himself in these Berkeleyan terms, talking instead of the importance of perspective, and of the difficulties which arise if we try to transcend the perspective in terms of which reality is rendered accessible to us. Elsewhere, and in deference to his philosophical influence, he makes use of a distinctly Kantian terminology.[1] Thus, the claims about perspective are articulated by reference to the *concepts* in terms of which we view reality, and scathing reference is made to Kant's notion of the thing in itself.

Nietzsche accepts without reservation that the thing in itself belongs to an epistemologically inaccessible realm. In this respect, his understanding of it corresponds to the conception of material substance which serves as the target of Berkeley's arguments. Thus, in a manner reminiscent of his predecessor, we find him complaining that this notion is 'inaccessible and undefinable for us' and 'incomprehensible'.[2] Berkeley, it will be remembered, claims that we shall accept the metaphysical picture under attack only at the cost of being unable to defend the possibility of knowledge and truth with respect to things. Nietzsche both accepts and develops this connection between metaphysics, knowledge, and truth, one consequence being that his criticisms of the thing in itself are transformed into criticisms of the conception of truth which, he believes, is its necessary by-product. According to this conception, truth is an unattainable ideal, something which must remain ever elusive to our thoughts.

Notwithstanding Nietzsche's criticisms of the offending conceptions of reality and truth – criticisms which imply that they should be rejected – his attitude to them remains ambivalent. Thus, his remarks sometimes seem to endorse the offending conception of reality, implying that there are some ultimate facts concerning reality in itself which are, however, inaccessible to us. It is in this connection that we find Nietzsche describing our concepts as distorting instruments and bewailing our inability to attain what he refers to as 'pure' truth. I shall argue that Nietzsche's commitment to 'pure' truth and the conception of reality it implies is indicative of the syndrome, and that it precludes him from defining a genuine alternative to the sceptical position he is so anxious to avoid. The charge is familiar from Chapter 1.

Perspectivism

The idea that our relation to the world is perspective-bound does not undermine our capacity for knowledge and truth. Given the tension to which I have alluded, however, it is understandable that Nietzsche's remarks in this context contain evidence also of a more radical theme – a theme which lends emphasis, rather, to our epistemological limitations, greeting with scepticism the possibility of our attaining knowledge and truth.

Take, for example, the claim: '(a)s if a world would remain after one deducted the perspective'.[3] According to one interpretation, Nietzsche is making the reasonable point that what there is to be found in reality depends for its discovery on the perspective which renders it accessible. Thus understood, the idea – somewhat unremarkable – is that the possibility of making discoveries about the world disappears if we remove the perspective by means of which those discoveries are made.[4] There is no implication, however, that the possibility of there *being* a world depends upon the existence of creatures who possess a perspective, nor that our access to it is in any sense indirect.

On a second interpretation, 'perspective' is to be taken from the point of view of that towards which it is directed as opposed to that which is doing the directing. Thus understood, the remark '(a)s if a world would remain after one deducted the perspective' gives expression to the difficulty confronted if one tries to reveal the world by removing the realm which is revealed through our perspective.[5] The point being made by Nietzsche, on this interpretation, can be related to an analogous point made by Berkeley when he describes the difficulties which arise if we try to reveal substance by abstracting from the things we perceive, the implication being that there is something contradictory to the idea that reality is something beyond anything upon which we could have a perspective. This second interpretation is going to be important in what follows. For the moment though, it suffices to note that there is no obvious sense in which the existence of the world is undermined hereby, nor does it follow that our relation to the world is indirect. Thus, to the extent that one might be tempted to conclude in this context that there is nothing but perspective, it would be necessary to emphasize that the use of the expression 'nothing but' here is both misplaced and misleading.

There are two more interpretations of Nietzsche's claim which carry more radical implications. According to a third interpretation, 'perspective' is understood from the point of view of that which has the perspective, and the claim is not simply that a perspective in this sense is required if one is to make discoveries about reality, but that it is required if reality is to *exist*. On this way of thinking, Nietzsche is claiming that there is nothing but perspective, and in doing so is advancing a version of Berkeley's claim that 'to be is to be perceived'. Finally, 'perspective' is to be understood again from the point of view of that to which the perspective provides access. The difference, however, is that it is not excluded that there is a further world lying beyond that which is revealed in our perspectives – a world, however, which remains epistemologically inaccessible to us. Thus when Nietzsche remarks '(a)s if a world would remain after one deducted the perspective', we are to understand him as claiming that, from our point of view, there is no world other than that which is revealed in the perspective we have upon reality. It is not ruled out, however, that there is some further world whose existence serves to undermine the knowledge claims we make about the realm to which we are confined.[6] In one obvious sense, this interpretation involves a rejection of the claim that there is nothing but perspective. In another sense, however, such a claim could have a point, namely, when used to lend emphasis to our epistemological limitations, in which case, the idea is that there is nothing but perspective *for us*.

There is evidence for all four of these interpretations in Nietzsche's essay. The following passage is typically ambiguous:

> It is even a difficult thing for him to admit that the insect or bird perceives an entirely different world from the one that man does, and that the question of which of these perceptions of the world is the more correct one is quite meaningless. For this would have to be decided previously in accordance with the criterion of the correct perception which means, in accordance with a criterion which is not available. But in any case, it seems to me that 'the correct perception' which would mean 'the adequate expression of an object in a subject' is a contradictory impossibility. For between two absolutely different spheres, as between subject and object, there is no causality, no correctness, and no expression; there is at most an aesthetic relation, I mean, a suggestive transference, a stammering translation into a completely foreign tongue – for which there is required, in any case, a freely inventive intermediate sphere and mediating force.[7]

The claim that subject and object are two absolutely different spheres is compatible with the idea that subjects can perceive or think about a mind-independent reality. Thus understood, the claim is intended simply to guarantee that there is an ontological difference between the subject who is engaged in the relevant mental act and the object towards which the act is directed, and it gives expression therefore to the previously noted idea that the possibility of making discoveries about reality requires that there be a discoverer on the scene.

However, there are two reasons for being sceptical about this interpretation. First, if this is all that Nietzsche was wanting to say, his claim would be true, albeit unremarkably so. Second, and more importantly, it is an interpretation which fits rather awkwardly with some of the other things he says in this extract – things which suggest that he is not simply concerned with distinguishing between a perceiving or thinking subject and the object perceived or thought about. Of particular relevance are his claims that an adequate expression of an object in a subject is a contradictory impossibility, that the relation between subject and object involves a stammering translation into a completely foreign tongue, and that between these two spheres there is no causality and no correctness. For these claims seem expressive, rather, of a concern with the distinction between the object as perceived or thought about and the object as it is in itself.

Nietzsche's insistence that there is no causality or correctness between subject and object and that an adequate expression of an object in a subject is a contradictory possibility is reminiscent of a similar theme which finds expression in Berkeley when he is challenging the materialist position, and it suggests likewise that objects are in principle inaccessible to subjects. It seems to imply also that the difficulty in question is a quite general one which applies to any mode of access to objects as opposed to being confined to a particular way of gaining access to them. And this is so whether we are talking about the modes of access of, say, humans as opposed to birds, or of the differing modes of access of a particular kind of creature – sensing as opposed to thinking in human beings, for example. By contrast, his talk of the relation between subject and object involving a stammering translation need not imply that we are concerned with an insurmountable distinction. Rather, the idea is that our relation to objects is indirect. If this is so, then it cannot be excluded that the stammering in question is less pronounced with respect to certain modes of access.

Nietzsche uses the idea that an adequate expression of an object in a subject is a contradictory impossibility to justify his claim that there is no criterion by means of which to measure our way of perceiving things against that of birds or insects. His way of giving expression to the relevant variations of perception is to say that birds and insects perceive 'an entirely different world' from the world we humans perceive. The claim that birds and insects perceive an entirely different world from the world we humans perceive, *can* be interpreted so as to be compatible with the ideas that these creatures share a common environment, and that the things it involves are epistemologically accessible to varying degrees. For example, it might be thought that Nietzsche is referring to the variations in perception which occur at the level of how things are perceived, when we are concerned, for example, with the perception of the secondary qualities of objects. However, this interpretation sits rather awkwardly with some of the other things he says, in particular, his claim that there can be no causality or correctness between subject and object. I have noted that our interpretation of this claim depends upon whether we give any weight to Nietzsche's talk of 'stammering translations' so as to allow that something of the object is accessible to the subject. If we do not make this concession, then it seems to follow not merely that our relation to things is indirect, but that it is inappropriate to suppose that any such relation exists. What is less clear is how this latter consequence is intended to square with Nietzsche's talk of the differing worlds of birds, insects, and humans.

Presumably we are to suppose that none of these worlds is properly described as a world of mind-independent things, for the reason that such things are said to elude them. How though are we to characterize their contents? Some of the things Nietzsche says suggest that he would be prepared to accept that the contents of these different worlds are determined by the creatures whose perspective is said to reveal these contents. He talks, for example, of a 'freely inventive intermediate sphere and mediating sphere' existing between subject and object – a mode of expression which, we shall see, involves reference to the activity of conceptualization. Indeed, it implies a reference to an invention of the kind which can be read into Kant's position and is reminiscent also of a related claim which finds occasional expression in the positions of Locke and Berkeley. If this *is* what Nietzsche is getting at, then provided that we accept that humans are inventive in a way that birds and insects are not, then we can begin to give a sense to the claim that their respective worlds are different.

Now if it is denied that there is anything beyond these worlds, and if it is claimed also that they are incommensurable with respect to one another, then we are forced to inquire after their origin. The focus upon invention and world-making suggests that their origin is to be traced back to the owner of the perspective upon them – that to be is to be perceived – in which case we are back with the third rather problematic interpretation of Nietzsche's perspectivism. By contrast, if one wishes to deny that our powers of invention can be stretched to accommodate the very existence of things, then one way of making good this denial is to allow that something comes to us from without. It is this something which the relevant worlds can be said to have in common.

The idea that something comes to us from without, something common to the different worlds of different creatures, returns us to a similar claim which finds expression in Locke and Berkeley. Furthermore, it is an idea which makes some sense of Nietzsche's talk of stammering translations, and which suggests also that it is quite wrong to suppose that the different worlds to which he refers are entirely incommensurable. How though are we to comprehend the relation between subject and object on the assumption that this stammering translation is operative? Locke, as I have said, uses the notion of material substance as a way of accounting for the sense in which things come to us from without – material substance being that to which the qualities we perceive belong. Furthermore, although he grants that we have no way of understanding how material things can causally affect us, much of what he says implies that this problem is not sufficient to undermine the belief that we are capable of engaging in thought with mind-independent things. Berkeley, by contrast, takes more seriously Locke's sceptical worries and prefers to ground these sensible properties in the mind of God. It remained unclear what God's role is intended to be in determining the nature of the things we perceive; evidence suggests, however, that, for Berkeley, these things are really just groupings of sensible qualities. The further important claim is that there is more to cognition than the passive reception of these qualities – hence the distinction between ideas and notions. We shall see that Nietzsche's way of thinking about this problem has its origins in the framework which is bequeathed to him by Berkeley, but is related more obviously to the modification and development it undergoes at the hands of Kant.

Nietzsche on truth and metaphor

Thus far, I have been trying to clarify the nature of Nietzsche's perspectivism. It has been possible to extract various insights from his remarks – some of which are comparable to those which were motivating Berkeley in his Lockean onslaught. Nevertheless, there is evidence also of a more extreme position, a position which excludes the possibility of our attaining truth and knowledge with respect to things. In this respect, Nietzsche is in danger of re-introducing the 'universal scepticism' it was Berkeley's purpose to avoid. It remains unclear whether he would be prepared to allow that we have some kind of grasp upon reality, and if so, how we are to comprehend the nature of this grasp.

We can begin to get an idea of how Nietzsche seeks to address these problems by examining his remarks on truth. He poses the following question:

> What then is truth? A moveable host of metaphors, metonymies, and anthropomorphisms: in short, a sum of human relations which have been poetically and rhetorically intensified, transferred, and embellished, and which, after long usage, seem to a people to be fixed, canonical, and binding. Truths are illusions which we have forgotten are illusions; they are metaphors that have become worn out and have been drained of sensuous force, coins which have lost their embossing and are now considered as metal and no longer as coins.[8]

Nietzsche's claims here are not easy to comprehend. Let me begin though by clarifying his use of the term 'metaphor' as it occurs elsewhere in the text, and in particular, the way in which he seeks to exploit this usage in the context of defining his own preferred metaphysical stance. We have seen already that Nietzsche wishes to question the idea that there could be an adequate expression of an object in a subject, where this is intended to rule out the possibility of there being knowledge of things in themselves. The remarks he makes about metaphor can be understood initially with this epistemological theme in mind, for we are told that perception gives us only metaphors of things rather than the things themselves:[9]

> To begin with, a nerve stimulus is transferred into an image: first metaphor. The image, in turn, is imitated in a sound: second metaphor. And each time

there is a complete overlapping of one sphere, right into the middle of an entirely new and different one. One can imagine a man who is totally deaf and has never had a sensation of sound and music. Perhaps such a person will gaze with astonishment at Chladni's sound figures: perhaps he will discover their causes in the vibrations of the strings and will now swear that he must know what men mean by 'sound'. It is this way with all of us concerning language: we believe we know something about the things themselves when we speak of trees, colours, snow and flowers, and yet we possess nothing but metaphors which correspond in no way to the original entities. In the same way as the sound appears as a sound figure, so the mysterious X of the thing in itself first appears as a nerve stimulus, then as an image, and finally as a sound.[10]

Nietszsche's claim that we possess nothing but metaphors for things is difficult to accept. For there seems to be a clear distinction between the employment of figurative and literal language, and although it makes sense to suppose that we can speak metaphorically about trees, colours, snow and so forth, it seems absurd to suppose that we cannot speak literally about them. It is an implication of his remarks here, however, that this is precisely what we must conclude – that, as he puts it, we possess nothing but metaphors for things.

We can begin to see what he is getting at by considering the meaning of the term 'metaphor'. The Greek word 'μεταφερείν' means to carry across, to move from one sphere to another (the German word is 'übertragen'). Now given what I have said already on Nietzsche's behalf, it seems plausible to suppose that he is trading upon the etymology of the term 'metaphor', and using it to characterize the relation between subject and object. That is to say, he is suggesting – somewhat metaphorically it must be said – that this relation involves the kind of creative transfer of meaning we associate with metaphor, the result being that the things we perceive bear little or no relation to the true nature of reality.

If this *is* what Nietzsche is wishing to claim, then it looks as if it is our *relation* to things which is metaphorical. It is metaphorical by virtue of involving a series of 'transfers' which, we are to suppose, distort and perhaps even eradicate the things to which we are supposedly related hereby. By contrast, it is an implication of Nietzsche's remarks above that it is the *claims* we make about things which are metaphorical, and on the face of it, the metaphysical considerations which have been rehearsed so far are insufficient to lend justice to this further conclusion. For even if we accept that our relation to things is indirect in the sense just described, it does not follow that our ways of talking about these things are metaphorical. On the contrary, it is more plausible and less fanciful to say that these ways of talking are merely false or meaningless.

The suggestion that our relation to things is metaphorical ties in with a further idea which is central to Nietzsche's overall picture, namely, that the subject is an artistic creator.[11] This idea relates back to his talk of there being an 'aesthetic relation' between subject and object – a relation which is held to involve a 'freely inventive intermediate sphere and mediating force'. Furthermore, it is an idea which can be read back into the suggestion – implicit in some of the things said by Locke and Berkeley – that it is *we* who construct the idea of a thing to which the qualities we perceive belong. Putting these claims together then, we arrive at the following picture. First, the 'transfers' which characterize the progression from object to subject involve the activity of the subject. Second, this activity can be compared to that which is operative when an artist uses materials to make a work of art, the difference being that, in the present context, it is a distortive activity. Third, the subject can be said to be making metaphors when engaging in such an activity. We are to assume no doubt that this activity is manifested both when the subject conceptualizes things and when he talks about the things he conceptualizes.

The idea that subjects do something to objects gives expression to Nietzsche's commitment to an aspect of Kant's metaphysical framework. According to this framework, what subjects do to objects is to conceptualize them, and conceptualization involves the imposition of form or structure on the matter of experience. Thus understood, conceptualization involves the *alteration* and *construction* of the matter of experience.[12] This matter serves to compromise the subject's powers of conceptual invention, and it is held to be ontologically dependent upon something that is independent of mind. For Kant this something is the realm of things in themselves.

It remains unclear whether Nietzsche is prepared to allow that something comes to us from without – something which serves as the object of the stammering translations to which he refers. In order to clarify this issue then, we need to look more closely at his conception of the relation between concepts and reality. He describes our concepts as displaying:

> (t)he rigid regularity of a Roman columbarium, an infinitely complicated dome of concepts upon an unstable foundation, and, as it were, on running water.[13]

And remarks also that:

> As a 'rational' being, he (the seeker after truth) now places his behaviour under the control of abstractions. He will no longer tolerate being carried away by sudden impressions, by intuitions. First, he universalizes all these impressions into less colourful, cooler concepts, so that he can entrust the guidance of his life and conduct to them. Everything which distinguishes man from the animals depends upon this ability to volatilize perceptual metaphors in a schema, and thus to dissolve an image into a concept.[14]

Nietzsche's talk of placing one's behaviour under the control of abstractions is distinctly pejorative in tone. Furthermore, given the contrast he makes between abstractions and impressions/intuitions, it is plausible to suppose that the abstractions in question are the 'less colourful' concepts to which he refers, concepts which, we are told, display the rigid regularity of a Roman columbarium. How though are we to understand the nature of the distinction with which he is operating here – that between concepts and intuitions/impressions? The term 'intuition' comes from Kant, and is used by him in the context of distinguishing between concepts and the matter of experience. In particular, we are told that it is the faculty of intuition that delivers this matter – it is that by virtue of which something comes to us from without.

Certainly, Nietzsche's claims here are suggestive of a commitment to the existence of this experiential component, and transgress those of his remarks which imply that our powers of conceptual invention are unconstrained in this respect. What is less clear, however, is how he conceives of the relation between intuitions – considered as that which is given to us in experience – and things in themselves. The doubts Nietzsche has expressed about whether there can be an adequate expression of an object in a subject suggest that he would be unwilling to allow that these intuitions provide for a more faithful representation of reality. Yet there is a distinct lack of pejorative tone in his discussion of intuitions. The implication then is that there is a mode of access to objects – a sensory mode of access – which is free of the distortions that frustrate our attempts to gain knowledge of things by conceptualization.

Nietzsche also describes intuitions as 'perceptual metaphors' – a description which suggests a quite different use of the term 'metaphor' than that which has been used to characterize the distortive nature of the subject/object relation. The following extract employs this terminology, and provides further insight into Nietzsche's conception of the relation between intuitions and concepts:

> Whereas each perceptual metaphor is individual and without equals and is therefore able to elude all classification, the great edifice of concepts displays the rigid regularity of a Roman columbarium and exhales in logic that strength and coolness which is characteristic of mathematics.[15]

The claim that each perceptual metaphor is 'individual and without equals' and able to 'elude all classification' can be related to another theme which is to be found in Nietzsche's essay, namely, that conceptualization involves the equation of dissimilar things. As he puts it:

> A word becomes a concept insofar as it simultaneously has to fit countless more or less similar cases – which means, purely and simply, cases which are never the same and thus altogether dissimilar.[16]

This theme is going to provide Nietzsche with a further justification for making reference to the notion of metaphor in this metaphysical context. For there is a sense in which metaphor, too, can be said to involve the equation of dissimilar things, when, for example, it involves the identification of the hitherto unseen similarities which exist between disparate objects. So, for example, the claim that men are wolves suggests that men resemble wolves in a certain respect. How though are we to comprehend what it means to say that conceptualization is metaphorical in this sense? In what sense does it involve the equation of dissimilar things?

According to the most obvious interpretation, the idea is that, in conceptualizing two things as, say, men, I am grouping together two things which, in reality, are different. But what does *this* mean? Is Nietzsche making the trivial point that the two men I conceptualize are numerically distinct? Or is he claiming, rather, that they have an individuality which eludes the level of concepts – that concepts, being general, fail to capture particularity? It is no implication of the first interpretation that there is something that our concepts fail to capture. By contrast, the second interpretation carries this implication quite explicitly. Given what has been said already on Nietzsche's behalf it seems undeniable that it is the second interpretation which captures Nietzsche's intent.[17]

Some tensions

My arguments so far have focused upon Nietzsche's worries about the possibility of gaining knowledge of things in themselves. I have said little, however, about his complaint elsewhere in the text that the postulation of an unknowable realm of things is quite without meaning – a complaint which echoes analogous remarks made by Berkeley in his attack upon the idea of material substance. We have seen that there are traces of this second theme to be found in the remarks Nietzsche makes about perspective. For at times, and in a manner reminiscent of his empiricist predecessor, he expresses scepticism about the question of whether there is anything beyond the perspective we have upon reality. This scepticism, I have suggested, can be variously interpreted. According to one reading it is intended to undermine the idea that there is anything towards which our perspectives are directed, suggesting a version of Berkeley's claim that to be is to be perceived. Understood in less radical terms, by contrast, it casts doubt upon the idea that there is anything beyond the realm which is revealed in the perspective we have upon reality – a realm of things in themselves, for example. On this second interpretation there need be no implication that the existence of a mind-independent reality is called into question, nor that our capacity for knowledge and truth is compromised.

The following extract, in which Nietzsche launches an attack upon the notion of the thing in itself, might be thought to lend support to this second interpretation. Yet it contains evidence also of a more insidious theme – one which casts doubt upon our aspirations to knowledge and truth:

> The 'thing in itself' (which is precisely what the pure truth, apart from consequences would be) is also something quite incomprehensible to the creator of language and something not in the least worth striving for. He only designates the relations of things to men, and expresses them with the boldest metaphors.[18]

The point of the identification Nietzsche makes between the thing in itself and pure truth is not immediately obvious, but the implication is that pure truth is what we would have if we could gain access to the thing in itself. Assuming then that the thing in itself is inaccessible to language, it follows that truth in this sense cannot be a property of our claims. The further suggestion, however, is that pure truth is as incomprehensible as the notion of reality it implies, and that it is not in the least worth striving for. Pursuing this latter line of thought then, it would be natural to conclude that it is no limitation of language that it fails to provide access to truth in this sense.

By contrast, Nietzsche's remark that language is concerned only with the relations of things to men, and that it involves the making of metaphors, suggests a rather serious limitation. To be sure, Nietzsche hints that it is unimportant that this limitation exists, doing so on the ground that the thing in itself is not in the least worth striving for. Notwithstanding this disclaimer, however, it is an implication of his remarks elsewhere that the thing in itself does nonetheless exist. It exists as something which remains ever elusive to thought and language and which serves to undermine the objective status of the claims we make about things.

If we accept on Nietzsche's behalf that it is a limitation of language that it fails to make contact with the thing in itself, then how are we to reconcile this claim with the accusation that the thing in itself is an incomprehensible notion? On the face of it, there is something of a difficulty involved if we accept both that the thing in itself exists as something which is inaccessible to thought and language and that it is an incomprehensible notion. At least, this is so on the assumption that it is incomprehensible by virtue of being elusive to thought and language. For one is committed to claiming both that the thing in itself is inaccessible to thought and language and that it is incomprehensible that it should be conceived of in this manner.

One way out would be to deny that the thing in itself – conceived of as something which remains ever elusive to thought and language – exists. One could do so on grounds which are similar to those employed by Berkeley when he attacks the idea of material substance, by arguing, for example, that there is no way of comprehending how such a thing could affect us, and no way of providing a coherent description thereof. Certainly, there is evidence that Nietzsche would be sympathetic to this Berkeleyan line of thought. For as I have said, he claims that there is no causality between subject and object, and that the very idea of a thing in itself is incomprehensible to the user of language. Arguing along these lines then, it would be possible for him to accept the identification between pure truth and the thing in itself whilst denying that it has any epistemological consequences for the status of the claims we make about things – in particular, their aspiration towards truth.

However, Nietzsche accepts quite explicitly that although the thing in itself and the pure truth with which it is to be identified are inaccessible and incomprehensible, their existence does serve to undermine the possibility of our being able to think and talk truly about things. Hence his insistence that truths are illusions. The claim that truths are illusions is given further substance with the introduction of an alternative conception of truth – 'anthropomorphic' truth – which is intended to be that by means of which we measure our beliefs 'concerning the relations of things to man'. We are to assume no doubt that this alternative conception of truth *is* worth striving for, for the reason that it is accessible to thought and language, and can therefore be a property of our thoughts and claims. Nietzsche complains, however, that anthropomorphic truth contains 'not a single point that would be true in itself or universally valid apart from human beings'. It fails to do so because it cannot accommodate the idea that a true thought corresponds to the way things really are, confined as it is to matters pertaining to our needs and interests. For this reason it lacks the worldly constraint which, for Nietzsche, is a prerequisite for a satisfactory conception of truth. Hence, it turns out to be as worthless and illusory as the paradigm of pure truth for which it was intended to be a sober substitute.

I shall be providing a more detailed examination of the concept of truth in Chapter 5, linking my discussion to the difficulties and insights which are motivating Nietzsche's argument. At this stage, we can note that it is an insight of his position that an adequate conception of truth must incorporate a worldly constraint so as to allow that our true thoughts and claims are constrained by the way things are. Nietzsche, however, rules out the possibility that the required worldly constraint could be defined by reference to a conception of reality which is other than the one he seeks to challenge on grounds of unintelligibility – a conception, for example, which allows that reality is accessible to thought and language. Arguing along these alternative lines, he would be in a position to accommodate the idea that a true thought is constrained by the way things are, and hence, can be true in the manner his argument demands. In support of this option, we can note that Nietzsche has given us no good reason for rejecting its possibility, and, given his criticisms of 'pure truth' and the conception of reality it implies, every reason for treating it as a viable alternative.

Why is Nietzsche unable to take this escape route? The difficulty, it seems, is the haunting spectre of the thing in itself, which, despite being inaccessible and incomprehensible, is that which enforces the philosophical judgement that our thoughts cannot be true. Thus, Nietzsche is telling us that concepts cannot capture reality in itself, and he is concluding from this observation that they cannot capture reality in any sense. The assumption here is that reality has to lie beyond the realm which is revealed in our concepts – an assumption which finds most explicit expression in what he says about the distortive nature of concepts, but which can be read also into some of the remarks he makes about perspective. As noted, however, there is equal evidence in his arguments to suggest that he is seeking to undermine this conception of reality, hence the accusation that it is inaccessible and incomprehensible, and that the kind of truth it brings with it is not in the least worth striving for.

Nietzsche and the syndrome

I want to argue now that there are significant comparisons to be made between the tensions exhibited by Nietzsche's position and those which find expression in the arguments of Locke and Berkeley, and that he is likewise in the grip of the syndrome. Nietzsche is concerned to comprehend the relation which exists between subject and object – a concern which, given a few Kantian assumptions, becomes the question of how we are to conceive of that which exists between concepts and things in themselves. We can compare this starting point to the empiricist's quest for an understanding of the relation between the things we perceive and substance. Nietzsche then conceives of things in themselves in such a way that they are set apart from our concepts, where this implies that they are distinct from anything to which we could gain access using conceptual resources. In this way, an insurmountable distinction is imposed between things in themselves and the realm revealed in our concepts – a distinction comparable to that which the empiricist imposes between substance itself and the qualities/ideas which are said to constitute the things we perceive.

Once this framework is in place, it follows that in order to gain access to things in themselves we must remove our concepts, where this task is equivalent to that of removing the realm of things they reveal. The difficulty, however, is that the removal of concepts in this sense, rather than giving way to the revelation of things in themselves, seems to reveal precisely nothing. In this respect, Nietzsche confronts a similar problem to that which prevents the empiricist from laying bare substance by removing the things we perceive. It is understandable therefore that he draws a sceptical conclusion which is comparable to Berkeley's attack on material substance, namely, that things in themselves are inaccessible, indefinable, and incomprehensible.

Having drawn this sceptical conclusion, Nietzsche proceeds to argue that no thought or statement can correspond to the way things really are, and cannot therefore be true. His justification for saying this is that the things to which they would have to correspond in order to be true are inaccessible to thought and language. It follows that truth cannot be a property of our thoughts and claims. He then falls back on what *is* so accessible, namely, the realm which is revealed in our concepts, and concludes that we are wrong to suppose that this realm is revelatory of things in themselves. It is with this point in mind that we can best appreciate his remarks about the distortive nature of concepts, and the complaint that they have an unstable foundation – that they rest on running water. The obvious point of comparison here is the empiricist's claim that the idea of a thing is a constructed idea – something that we impose upon the qualities we perceive so as to make sense of their unification. The upshot of Nietzsche's argument is that the pretension of thought and language to represent reality is unsustainable – or, to use his more gripping terminology, that truths are illusions.

Nietzsche then defines an alternative conception of truth – anthropomorphic truth – which is intended to be an acceptable substitute for the pure truth to which we are unable to aspire. It is acceptable in the sense that it does not involve reference to the conception of reality which has been challenged by the previous line of argument, namely, the conception according to which reality is that which no concept can capture. It turns out, however, that this alternative notion of truth cannot accommodate the sense in which a true thought is constrained by the way things really are. As Nietzsche puts it, it contains 'not a single point that would be true in itself or universally valid apart from human beings'. Accordingly, it is not truth properly so-called. The result, of course, is that the 'pure' conception for which anthropomorphic truth was intended to be a sober substitute appears to be more significant than the previous sceptical arguments would suggest, as does the 'non-conceptual' reality in terms of which it is defined. The tension in Nietzsche's account here is comparable to that which leads Locke to suppose that the 'ill-grounded' notion of substance is, after all, of chief importance.

Given what I have said already on Nietzsche's behalf, it looks as if the problematic step in his argument occurs when he imposes an insurmountable distinction between things in themselves and the realm revealed in our concepts. It is this distinction which forces him to conclude that things in themselves lie beyond the conceptual realm, and that what is revealed in this realm lacks any objective significance. Hence the claims that concepts are distortive instruments, and that we are incapable of thinking truly about things. At this point, we can identify several reasons for being sceptical about the position at which Nietzsche has arrived – reasons which echo those identified in the positions of Locke and Berkeley. The first reason – to which I have alluded already – is that Nietzsche's position is motivated in part by a wish to expose as spurious the belief that we are capable of thinking truly about things. The assumption here is that things in themselves have to elude the realm which is revealed in our concepts. Elsewhere in his argument, however, he seeks to call into question this conception of a thing, doing so on the ground that it is unintelligible.

A second difficulty arises when we press the question of how Nietzsche conceives of the relation between the things revealed in our concepts and things in themselves. His claim that there is no causality and no expression between these terms suggests that they constitute two ontologically distinct realms. Assuming that this is so, however, we face several alternatives, none of which lends credence to the dualistic framework at issue. According to the first alternative, things as conceptualized are ontologically self-sufficient but they are to be set alongside a further realm of things in themselves. Such a position, which calls to mind Berkeley's conception of the relation between material substance and the things we perceive, forces the question of whether there is any point in postulating a further realm of things in themselves – a question which becomes more pressing when set alongside Nietzsche's criticisms of such a framework. One possibility is that the thing in itself is really just a placeholder for God. The position then is that God is to be dualistically opposed to anything of which we could have determinate experience or thought. Arguing along these lines, one could mount a case for supposing that the pure truth with which Nietzsche is concerned is the truth which is operative when we attain a God's eye view upon reality, and his criticisms of such a conception could be interpreted as an attack upon the very idea of there being such a viewpoint. Such a position, if defensible, would offer the resources for concluding that reference to God constitutes, at best, an irrelevant extra to the world of things, and hence that the thing in itself is of no great importance to an understanding of the things we conceptualize. Crucially, however, there would be no justification for supposing that truth is an unattainable ideal. All that would follow is that it is unattainable only if understood in theological terms, the further implication being that these terms are unwarranted. I shall return to this theme in my discussion of Kant and Hegel.

According to a second alternative, things as conceptualized are held to be ontologically dependent upon things in themselves. This option allows one to concede the significance of the role played by things in themselves, and a version of it can be read into Locke's insistence that the idea of material substance is an inextricable component in our ideas of things and Berkeley's claim that the things we perceive are sustained in existence by God. However, when combined with the complaint that things in themselves are in principle inaccessible, it is difficult to see how this dependency claim can be made good. Indeed, it looks as if we shall be left with a realm of groundless appearances and a return of the problem which faces the empiricist when he claims that things are just groupings of sensible qualities.

As a final court of appeal, we might return to Nietzsche's talk of stammering translations so as to allow that there is some kind of relation between things in themselves and things as conceptualized, albeit one which involves a distortion of things in themselves. The dualistic version of this claim confronts the difficulties I have already rehearsed, implying as it does that the things we perceive are to be ontologically grounded in a further realm whose intelligibility and existence is in question. By contrast, if we resist this dualistic framework so as to allow that things in themselves are accessible to us, then talk of stammering translations becomes either a concession to our fallibility or a preparedness to acknowledge that some of the qualities we take objects to possess have a nature which is determined by our particular mode of access to them – a sensory mode of access, for example.[19]

There is a third difficulty arising from Nietzsche's unwillingness to reject the offending conception of reality, namely, that once it is assumed that things in themselves are inaccessible to thought, then the problem arises of how to account for the allegedly mistaken belief that we are capable of thinking truly about things. Nietzsche gives expression to this mistake by claiming that truths are illusions we have forgotten are illusions, that they are metaphors which have been drained of sensuous force. Presumably he would have to say that it is the erroneous workings of mind which lead us to suppose that our concepts reveal things in themselves, and hence, that we can think truly about things. Again, however, we have to press the question of how best to comprehend the metaphysics behind this picture. The idea that things in themselves are ontologically distinct from the things we conceptualize, when taken in conjunction with Nietzsche's criticisms of this framework, leads us back to the conclusion that the things we perceive are ontologically self-sufficient, in which case there is no scope for insisting that they are to be set apart from things in themselves, and no scope for concluding that it is an error to suppose that our concepts reveal things in themselves. By contrast, if we insist that things in themselves *are* to be set apart from the things we conceptualize, then we can grant that it is an error to suppose that we can conceptualize them. At this point, however, it would be necessary to explain why we should accept this dualistic framework, and if we do accept it, how we could even begin to trade upon the workings of the mind in an account of how we arrive at the belief that we are capable of thinking truly about things.

I conclude that Nietzsche is imposing conditions upon the concept of a thing which it cannot meet, and using its failure to meet those conditions in order to conclude that our concepts are distorting instruments, and hence that our thoughts cannot be true. What he should be doing, rather, is renouncing the conception of a thing which is implied by the framework he seems unable to reject, namely, that according to which things in themselves are to be located beyond the realm revealed in our concepts. However, a rejection of this faulty conception of a thing does not bring with it a rejection of things in themselves *per se*. As I have suggested, the supposition that this conclusion is inevitable – that an 'anthropomorphic' alternative constitutes the only available conceptual space in this context – is simply a further expression of the framework which gives rise to this problematic conception of a thing in the first place, the framework expressive of the syndrome.

It is Nietzsche's inability to shake off the syndrome which explains why it is so difficult at times to work out his philosophical commitments. According to my diagnosis, his position contains these ambiguities because the framework to which he continues to adhere serves to vindicate the object of his attack. It follows therefore that he is led to make claims which are expressive of the position he is seeking to undermine elsewhere, whilst the position he should really be defending remains elusive to him. The obvious example here is his claim that it is a limitation of language and thought that it fails to make contact with things in themselves, and his insistence elsewhere that a non-conceptual order of things in themselves is unintelligible.

The alternative, if Nietzsche is to effect a genuine rejection of the offending metaphysical framework, is to replace it with one which can make sense of our capacity to conceptualize things, where there is no implication that there exists some further realm of things in themselves which undermines the objective status of our thoughts. The upshot is that it will no longer be necessary to hanker after a conception of reality which belies one's intuitive and philosophical convictions, and to do so after having despaired of its reductive counterpart on the ground that it is equally problematic. At this point, the possibility emerges that one's understanding of the concept of truth can undergo an analogous modification. I shall return in Chapter 5 to the question of how this modification might proceed.

Concepts and reality: some distinctions and options

Let me now use the conclusions I have reached to clarify how the term 'concept' has been used here, and to give a hint of the direction my argument will take in subsequent chapters. Perhaps the most obvious way of addressing the question of how we are to understand the term 'concept' is by introducing a Fregean framework. Working within such a framework, we are given two options by means of which to address this question. According to the first option – which involves a more technical use of the term 'concept' – concepts are the references of predicates, and as such, refer to the qualities of things, qualities which are independent of mind. According to the second option, they are at the level of Fregean senses, where this implies that they are to be treated as modes of presentation or conceptions. That is to say, they are that in virtue of which the world is presented to us in a particular way when we form a conception of some aspect of it, there being no implication that the world thus presented is confined to concepts in the first sense. Thus, I have the concept of a cat if I have a conception of what it is to be a cat, and I have a conception of what it is to be a cat if I am capable of entertaining thoughts about cats. Concepts in the second sense then are to be understood by reference to the mind, for they involve the capacity we have, situated in the world as we are, to exercise conceptions of things.

Presumably, Nietzsche would be happy to allow that concepts are conceptions given that he is concerned with our capacity to conceptualize things. Where though does he stand with respect to the idea that concepts are that in virtue of which the world is presented to us in a particular way when we form a conception of some aspect of it? The question is difficult to answer because Nietzsche seems to be working with various conceptions of the relation between concepts and reality. Much of what he says implies that there is an insurmountable gap between these two terms, for example, his claim that there is no causality and no expression between subject and object. Furthermore, he suggests at times that conceptualization involves the equation of dissimilar things – a suggestion which implies that the relation between concepts and reality maps onto that which exists between general and particular. Pursuing this line of thought, it would seem more appropriate to treat concepts as the references of predicates, in which case we have arrived at a position which manages to combine both aspects of the Fregean way of thinking about concepts.

Nevertheless, there is equal evidence to suggest that Nietzsche would wish to reject the idea that concepts and reality are to be dualistically opposed in this manner. This rejection takes two forms in his arguments. First, there are remarks which, although sceptical about our capacity to gain knowledge and truth, do not exclude the possibility that concepts are that in virtue of which some aspect of the world is presented to us in thought. Of particular relevance here are his claims that the relation between concepts and reality is an aesthetic one, that it involves a stammering translation into a completely foreign tongue, and that, at most, there can be an inadequate expression of an object in a subject. However, it is an implication of all of these claims that conceptualization involves a distortion of what there is.

Second, there are places where Nietzsche seems to want to reject the idea that things in themselves elude the grasp of concepts, doing so on the ground that such a position is unintelligible. The idea that it is unintelligible to view things in themselves in these terms is compatible with allowing that they *are* revealed in our concepts. Furthermore, if one is prepared to go this far, it is but a small step to a rejection of the claim that conceptualization involves distortion. As we have seen, Nietzsche refuses to take this final step. He is unable to do so, according to my diagnosis, because he has failed to overthrow the framework which underlies the conception of reality he wishes to undermine – the framework which imposes an insurmountable distinction between concepts and reality.

We can conclude that there are several ways of conceiving of the relation between concepts and reality. According to the first option, things in themselves are inaccessible to concepts. This picture is expressive of the perspective to which Putnam refers as 'externalist' – externalist in the sense that it involves the claim that an adequate conception of reality requires that we transcend our concepts, by adopting a God's eye point of view, for example.[20] From Berkeley's perspective, this position finds expression in Locke's philosophy, the criticisms he raises in this context being similar to those which arise in Nietzsche's onslaught upon things in themselves. It is not absurd also to suppose that it resurfaces in Berkeley's own preferred position – at least, it does so on the assumption that his immaterialism inherits the offending dualistic framework.

It is incumbent upon one who accepts this externalist position to give an account of the ontological status of the things we conceptualize. The most obvious line to take – familiar from what I have said on Nietzsche's behalf, is that the nature of these things is determined by us – that things *qua* things are constructions of consciousness which correspond in no way to things in themselves. The more moderate version of this position has it that the mind acts upon material which comes to it from without, the point being to guarantee that some kind of link – however tenuous – is preserved with mind-independent reality. It is with this version in mind that we can best appreciate Nietzsche's talk of stammering translations and his claim that the activity of the subject is comparable to that of an artist when he works upon and enforms his materials. As I have stressed, however, if it is claimed also that there can be no causality between the realm of things in themselves and things as conceptualized, then it will be difficult to avoid the conclusion that there is nothing which comes to us from without – that things are constructions of consciousness in the most radical sense. Described in these terms, the position seems absurd. Nevertheless, it can be read into some of Nietzsche's headier protestations, when, for example, he is distinguishing between the different 'worlds' of birds, insects, and men. Presumably Locke would be committed to such a position if he were to dispense with the notion of material substance, as would Berkeley if he made no reference to God.

We have seen that, as far as Berkeley is concerned, the slogan that to be is to be perceived is not intended to undermine the sense in which the things we perceive are independent of our minds. On the contrary, it promises to provide a sober alternative to the position according to which these things lie on the far side of thought. As he puts it, 'the supposition that things are distinct from Ideas takes away all real Truth, and consequently brings in a Universal Scepticism, since all our knowledge is confin'd barely to our own Ideas'.[21] Berkeley is making an important point here, and this is so even if we accept that he fails on his own terms to make good the required anti-sceptical aim. Indeed, we shall see that it is similar to a point made by Hegel in the context of criticizing what he takes to be the 'subjective idealism' of Kant's position. For, like his idealist predecessors, Hegel is adamant that we avoid the supposition that things are distinct from ideas, and further, that his own preferred version of idealism serves to re-introduce us to things in a manner unrivalled by any previous option.

The position Hegel has in mind promises to kill off the syndrome which plagues the positions described previously, involving as it does a rejection of the claim that things in themselves are inaccessible to our concepts. As such, it represents the kind of option towards which Locke, Berkeley, and Nietzsche are gesturing in their more sober moments. The idea that things in themselves are revealed in our concepts stands opposed to the picture according to which conceptualization is a matter of distortion. Hence it is inappropriate to present this position by means of the kind of metaphor which accompanies the position against which it is defined – a metaphor according to which conceptualization is a matter of imposing shape upon formless matter, or, more radically, upon nothing at all. The alternative is to utilize a metaphor which captures the sense in which conceptualization involves revelation rather than distortion. One such metaphor is that of the fishnet.[22] According to this metaphor, conceptualization is a matter of fishing, and the things we conceptualize are the things we catch in our nets when we go fishing. The main point behind this metaphor is to lend emphasis to the idea that although one can only think about objects one has concepts for, these objects can be there anyway, there being no implication that the activity of conceptualization serves to distort or to construct their nature. This aspect of the metaphor is undisturbed by the fact that we might succeed in catching nothing at all – that we can think of types without their being such objects in reality. For all that follows from this concession is that externalism about thought-content is not universally true. It seems fair to say that this metaphor captures an important aspect of every one of the positions with which I have been concerned.

My arguments suggest that this second way of thinking about conceptualization is the correct way – at least in so far as we are concerned with our capacity to conceptualize things. It remains open, however, that the first way of thinking has a point in some contexts – one possible context being our capacity to conceptualize God. We shall see that this theological theme resurfaces in Kant, and that, as in the case of Berkeley, the concept of the thing in itself is used interchangeably in two quite different contexts – in the first context, it serves as a placeholder for God; in the second, it is that by virtue of which the things we conceptualize can be said to be independent of our minds. It follows therefore that the questions of our relation to God and our relation to things are not adequately separated – a conflation which, when wedded to the claim that God is inaccessible to thought, leads all too quickly to the conclusion that we are incapable of exercising conceptions of mind-independent things. This conflation, I shall argue, is indicative of just one of the tensions which re-emerge in Kant's position – tensions which are expressive of the syndrome and which compromise his ability to put to rest the spectre of universal scepticism. It is to Kant's arguments that I now turn.

3 Concepts and reality

Kant

Nietzsche and Kant

Kant's conception of the relation between concepts and reality is not easy to determine. Much of what he says lends support to Nietzsche's claim that there is no sense to be made of the idea that reality in itself is that which no concept can capture. His reasons for accepting this point, however, are subtly different. He begins by insisting that we respect the conditions – both conceptual and sensible – under which objects must be given to us if we are to conceive of them as genuine items of knowledge. Yet there are places where he allows that the range of our concepts is unhindered by the sensible conditions which must be respected if their objects are to be genuine candidates for knowledge. Thus, he tells us that our concepts are 'not limited by the conditions of our sensible intuition, but have an unlimited field. It is only the *knowledge* of that which we think, the determining of the object, that requires intuition'.[1] The further suggestion is that reality in itself falls within this 'unlimited field'. On the face of it then, Kant is prepared to resist the claim that our concepts are subjective forms which distort the nature of reality. Furthermore, it is a resistance that offers him a quite different justification for denying that reality in itself is that which no concept can capture, namely, that concepts *are*, after all, adequate to the task of making contact with it. Elsewhere, however, he insists that 'the pure concepts of the understanding can *never* admit of *transcendental* but *always* only empirical employment'.[2]

A further difficulty arises when we try to determine the extent to which Kant can be said to have put to rest the problem of external world scepticism. The suggestion that our concepts have an unlimited field puts him in a good position to set aside the problem of scepticism, at least in so far as that problem can be said to arise from the assumption that our concepts can make no contact with things in themselves. Yet Kant stops short of claiming that there can be *knowledge* of things in themselves. He does so on the ground that there are sensible conditions which must be met if this epistemological goal is to be realized. Nevertheless, he remains steadfast in his conviction that external world scepticism is avoided on his way of thinking.

Kant's conception of empirical knowledge is bound up with his view of the relation between concepts and intuitions, and an understanding of his positive position will allow me to expand upon some of the more impressionistic remarks I made in connection with Nietzsche's conception of this relation. As we have seen, there is evidence in Nietzsche to suggest that intuitions provide us with a more direct access to reality than that afforded by concepts – a suggestion which is in conflict with his criticisms elsewhere of the very idea of a non-conceptual form of reality. Much of what Kant says can be understood as a way of taking issue with this conception of an intuition. We shall see, however, that his positive verdict on this score is unclear, and that there remains a tension in his position which is reminiscent of that to be found in Nietzsche.

Given this residual tension, it is going to be difficult to adjudicate on the question of where Kant stands with respect to Nietzsche's claim that subject and object are two completely different spheres. As I have noted, this claim admits of various interpretations, not all of which are incompatible with the idea that a subject is capable of singling out a mind-independent object. Kant himself seeks to render intelligible this latter idea, albeit from within a framework which, on one reading, can be said to involve a rejection of the more problematic aspects of Nietzsche's position. Viewed from this perspective, he can be understood as wishing to deny Nietzsche's related claim that an adequate expression of an object in a subject is a contradictory impossibility. However, there is an alternative strand in his position which gives the lie to this interpretation, a strand which suggests that he too must hold that an expression of this kind is impossible.

Transcendental idealism: an overview

Kant is concerned to uncover what he refers to as the '*a priori* conditions of the possibility of experience'. The notion of experience, as he understands it, is a form of empirical knowledge, and the a priori conditions with which he is concerned are intended to be necessary conditions of it. So Kant is concerned to uncover the necessary conditions for the possibility of empirical knowledge. He claims that such knowledge springs from 'two fundamental sources of the mind', or 'two powers or capacities'.[3] These powers or capacities are sensibility and understanding. Sensibility is that by virtue of which an object is given to us from without. As Kant puts it, it is 'the capacity (receptivity) for receiving representations through the mode in which we are affected by objects'.[4] Sensibility is the only way in which an object can be given to us,[5] and it is referred to as the faculty of intuition.[6]

Kant distinguishes between empirical and pure intuition. Empirical intuition occurs when we are affected by an object through sensation, sensation being the matter of appearance. This matter of appearance is merely 'the effect of an object upon the faculty of representation', and, as such, represents no object at all.[7] It follows therefore that intuitions, taken by themselves, are insufficient for cognition of objects, such cognition requiring the contribution of the faculty of understanding. Pure intuition is that by virtue of which the matter of appearance is ordered in certain relations, and is referred to as the form of sensibility.[8] In the Transcendental Aesthetic Kant tells us that there are two pure forms of sensibility, namely, space and time.[9] These forms contain nothing that belongs to sensation, they are that without which there would be no objects of experience,[10] and in this latter respect constitute the necessary sensible conditions for empirical knowledge. However, Kant is not claiming that these sensible conditions apply to any kind of empirical knowledge of objects. For he allows that there are knowing beings who do not share our form of sensibility – beings who are not 'bound by the same conditions as those which limit our intuition and which for us are universally valid'.[11] Nevertheless, he insists that spatio-temporal awareness is a necessary condition for human awareness of objects.

Turning now to understanding, understanding is the faculty by virtue of which we are able to *think* the object of experience by bringing it under concepts, and it is referred to as the faculty of concepts. Just as there are empirical and pure intuitions, so, too, there are empirical and pure concepts. Empirical concepts are based on empirical intuitions, they presuppose the presence of the object,[12] and are therefore knowable only a posteriori.[13] Pure concepts, or categories, as Kant calls them, are those without which we would be unable to conceptualize empirical objects. They determine the form of empirical concepts, and, like pure intuitions, are knowable a priori. The concepts of causality and substance fall into this category, and much of Kant's discussion is focused upon these two cases. Whereas an intuition 'is that through which [an object] is in immediate relation to us',[14] concepts relate to objects mediately 'by means of a feature which several things may have in common'.[15] Thus understood, the distinction between concept and intuition maps onto that between general and particular.

Sensibility and understanding cannot exchange their function, and it is only through their union that we can have experience of determinate objects with a view to gaining knowledge of them:

> (w)ithout sensibility no object would be given to us, without understanding no object would be thought. Thoughts without content are empty; intuitions without concepts are blind.[16]

Kant emphasizes that we must not confound the contribution of either capacity with the other.[17] Finally, whereas he is prepared to allow that there could be knowing subjects who do not share the spatio-temporal awareness which is a necessary feature of human experience, he does not make the same concession as far as the categories are concerned. On the contrary, he claims that the categories 'relate to objects of intuition in general, whether that intuition be our own or any other, provided only that it be sensible'.[18] The claim then is that any empirical knowledge, not just that of humans, requires the application of the categories.

Thus far, we have been told that the joint operation of sensibility and understanding is required if we are to have experience and knowledge of empirical objects. Kant claims, however, that the notion of an object is to be taken in a twofold sense, namely, as appearance and as thing in itself.[19] Considered as an appearance, an object is what one gets with the synthesis of concept and intuition. Thus understood, an appearance is an object of experience.[20] Considered as a thing in itself, by contrast, an object is the ground of that which appears.[21] Kant claims that there is nothing inherent in the categories which precludes them from gaining application to things in themselves, but he stresses that it is only through intuition that they acquire the content required for knowledge. He suggests also that we cannot know things in themselves, the categories not being 'of themselves adequate to the knowledge of things in themselves'.[22] For the moment we can leave aside questions pertaining to the precise import of this negative claim. However, we can make a note of Kant's insistence that we must be able to conceive of the existence of things in themselves lest we be forced to conclude that there can be appearance without anything that appears.[23]

Kant's belief that we can have knowledge only of appearances and not of things in themselves leads to the form of idealism he seeks to defend. He describes transcendental idealism as the position according to which:

> appearances are to be regarded as being, one and all, representations only, not things in themselves, and that time and space are therefore only sensible forms of our intuition, not determinations given as existing by themselves, nor conditions of objects viewed as things in themselves.[24]

Transcendental idealism is opposed to transcendental realism, transcendental realism being the view that outer appearances are things in themselves 'which exist independently of us and of our sensibility, and which are therefore outside us'.[25] Kant claims, in a manner reminiscent of Berkeley, that the transcendental realist is wrong to assume that objects of the senses, in order to be external, 'must have an existence by themselves, and independent of the senses', and that he is forced hereby to conclude that 'our sensuous representations are inadequate to establish their reality'.[26] From Kant's point of view this latter conclusion is tantamount to empirical idealism, which he understands as the view according to which we can never be certain of the existence of external objects.[27]

By contrast, Kant tells us that the transcendental idealist is an empirical realist. He is an empirical realist in the sense that he may admit the existence of external objects without 'assuming anything more than the certainty of his representations'. Unlike the transcendental realist and the empirical idealist, then, he has no need to resort to inference in order to arrive at the reality of outer objects.[28] Finally, Kant distinguishes between two senses of the expression 'outside us'. In the first sense, it signifies 'what *as thing in itself* exists apart from us'. In the second sense, it signifies 'what belongs solely to outer appearance'. When Kant talks of objects existing outside of us, he is using that expression in the second sense. Thus understood, objects are *empirically external* and are to be understood as 'things which are to be found in space'. By contrast, he is denying that objects are external 'in the transcendental sense', meaning by this that they exist as the unknown causes of our outer intuitions. He makes this denial on the grounds that we could never be in a position to establish the existence of such objects, and that such objects are not what we are thinking when we represent corporeal things. The objection is familiar from Berkeley and Nietzsche.

The upshot of Kant's position is that we can have knowledge only of things which are subject to the conditions of possible experience. We cannot, however, have knowledge of things in themselves. Nevertheless, Kant claims that we are compelled to transcend these empirical conditions by means of the pure concepts of *reason* whose employment is not confined to objects of possible experience.[29] These pure concepts of reason are transcendental ideas. They are that by means of which we can conceive of things in themselves, they are 'imposed by the very nature of reason itself', they are 'transcendent, and overstep the limits of all experience'. Hence, 'no object adequate to the transcendental idea can ever be found within experience',[30] our use of such ideas can never yield knowledge, and tends to lead instead to contradiction and fallacy. Kant refers to the mode of thinking which yields these inevitable contradictions as dialectic. Transcendental ideas are by no means 'superfluous and void', however, for although they cannot determine any object, they may be 'of service to the understanding as a canon for its extended and consistent employment'. They also make possible a transition from the concepts of nature to the practical/moral concepts.[31]

Kant's idea that we are compelled to transcend the limits of possible experience is tied up with his further claim that we can form the idea of an intellect which does not involve the application of concepts to objects of experience. Such an intellect would involve 'a special mode of intuition, namely, the intellectual, which is not that which we possess, and is something of which we cannot even comprehend the possibility'.[32] What we can say, however, is that it does not involve being affected from without. This point is important, illustrating as it does that although we can form no positive conception of such an intellect, we are capable nonetheless of comprehending it in negative terms. For such an intellect then, the distinction between thinking and sensing would collapse, and objects would become actual simply by virtue of being thought about. As Kant puts it at B72, intellectual intuition gives us 'the existence of its object – a mode of intuition which, so far as we can judge, can belong only to the primordial being'.

Kant relates the notion of an intellectual intuition to that of a thing in itself as follows. First, he makes a distinction between a noumenon in the negative sense and a noumenon in the positive sense. A noumenon in the negative sense is 'a thing so far as it is *not an object of our sensible intuition*', that is, a thing which is to be abstracted from our mode of intuiting it.[33] A noumenon in this sense coincides with the notion of a thing in itself, considered as something which is thought without reference to our mode of intuition, and which serves as a ground for the things we are capable of experiencing.[34] Furthermore, it is natural to suppose that this negative conception of a noumenon is to be related to the corresponding negative conception of an intuitive intellect. A noumenon in the positive sense, by contrast, is 'an *object* of a *non-sensible* intuition', an 'entity that allows of being known in a certain manner', namely, the manner appropriate to one who possesses the capacity for intellectual intuition. Kant emphasizes that a noumenon in the positive sense is just as incomprehensible as the mode of cognition that would render it accessible, the implication being that we are not entitled to assume that there is anything in reality corresponding to such a notion.

Things in themselves

Notwithstanding the obscurities surrounding Kant's notion of the thing in itself, it is undoubtedly a crucial component of his position. Indeed, he believes that it is only by accepting it that one can avoid those versions of idealism which fail to make sense of our capacity to engage in thought with mind-independent things. Thus, we are told in the third note to section 13 of the *Prolegomenon* that Berkeley's idealism is an idealism concerning the existence of things in themselves, and that in this respect it stands opposed to his own version according to which things in themselves exist. We can leave on one side the fact that Kant's representation of Berkeley fails to take account of the role played by God in his position – a role which might be thought to provide a reasonable enough place-holder for things in themselves. The important point to grasp is that the thing in itself is intended to be the ingredient which, to use Berkeley's words, avoids the position according to which 'we are confin'd barely to our own ideas'. Henry Allison's way of making a similar point is to say that things in themselves are required if we are to avoid a 'subjectivistic, psychologistic, phenomenalist' reading of Kant,[35] the implication being that such a reading would fail to engage with Kant's philosophical aim.

It is reasonable enough to insist that there are things in themselves if the point is simply to avoid phenomenalism. And much of what Kant says suggests that his aim in introducing this notion is precisely to satisfy this demand. Thus, he tells us that.

> Though we cannot know these objects as things in themselves, we must be in a position at least to think them as things in themselves; otherwise we should be landed in the absurd position that there can be appearance without anything that appears.[36]

And:

> The word *appearance* must be recognised as already indicating a relation to something, the immediate representation of which is, indeed, sensible, but which, even apart from the constitution of our sensibility ... must be something in itself, that is, an object independent of sensibility.[37]

Finally, we are told in the *Prolegomenon* that:

> The thing, which is *unknown* to us ... is not therefore less real. Can this be termed idealism? It is the very contrary.[38]

What is less clear is how Kant conceives of the relation between appearance and thing, and whether he has succeeded in defining a position which sidesteps the syndrome. Certainly, there is evidence to suppose that he stands opposed to the picture according to which appearances are to be dualistically opposed to things in themselves. For it is an implication of the above quotations that the appearances to which we have access presuppose things, and that it is things in themselves that appear. Second, he insists that we are not entitled to suppose that there are noumena in the positive sense, a noumenon in the positive sense being an 'object of a non-sensible intuition' which, we are to suppose, stands dualistically opposed to the things of which we have experience.[39] Thus, he tells us that:

> (t)he division of objects into phenomena and noumena, and the world into a world of the senses and a world of the understanding, is therefore quite inadmissible in the positive sense'.[40]

Finally, he claims that it is the doctrine of the noumenon in the negative sense which is relevant to the distinction he wishes to make between appearance and thing. A noumenon in the negative sense, he tells us, is a placeholder for 'things which our understanding must think without reference to our mode of intuition, therefore not merely as appearances but as things in themselves'.[41]

Putting these points together, we have evidence for concluding that Kant is neither a phenomenalist nor a noumenalist.[42] That is to say, he is committed neither to the claim that appearances are mental items nor to the claim that things in themselves are to be dualistically opposed to appearances. The alternative is to suppose that he is gesturing towards a non-dualistic conception of the relation between appearance and thing – a conception which grants us the right to allow that we are capable of conceptualizing mind-independent things.

The following extracts tell in favour of such an interpretation:

> Appearance ... always has two sides, the one by which the object is viewed in and by itself (without regard to the mode of intuiting it – its nature therefore remaining always problematic), the other by which the form of the intuition of this object is taken into account.[43]

> If we entitle certain objects, as appearances, sensible entities (phenomena), then ... we thus distinguish the mode in which we intuit them from the nature that belongs to them in themselves.[44]

> If the senses represent to us something merely as it appears, this something must also in itself be a thing. [45]

Finally, we are told that the concept of an object is to be

> (t)aken in a twofold sense, namely as appearance and as thing in itself.[46]

According to the most natural reading of these claims, Kant is denying that appearance and thing are to be treated as two dualistically opposed entities. Rather, the claim is that there is one entity which is to be conceived of in two ways, namely, as appearance and as thing in itself.[47] Conceding this much is not particularly helpful, however, raising as it does the question of how we are to comprehend the nature of the relation which exists between appearance and thing in itself once it has been acknowledged that we are not dealing with two distinct entities.

One way of giving expression to Kant's line of thought is to say that he is concerned with the distinction which obtains between things considered as objects of possible experience and those same things as they are in themselves. The further claim is that, considered in themselves, their nature remains 'unknown' and 'always problematic'. The idea that the things we experience can be considered in themselves seems both unexceptional and correct, implying as it does simply that these things have a mind-independent nature – a way they are in themselves. Furthermore, it seems perfectly reasonable to suppose that there are unknown facts about these things. Indeed, it is only by making such a concession that we shall preserve the right to allow that they have natures which are genuinely independent of us. By contrast, the further suggestion that these natures must remain unknown is more difficult to interpret and to accept. Perhaps the most worrying problem we face in conceding that things have unknowable natures is that we appear to be returned to a version of the dualistic relation this way of thinking might have been thought to avoid. For although we have avoided any reference to distinct kinds of entity – knowable phenomena and unknowable noumena – we now have two realms of facts about phenomena: knowable facts which relate to those phenomena *qua* objects of experience and unknowable facts which relate to them when they are considered in themselves.[48]

Is it possible to concede that there are unknowable facts about the things we experience whilst maintaining the non-dualistic framework under consideration? Certainly, it would be odd to suppose that facts of this ilk are of interest to the scientist, for he is concerned with things that are accessible to investigation and explanation. Indeed, Kant himself allows that the scientist is concerned exclusively with the realm of appearance.[49] Hence, if we are going to defend the possibility of there being unknowable facts about things, these facts must lie beyond the scope of scientific investigation.

One way of making good the required non-dualistic aim comes with the following line of thought.[50] The scientist, so the argument goes, is concerned exclusively with the dispositional properties of things. This is not to say that he is concerned only with what we might refer to as sensory dispositional properties – properties like colour which can be understood only in terms of how they are disposed to affect us. Rather, the point is that the non-sensory properties with which he is concerned are to be understood also in dispositional terms, namely, in terms of how they are disposed to affect or to interact with other mind-independent properties or things.[51] The further claim is that this applies not only to the macroscopic properties of things but also to their microscopic, subatomic properties. On this way of thinking then, even if we concede that the most fundamental laws of physics governing the actions between microscopic entities are hypotheses that cannot presently be further grounded, any new theories that promise to account for these regularities in terms of more fundamental ones will be of the same basic form – concerning interactions between more basic things. What the scientist cannot do, however, is provide an account of the *ground* of these dispositions. According to this way of thinking, then, dispositions go all the way down as far as science is concerned. The implication though is that there are further facts about things – facts concerning the grounds of their dispositional properties – which must remain ever elusive to science.

Certainly, if this line of thought could be defended then we should have a way of vindicating the idea that there are properties of things which remain elusive to scientific investigation and which are in principle unknowable. Nevertheless, it raises various difficulties. One difficulty is that it cannot be assumed that the scientist's focus upon dispositional properties should be read as a limitation upon the explanatory scope of his inquiry, for there are good scientific grounds for supposing that dispositions go all the way down. It is a presupposition of classical Newtonian mechanics, for example, that the nature of a thing is to act on other things and – more controversially perhaps[52] – to be acted back upon by them, the implication being that to attribute a property to a body or physical system that can never be felt by other systems is to indulge in idle metaphysics. On this way of thinking then – a way of thinking which is embraced by Leibniz – we are required to explain what a thing is in terms of what it does, it being a necessary condition for a thing to be of interest to physics that it acts on other things.[53] Indeed, there is good evidence to suppose that Kant himself was sympathetic to this line of thought, and that he would be happy to concede that physics has no need for properties other than powers.[54]

One reason why philosophers have clung to the idea that dispositions require a non-dispositional ground is that they believe that we can forsake this idea only at the cost of succumbing to a form of phenomenalism. Assuming that this is so then, it looks as if we have a motive for insisting upon the concept of the thing in itself – a motive, moreover, which relates quite obviously to Kant's anti-phenomenalist concerns. The argument can be summarised as follows.[55] We distinguish, at the macroscopic level, between those properties which are peculiarly sensory – properties like colour, for example – and those which are intrinsic to things. The sensory properties are to be understood in dispositional terms – that is to say, in terms of how they affect suitably endowed human subjects. The latter, by contrast, provide a categorical ground or base for these dispositions – a ground which allows us to make sense of the idea that the relevant sensory properties belong to mind-independent things. The further claim is that if we deny the existence of this ground we shall be forced into a version of phenomenalism. For in the absence of a ground for the dispositional properties of things, it follows that there is nothing more to an object having a property than its being disposed to affect suitably receptive subjects with certain experiences.

The idea that the properties we perceive have a mind-independent ground is familiar from Locke – the ground in this case being supplied by material substance. What is unclear, however, is that this concession forces us to abandon the idea that dispositions go all the way down. We can avoid this implication by insisting upon a distinction made previously, namely, that which obtains between dispositional properties which are peculiarly sensory and those which are not. Armed with this distinction, we can argue that the ground which permits us to avoid phenomenalism is supplied by those dispositional properties of things which are understood not simply in terms of how they are disposed to affect *us,* but, rather, in terms of how they are disposed to affect other mind-independent things. It is the satisfaction of this requirement, so the argument goes, that allows us to make sense of the idea that things are genuinely mind-independent. For it captures the sense in which things are *there anyway,* interacting with one another regardless of whether we happen to be on the scene.

Certainly, this move is compatible with Locke's position provided that we attend to its non-sceptical strand. For the idea is simply that the mind-independent things we perceive and investigate are to be understood in causal terms – terms with which Locke is concerned when he talks about real essences. Understood with this interpretation in mind, it really is possible to explain what a thing is by reference to what it does, there being no implication that, in doing so, we are bypassing its real essence. By contrast, if we attend to the sceptical strand in Locke's position – that which has it that the real essence of a thing is inaccessible to us – the implication is, rather, that the causal ground of a thing must remain ever elusive to us. On this second way of thinking, it follows that the properties of things to which we have access *do* require a further causal ground, the inaccessibility of this ground implying that the things we perceive cannot be understood in properly mind-independent terms. At this point, the postulation of such a ground becomes useless to the task of defining a non-phenomenalist position – hence Locke's reluctance to embrace such a position – and the conclusion seems forced on us that the dispositions to which we are confined are to be characterized in purely sensory terms. Thus, a denial of the claim that dispositions go all the way down in this sense returns us full circle to the position which made it so tempting to postulate a non-dispositional ground in the first place. We have not advanced.

We can conclude that there are no good scientific grounds for insisting that the dispositional properties of things require a non-dispositional ground, and no requirement that such a ground be used as a way of lending credence to the idea that there is an aspect of things which must remain unknowable. Viewed from this perspective, such an aspect is irrelevant to an understanding of the nature of the things we perceive – something which functions at best as an idle mechanism, and at worst as something which threatens to undermine their objective status. Given Kant's non-phenomenalist aspirations and his commitment to the idea that the scientist has no need for properties other than powers, it is difficult to see how he could defend such a position whilst remaining true to a non-dualistic conception of the relation between appearance and thing.

There is one final way in which the Kantian could seek to lend justice to the idea that the things we perceive have an unknowable aspect. According to this defence, the idea is not that things possess properties other than those they possess *qua* objects of knowledge. Rather, it is that the things of which we have knowledge can be considered in abstraction from the way in which they figure in our knowledge of them.[56] The difficulty with this response is that it is not obvious how we are to interpret the required process of abstraction. Kant himself suggests that we are to abstract from the sensible conditions in terms of which we view things, a recommendation which is perfectly in order if taken to mean that there are experiential properties of things which do not accrue to their intrinsic nature – properties which are peculiarly sensory in the sense previously defined, for example. We shall see, however, that Kant seems to have something much stronger in mind, and that the relevant abstractive exercise involves the removal not merely of those properties which are peculiarly sensory, but also of those which we would ordinarily take to be intrinsic to the things themselves – their non-sensory dispositional properties, for example. This demand goes quite naturally with the idea that things in themselves elude the scope of scientific enquiry. It accords also with a further strand in Kant's argument – one which carries a more explicit commitment to a dualistic conception of the relation between appearance and thing. It is to this strand that I now turn.

Some tensions

Evidence for a dualistic interpretation is to be found in those places where Kant implies that the thing in itself *can* be viewed in positive terms, and that, conceived as such, it is to be set apart from the appearances to which we are confined at the level of experience. One such piece of evidence occurs in the preface to the second edition of the *Critique* where he refers to the thing in itself as 'real *per se*, but as not known by us'. Such evidence is hardly decisive, particularly when set against the frequently occurring passages which suggest a quite different picture. It becomes more compelling, however, when situated alongside other parts of the text which convey a similar dualistic message.

Passages such as the following lend support to the so-called 'two-world' view:

External objects (bodies), however, are mere appearances, and are therefore nothing but a species of my representations, the objects of which are something only through these representations. Apart from them they are nothing.[57]

We have sufficiently proved ... that everything intuited in space or time, and therefore all objects of any experience possible to us, are nothing but appearances, that is, mere representations, which, in the manner in which they are represented, as extended beings, or as series of alterations, have no independent existence outside our thoughts. This doctrine I entitle *transcendental idealism*. The realist in the transcendental meaning of this term, treats these modifications of our sensibility as self-subsistent things, that is, treats *mere representations* as things in themselves.[58]

But this space and this time, and with them all appearances, are not in themselves *things*; they are nothing but representations, and cannot exist outside our mind.[59]

To call an appearance a real thing prior to our perceiving it, either means that in the advance of experience we must meet with such a perception, or it means nothing at all. For if we were speaking of a thing in itself, we could indeed say that it exists in itself apart from relation to our senses and possible experience. But we are here speaking only of an appearance in space and time, which are not determinations of things in themselves but only of our sensibility. Accordingly, that which is in space and time is an appearance; it is not anything in itself but consists merely of representations, which, if not given in us – that is to say, in perception – are nowhere to be met with.[60]

If, in connection with transcendental theology, we ask, *first,* whether there is anything distinct from the world, which contains the ground of the order of the world and of its connection in accordance with universal laws, the answer is that there *undoubtedly* is. For the world is a sum of appearances; and there must therefore be some transcendental ground of the appearances, that is, a ground which is thinkable only by the pure understanding … . If, *thirdly,* the question be, whether we may not at least think this being, which is distinct from the world, in *analogy* with the objects of experience, the answer is: certainly, but only as object in *idea* and not in reality, namely, only as being a substratum, to us unknown, of the systematic unity, order, and purposiveness of the arrangement of the world.[61]

For this something[62] is not extended, nor is it impenetrable or composite, since all these predicates concern only sensibility and its intuition, in so far as we are affected by certain (to us otherwise unknown) objects. By such statements we are not, however, enabled to know what kind of an object it is, but only to recognize that if it be considered in itself, and therefore apart from any relation to the outer senses, these predicates of outer appearances cannot be assigned to it. On the other hand, the predicates of inner sense, representations and thought are not inconsistent with its nature.[63]

One might argue that these quotations are indecisive in demonstrating the cogency of a 'two-world' interpretation of Kant's position. The evidence which proliferates in the first edition of the *Critique* can be written off on the ground that one of Kant's motives for re-writing sections for a second edition was the failure of readers to appreciate the difference between his idealism and that of Berkeley. Second, Kant's mode of expression – for example, that representations exist 'in us' or 'in our mind' – is too vague to commit him to any particular position, idealist or otherwise. Finally, the references to transcendental theology might be said to have no relevance for an understanding of things in themselves *qua* ground of appearances, and could do so only on the assumption that there is no distinction between the negative and positive senses of the notion of a noumenon.

The complaint that it is unjustified to focus exclusively upon first edition claims is fair enough. The difficulty, however, is that there is evidence for a 'two-world' interpretation to be found in the second edition. Hence, in the context of setting out transcendental idealism, Kant tells us that objects of experience are 'nothing but appearances', 'mere representations', and that they have 'no existence outside our thoughts'. To be sure, one might repeat that these modes of expression are too vague to commit Kant to any particular philosophical position. On the face of it, however, such expressions could be termed vague only to one who is already convinced that the 'two-world' interpretation is misguided. To one who is not so convinced, by contrast, they provide clear enough evidence to suggest that there is, at the very least, a serious tension in his position with respect to the issue of how we are to comprehend the relation between appearance and thing. Once it is acknowledged that such a tension exists – and one could ignore it only by clinging to the absurd idea that Kant's position is immune from error and difficulty – the remarks he makes about transcendental theology can be assessed accordingly. For, as in the case of Locke and Berkeley before him, it looks as if Kant is oscillating between two quite different positions. According to the first position, appearances are of things, and reference to the ground of appearance is to be understood as reference to that by virtue of which we avoid phenomenalism. According to the second position, by contrast, the ground of appearances is something which stands opposed to the things we perceive – something like the separable substratum which figures in Locke and Berkeley. Unlike Locke's substratum, however, this ground is not to be understood in causal terms. Indeed, it seems more appropriate to liken its activity to that which characterizes Berkeley's immaterial substance. For as the quotation from A359 makes clear, Kant is not ruling out the possibility that this separable substratum is a thinking thing.

Once this second framework is in place, the question of how we are to view the status of the things we experience becomes pressing, and it becomes compelling to take at face value Kant's claim that they are 'mere representations'. It becomes compelling also to suppose that the tension in his position echoes that which finds expression in Berkeley's treatment of the notion of God. For it will be remembered that Berkeley never makes it clear how we are to conceive of the relation between God and the things we perceive. Finally, we can note that, in both Berkeley and Kant, it is claimed – not entirely consistently – that this separable entity, whether it be termed 'God' or 'the thing in itself', is something we cannot really comprehend.

The categories

We have seen that there are two metaphors in terms of which to comprehend the activity of conceptualization. According to the first metaphor, it is comparable to what happens when a cookie cutter imposes shape upon a lump of raw pastry, the raw pastry being a placeholder for the matter of experience. On this picture then, the work of the conceptualizing mind is work of construction. According to the second metaphor, by contrast, conceptual activity is to be likened to fishing. That is to say, it is comparable to what happens when nets are cast into the ocean to reveal the fish lurking in its depths. The implication here is that conceptualization involves discovery, and, to the extent that it can be said to involve the mind's work, it is work of construal rather than construction.[64]

Nietzsche remains committed to the first metaphor – hence his suggestion that the activity of conceptualization is comparable to what goes on when an artist shapes his material into a work of art. Yet his objections to the idea that reality in itself lies beyond the realm revealed in our concepts suggest that the second metaphor would be more appropriate to his philosophical aims. I have noted that there is an element of Kant's position which is lacking in Nietzsche, for Kant implies on occasion that there is nothing in concepts or categories *per se* which precludes them from applying to things in themselves. As he puts it, our concepts are 'not limited by the conditions of our sensible intuition, but have an unlimited field'.[65] Taking account of this concession then, it looks as if Kant is committed to denying that concepts shield us from things in themselves, and is in a position therefore to reject the first cookie cutter metaphor.

When Kant tells us that our concepts have an unlimited field he adds that 'it is only the *knowledge* of that which we think, the determining of the object, that requires intuition', and that the categories are not in themselves adequate to the knowledge of things in themselves. Thus, although he is prepared to make this concession with respect to the scope of our concepts, he stops short of allowing that we can, by their means, gain *knowledge* of things in themselves. Notwithstanding this limitation, however, it is unclear that it could be said also on Kant's behalf that concepts serve to distort things in themselves. On the contrary, it would seem to be the fact that we can know things only relative to our sensibility – that we require to be affected by them – which imposes a limitation upon our cognition. On this interpretation then, things can be termed appearances not with respect to their conceptual form, which, on this way of thinking, is capable of revealing the true nature of a thing. Rather, they are appearances only in so far as they are considered in sensible terms.

Much of what Kant says suggests that these sensible terms extend to all the properties which attach to a thing *qua* object of possible experience, the implication being that the idea of conceptual form is already presupposed in this way of thinking about things. Given that this is so, it is not obvious what we are to make of the idea that, from a conceptual point of view, things are not to be viewed as mere appearances. A possible response to this difficulty emerges if we look at the Schematism. For the main point of this section is to stress that the categories, when understood in non-experiential terms, are quite empty, and further, that they require to be temporalized if they are to be applied to objects of experience. Thus, we are told that the concepts or categories 'must contain *a priori* certain formal conditions of sensibility, namely, those of inner sense' – conditions which, Kant continues, 'constitute the universal condition under which alone the category can be applied to any object'.[66] He concludes that sensibility 'realises understanding in the very process of restricting it'.[67] Now the formal condition in question is temporality, and given that temporality, for Kant, is a subjective form which does not apply to things in themselves, it is natural to suppose that schematized concepts are subjective, not by virtue of their nature as concepts, but by virtue of their temporality. According to this way of thinking, then, things are mere appearances when considered from a conceptual point of view, because the concepts in question are time-involving, and time does not apply to things in themselves.

The difficulty with this response is that there are places in the text where Kant implies that it is the nature of concepts *per se* which precludes them from revealing things in themselves – his claim at B303, for example, that 'the pure concepts of the understanding can *never* admit of *transcendental* employment but *always* only of *empirical* employment'. It is possible to play down the force of this claim by insisting that Kant is focusing upon the empirical limitations to which *we* are subject when conceptualizing things. The problem, however, is that there is further textual evidence to suggest that concepts are, after all, subjective forms whose nature remains elusive to things in themselves. We are told, for example, that concepts have 'their first seeds and dispositions in the human understanding'[68], and that:

> (t)he order and regularity in the appearances, which we entitle *nature,* we ourselves introduce. We could never find them in appearances, had we not ourselves, or the nature of our mind, originally set them there.[69]

> Thus the understanding is something more than a power of formulating rules through comparison of appearances; it is itself the lawgiver of nature … However exaggerated and absurd it may sound, to say that the understanding is itself the source of the laws of nature, and so of its formal unity, such an assertion is none the less correct, and is in keeping with the object to which it refers, namely, experience.[70]

> Categories are concepts which prescribe laws *a priori* to appearances, and therefore to nature, the sum of all appearances … .The question therefore arises, how it can be conceivable that nature should have to proceed in accordance with the categories which yet are not derived from it, and do not model themselves on its pattern.[71]

> That the *laws* of appearances in nature must agree with the understanding and its *a priori* form, that is, with its faculty of *combining* the manifold in general, is no more surprising than that the appearances themselves must agree with the form of *a priori* sensible intuition. For just as appearances do not exist in themselves but only relative to the subject in which, so far as it has senses, they inhere, so the laws do not exist in the appearances but only relative to this same being, in so far as it has understanding.[72]

Again, it is possible to play down the force of these claims. We could argue, for example, that Kant's talk of the understanding being the lawgiver of nature is not intended to imply that the objects we conceptualize owe their existence to us, nor that the laws which govern them have their origin in us. In support of the first point, we could remind ourselves of Kant's insistence that 'representation does not produce its object as far as existence is concerned'.[73] In support of the second, we could allow that the mind's work to which Kant refers in this context is to be viewed as work of construal rather than construction. Understood with this latter interpretation in mind, Kant's point is that it is our capacity to conceptualize things which allows us to discern the laws that obtain in mind-independent nature. The further related point is that concepts have their first seeds and dispositions in the human understanding only in the innocuous sense that conceptualization is something that *we* do.

It has to be admitted that these claims are rather unconvincing. To begin with, Kant's claim that representation does not produce its object as far as existence is concerned does nothing to tell against a conception of concepts according to which they are subjective forms which are imposed upon the matter of experience. For it remains open that the existence of the object in this context is to be understood in non-conceptual terms. Second, it is difficult to resist the conclusion that, in the above-quoted extracts, Kant *is* quite unambiguously suggesting that conceptualization involves construction. As he puts it, the categories are not derived from nature, laws do not exist in appearances, and their source is in the understanding.

In order to clarify these issues, we need to examine the remarks Kant makes elsewhere about the nature of concepts.[74] In his 1800 *Logic* he tells us that a concept is a 'general presentation or a presentation of what is common to several objects'.[75] Second, he claims that 'in every concept there is to be distinguished matter and form. The matter of concepts is the *object;* their form is their *generality*'.[76] We are told further that form in this sense is always *made* and this is so whether we are concerned with pure or empirical concepts. A pure concept is 'one that is not abstracted from experience but springs from the understanding even as to content'. By contrast, an empirical concept 'springs from the senses through comparison of the objects of experience and receives, through the understanding, merely the form of generality'.[77] Thus, Kant is telling us that the form of any concept is made, meaning by this that it is the understanding that determines its form, and he expands upon this claim by making reference to the logical acts of the understanding by virtue of which concepts are 'generated as to their form'.[78] The acts in question are comparison, reflection, and abstraction. Thus:

> In order to make our presentations into concepts, one must be able to *compare*, *reflect*, and *abstract*, for these three logical operations of the understanding are the essential and general conditions of generating any concept whatsoever. For example, I see a fir, a willow, and a linden. In firstly comparing these objects, I notice they are different from one another in respect of trunk, branches, leaves, and the like; further, however, I reflect only on what they have in common, the trunk, the branches, the leaves themselves, and abstract from their size, shape, and so forth; thus I gain a concept of a tree.[79]

It seems clear from what Kant is saying here that the object which serves as the matter of an empirical concept like that of a tree is the tree itself. Thus, the role of the understanding is to compare and reflect upon these objects and thereby to abstract those qualities by virtue of which something counts as a tree. If this is right then his point is that empirical concepts are abstracted from experience in the sense that the objects they involve are given in experience.

Things are quite different with the pure concepts or categories, however, for Kant holds that the matter of these concepts cannot be given in experience in the way that it is for empirical concepts. As he puts it, they are 'not abstracted from experience but spring from the understanding even as to content'. One of the things this seems to mean is that the matter of pure concepts like that of substance and causality are not given in experience in the way that that of the concept *tree* is. I have suggested that the matter of the concept *tree* is given in experience in the sense that trees are things we can experience. The implication then is that we are not capable of experiencing things like substances and causality. One difficulty with this line of thought is that there is an important sense in which Kant is committed to claiming that we *are* capable of experiencing substances and causality – a sense, moreover, which offers him the resources for distinguishing the categories from the ideas of reason. Thus, in his 'Vienna Logic', in response to the question of whether the objects of the categories can be experienced, he claims unequivocally: 'Yes. This happens through examples. An example of causality is: fire destroys wood'.[80] At the same time, however, he insists in the first *Critique* that experience cannot tell us that something *must* be so, and that necessity is an essential component of the concept of causality. Thus, Kant believes that in one sense we are capable of experiencing causality – the sense in which we can observe the fire destroying the wood, and that in another sense we are not – the sense in which experience can never present us with a necessary connection. The further claim is that it is the understanding which furnishes us with this extra and essential component of the concept.

We are returned then to the question of what it means to say that the categories 'spring from the understanding even as to content' and whether this commits Kant to claiming that conceptualization involves the constructive work of mind. We have been told already that abstraction, reflection, and comparison are said to be involved in the acquisition of any concept whatsoever. The claim then is that these acts of mind are operative in the acquisition of the categories. We have seen also, however, that, in the case of the categories, these acts of mind cannot be said to operate on objects of experience. The alternative, given Kant's insistence that the matter of the categories is supplied by the understanding, is to suppose that the process of abstraction effected by the mind gains application to itself – that, as he puts it in the *Inaugural Dissertation,* the categories are 'abstracted from the laws inherent in the mind'.[81]

There are many questions to be raised about the kind of position at issue here – questions which need not worry us. The crucial issue is that of whether Kant is forced to conclude that conceptualization involves the constructive work of mind. Certainly, the remarks we have considered tell in favour of such an interpretation. For it is an implication of what he says that the categories are *not* derived from nature, and that the sense in which they have their source in the understanding is not intended to be compatible with the idea that the things they reveal have a mind-independent nature. Of course, the evidence is far from decisive, not least because it is left entirely mysterious how we are to understand the nature and origin of these mental laws. What does seem clear, however, is that there is no straightforward sense in which Kant can be said to be working unambiguously with a conception according to which concepts are revelatory of things, and every reason for thinking that his position involves a serious tension.

Experience

Notwithstanding the tensions in Kant's position, he clearly wishes to avoid the subjective idealism he finds in Berkeley, hence his insistence that representation does not produce its object as far as existence is concerned. We must consider then whether his conception of experience affords him the right to maintain this anti-subjectivist stance, and, if so, whether there is scope for dispelling the force of the aforementioned difficulties.

Kant believes that it is by virtue of our capacity for receptivity that objects are given to us from without. The representations in terms of which these objects are given to us are referred to as 'intuitions', an intuition being 'that through which (an object) is in immediate relation to us'.[82] As he puts it, '(o)bjects are *given* to us by means of sensibility, and it alone yields us *intuitions*'.[83] The further crucial claim is that intuitions, taken in themselves, do not involve cognition of the objects they reveal, such cognition requiring that those objects be conceptualized. Thus 'without sensibility no object would be given to us, without understanding no object would be thought'.[84] Finally, Kant tells us that space and time are the 'two original forms of sensibility',[85] that they constitute 'the necessary conditions under which alone objects can be for us objects of the senses',[86] and that they apply to things only with regard to the constitution of our sensibility.[87]

In order to tackle the question of whether Kant's conception of the given element of experience can afford him the right to avoid subjective idealism, let me assume initially that he is operating with a non-dualistic conception of the relation between appearance and thing. According to a non-dualistic conception, we are to take the notion of an object in a twofold sense so as to allow that it can be considered both as appearance and as thing in itself. Now once it is denied that things in themselves lie in a realm which is external to that revealed in our concepts, then it becomes possible to allow that it is these things which provide the external constraint upon thought. They provide an external constraint, not by virtue of existing in a realm which lies beyond any possible content of thought, but, rather, by virtue of existing independently of our particular acts of conceiving of them. Certainly, this interpretation squares with at least some of the things Kant says. For he is quick to point out that intuitions – considered in non-conceptual terms – do not constitute a representation of a determinate object. As he puts it, sensation is merely 'the effect of an object upon the faculty of representation'.[88] On the face of it, then, Kant is telling us that it would be misguided to suppose that sensation represents objects, and quite wrong therefore to suppose that non-conceptual intuitions could account for our capacity to be in touch with genuine things. The further implication is that it would be equally misguided to suppose that they provide for a more faithful representation of things in themselves.

This interpretation finds confirmation in the second sense of the term 'intuition' which runs through Kant's work. According to this second sense, intuitions are already concept-involving, and for this reason can be said to be representations of determinate things.[89] It is with this conception in mind that we can best appreciate Kant's claim that space is the form of intuition, for it is made quite clear that space, thus conceived, is that which relates us to the things we perceive. Thus, we are told that:

> By means of outer sense, a property of our mind, we represent to ourselves objects as outside us, and all without exception in space. In space their shape, magnitude, and relation to one another are determined or determinable.[90]

And:

> How, then, can there exist in the mind an outer intuition which precedes the objects themselves, and in which the concept of these objects can be determined *a priori?* Manifestly not otherwise than in so far as the intuition has its seat in the subject only, as the formal character of the subject, in virtue of which, in being affected by objects, it obtains *immediate representation,* that is, *intuition,* of them.[91]

I shall return to the important claim that space, *qua* form of intuition 'has its seat in the subject only'. First though, let me be absolutely clear about the position under present consideration. According to this position, intuitions are representations of things. These things are represented through the operation of our distinctive cognitive forms – sensible and intellectual – the sensible form of which guarantees that they be given to us in spatio-temporal form. They provide an external constraint upon thought in the sense that they exist independently of particular acts of conceiving of them, there being no implication that we have a constructive role to play with respect to their nature and existence.

The main difficulty with this way of thinking about intuitions is that it flies in the face of Kant's repeated insistence that things in themselves are to be set apart from the realm of appearance, and that, considered as such, they are unknowable. Working with this alternative conception in mind, and assuming that Kant is committed hereby to a dualism of appearance and thing, we are compelled to conclude that the source of the given element of experience is unknowable. The further implications are that we are left with no way of explaining how this source can affect us and no way of guaranteeing that it even exists. At this point, Kant's insistence that his position constitutes an advance upon that of his idealist predecessor begins to look rather dubious.

Further evidence of this tension comes to light if we reflect upon Kant's conception of the status of space and time. He tells us that:

It is, therefore, only from the human standpoint that we can speak of space, of extended things.[92]

And:

What we have meant to say is that all our intuition is nothing but the representation of appearance; that the things which we intuit are not in themselves what we intuit them as being, nor their relations so constituted in themselves as they appear to us, and that if the subject, or even only the subjective constitution of the senses in general, be removed, the whole constitution and all the relations of objects in space and time, nay space and time themselves, would vanish.[93]

He concludes:

Everything that is represented through a sense is so far always appearance.[94]

It is not that by our sensibility we cannot know the nature of things in themselves in any save a confused fashion; we do not apprehend them in any fashion whatsoever.[95]

The idea that the things we intuit are not in themselves what we intuit them as being is suggestive again of a non-dualistic conception of the relation between appearance and thing. Taken alongside the other claims Kant makes here, however, a very different picture emerges – one which is explicitly and predominantly dualistic. We are told, for example, that all our intuition is nothing but the representation of appearance, that it is only from the human standpoint that we can speak of extended things, that these things vanish with the removal of the subject, and that by our sensibility we do not apprehend things *in any fashion whatsoever.* The implication here is that the things we intuit are not in themselves things and are not things in themselves. Taking account of this alternative picture, then, it looks as if Kant is forced into one of the following positions, none of which can lend credence to his realist aspirations. According to the first position, the things we intuit – the things constituted by the joint operations of sensibility and understanding – are mere appearances whose nature and existence as things is determined by us. On this way of thinking then, we really are 'confin'd barely to our own ideas'. The second position promises to do justice to the idea that there is a genuine constraint upon thought, for it involves the claim that this constraint is provided by things in themselves. Given that we do not apprehend these things *in any fashion whatsoever,* however, we have no account of how we could be affected by them and no guarantee that they even exist. The putative constraint is empty. Finally, and this option serves to combine elements of the previous two, it is claimed that the things which constrain our thinking are *qua* spatio-temporal causally interacting things constructed by us, but the material from which the construction proceeds has its source in things in themselves. This final position inherits all of the difficulties previously rehearsed.[96]

We can conclude that Kant's conception of the given element of experience affords him the right to avoid a phenomenalist position only if it is articulated from within a non-dualistic way of thinking of the appearance/reality relation. By contrast, if we take heed of the not infrequent places where a dualistic framework predominates, then we are forced to conclude that Kant is not, after all, in a position to allow that representation does not produce its object as far as existence is concerned, and has failed to provide a version of idealism which can guarantee that, in perceiving things, we are not 'confin'd barely to our own ideas'.

Intellectual intuition

We have seen that, for Kant, an intellectual intuition is a placeholder for a mode of cognition for which there can only really be a negative characterization. Thus understood, it is a mode which does not involve being affected from without, and which is such that the distinction between thinking and being no longer exists.

Although much of what Kant says suggests that this mode of cognition is something we cannot properly comprehend, it is possible to interpret it in terms which are compatible with a non-dualistic conception of the appearance/reality relation and which do not rule out the possibility that it is a cognition to which we could hope to aspire.[97] According to one such interpretation, we are to take seriously Kant's claim that intellectual intuition involves a mode of cognition which does not involve being sensorily affected so as to allow that he is gesturing hereby towards the possibility of an absolute conception of reality in the sense intended by Bernard Williams, where there is no implication that this absolute conception is in principle unattainable. The idea here is that we can abstract from those features of experience which are a function not merely of the thing experienced but also of the subject who is doing the experiencing, the most obvious example being those features whose nature is determined by the contingencies of a particular sensory modality, the colour of an object, for example. In such a case, it makes sense to suppose that the relevant experienced property is an appearance. It is an appearance in the sense that it belongs not to the nature of the thing as it is in itself, but rather to its nature as it appears to a subject with a visual apparatus.[98]

According to a second interpretation – one which begins from Kant's suggestion that an intellectual intuition involves a collapse of the distinction between thinking and being – we deny that there is an external constraint upon thought in the manner envisaged by one who holds to a dualistic conception of the relation between appearance and thing. That is to say, we reject the idea that thought is constrained by something which is inaccessible to thought in the way that Kant's thing in itself is on one interpretation. Thus understood, the distinction between thought and being is collapsed only in the innocuous sense that it is denied that these two terms are to be dualistically opposed. The further implication is that an absolute conception is, after all, a realizable ideal.

Both of these ways of understanding the notion of an intellectual intuition find some kind of expression in Kant. The first line of thought is implicit in the distinction he makes between our sensible mode of intuiting things and the nature which belongs to those things in themselves; the second in his insistence that concepts and intuitions are internally related, and that it is only by virtue of such a relation that we can be said to be related in thought to determinate things.

Nevertheless, there are further elements of Kant's position which are more difficult to accommodate in this manner – in particular, his commitment to the idea that the appearance properties of things comprise not merely their secondary properties, but also those which we would ordinarily take to be intrinsic to them. The implication here is that an absolute conception of reality requires that we set aside not merely the medium-sized things with which we interact on a day-to-day basis, but also the more theoretical entities which form the province of scientific inquiry. Bearing these points in mind, and taking heed of his insistence that the notion of an intellectual intuition is something we cannot properly comprehend, it is difficult to avoid concluding that the absolute conception Kant has in mind is something approximating to a God's eye view.

This second interpretation of Kant's notion of an intellectual intuition fits neatly with a commitment to a dualistic conception of the appearance/reality relation, implying as it does that there is a level of reality which is inaccessible to us and which is to be set apart from anything of which we could have experience and knowledge. There is, however, a further train of thought at work here – one which comes to light when we reflect upon Kant's interest in providing a sketch of what is involved in the notion of a divine intellect. Now I have noted already that some of Kant's remarks about the thing in itself invite a theological interpretation, for he toys with the idea that there is a transcendent ground to the world – something which is to be set apart from it and which grounds the order it exhibits. He speculates further that we treat this ground as a subject – as he puts it, the predicates of inner sense, representation, and thought are not inconsistent with its nature. Understood with this latter theme in mind, the claim Kant makes at A383 – that the corporeal world vanishes with the removal of the subject – no longer carries a commitment to phenomenalism. Rather, it suggests a theological version of the claim that to be is to be perceived – a claim which, as noted in my discussion of Berkeley, implies that God is causally responsible for the things we perceive – that *to be is to be caused to exist by God.*[99] The further implication is that an intuitive understanding involves a conflation of thought and being in the strongest sense. That is to say, it implies not merely that things in themselves are accessible to cognition, but, rather, that it is the activity of thinking which brings them into existence.

This theological theme need not be incompatible with a commitment to a nondualistic conception of the appearance/reality relation. For as I suggested in my discussion of Berkeley, we can make a distinction between the question of the relation in which we stand to God and that of the relation in which we stand to things. Understood from this perspective, we can grant Kant's interest in offering a partial and highly speculative description of the manner in which God stands to the world, whilst allowing that it has no bearing upon the metaphysical and epistemological status of the things we experience.

Certainly, there is nothing incoherent to such a suggestion. Furthermore, it ds to be taken seriously when set alongside all the evidence there is to suggest that Kant is committed to a non-dualistic conception of the appearance/reality distinction. Once we take heed of the various tensions in his position, however, it becomes more difficult to maintain such a stance. For these tensions cannot be written off simply by allowing that any remnant of dualism in his position is simply an expression of his interest in the God/world relation. On the contrary, the dualism in question has quite obvious repercussions for an understanding of the objective status of the things we perceive, implying as it does that these things are mere appearances which cannot be intelligibly related to things in themselves. It is no coincidence, I think, that a similar tension is to be found in Berkeley's position. For, as we have seen, he never makes it absolutely clear how we are to comprehend the metaphysical role played by God – whether He is central to an account of the nature of the things we perceive, or alternatively, whether these things can be understood in terms which require no reference to the law of a divine Being.

Some concluding remarks

We can conclude that there are significant similarities to be drawn between Kant's position and that of the other philosophers I have discussed. All of them have an interest in the subjective conditions which must be met if we are to have experience and knowledge of things, whilst wishing to avoid the implication that the world thus revealed is a world of mere appearance. In Kant's scheme of things the details of this first requirement are laid out in his account of the sensible and intellectual conditions which must be met if there is to be determinate experience and knowledge of things. The second requirement finds expression in his claim that transcendental idealism is a species of realism.

The idea that transcendental idealism is a species of realism suggests that the realm of appearance – which, for Kant, is the realm of causally related spatio-temporal things – is a realm of mind-independent things. And once this position is granted, it becomes both pointless and counterproductive to suppose that there is a further realm of things in themselves. We have seen that both Nietzsche and Berkeley agree that a commitment to a further realm of this kind can be criticized on such grounds. Furthermore, there is a similar attitude to be found in Kant, when, for example, he implies that it is a mistake to suppose that things in themselves are to be dualistically opposed to appearances, and insists that the realm beyond appearances is quite empty. Nevertheless, and as in the case of these other philosophers, there is equal evidence to suggest that he is endorsing a quite different position. For as I have shown – and it is at this point that the syndrome gets a grip – he implies on occasion that things in themselves *are* to be dualistically opposed to appearances, and that the claim that the realm beyond appearances is empty serves simply as an expression of *our* epistemological limitations.

It follows that there are good and bad things to be found in all of the philosophers examined so far, and that, ultimately, their insights are hindered by an implicit commitment to a framework which goes against their better philosophical judgements. In the following chapter I shall consider how Hegel seeks to dispense with this framework once and for all so as to define a form of idealism which satisfies the required realist aim. It remains to be seen whether he succeeds in this enterprise, or whether he is forced yet once more into the long line of idealists whose anti-sceptical pretensions turn out to be empty.

4 Concepts and reality
Hegel

Things in themselves

Hegel's absolute idealism has been described as transcendental idealism without the thing in itself.[1] It has been claimed, however, that it is a form of idealism which, to use Rorty's words, is a 'patsy for realistic reaction'.[2] It is a patsy for realistic reaction because the removal of the thing in itself, according to this interpretation, leaves one with no way of accounting for the sense in which we are capable of engaging in thought with mind-independent things. The claim then is that Hegel's idealism is tantamount to subjectivism or phenomenalism – a claim which, if justified, suggests that Hegel has not succeeded in overthrowing the framework which pervades the arguments of his predecessors, and hence, that he is equally in the grip of the syndrome.

Certainly, Hegel rejects Kant's notion of the thing in itself. He also retains enough of Kant's epistemology to warrant describing his position as transcendental idealism without the thing in itself. Nevertheless, Hegel believes that a rejection of the thing in itself, *as that notion is understood by Kant,* is a move which is required if we are to provide a genuine solution to scepticism. He believes also that its residual presence in Kant renders inevitable a subjective form of idealism. From a Hegelian perspective then, Kant's position is no better than the alternative forms of idealism it was intended to supersede.[3]

Hegel's criticisms of Kant's notion of the thing in itself are similar to those which find expression in Nietzsche's writings and can be traced back ultimately to Berkeley's criticisms of Locke's conception of substance. Thus, Hegel agrees that there is no sense to be made of the idea that reality in itself is that which lies beyond the realm revealed in our concepts – that it is inaccessible and indefinable. Furthermore, he reaches this conclusion via a consideration which is taken seriously by Nietzsche and Berkeley, namely, that once we remove our concepts so as to reveal reality in the manner demanded by this model, we shall find that there is nothing there. Here, for example, is what he says in *The Encyclopaedia Logic:*

> The *thing-in-itself* (and here 'thing' embraces God, or the spirit, as well) expresses the ob-ject, inasmuch as *abstraction* is made of all that it is for consciousness, of all determinations of feeling, as well of all determinate

thoughts about it. It is easy to see what is left, namely, what is *completely abstract,* or totally *empty,* and determined only as what is 'beyond'; the *negative* of representation, of feeling, of determinate thinking, etc. ... We must be quite surprised, therefore, to read so often that one does not know what the *thing-in-itself* is; for nothing is easier to know than this.[4]

And in *Faith and Knowledge,* he describes as follows the position which arises with this conception of the thing in itself:

> On one side there is the Ego, with its productive imagination or rather with its synthetic unity which, taken thus in isolation, is formal unity of the manifold. But next to it there is an infinity of sensations and, if you like, of things in themselves. Once it is abandoned by the categories, this realm cannot be anything but a formless lump ... . Objectivity and stability derive solely from the categories; the realm of things in themselves is without categories; yet it is something for itself and for reflection. The only idea we can form of this realm is like that of the iron king in the fairy tale whom a self-consciousness permeates with veins of objectivity so that he can stand erect. But then formal transcendental idealism sucks these veins out of the king so that the upright shape collapses and becomes something in between form and lump, repulsive to look at.[5]

Kant agrees that no positive content can be given to the notion of a thing in itself once it has been set apart from anything of which we could have determinate experience. Nevertheless, there is evidence in his work to suggest a commitment to this dualistic way of thinking – a commitment which belies his insistence at times that such a framework be avoided. Hegel has no problem with things in themselves *per se.* What he objects to is the idea that they are to be conceived of as lying beyond the realm revealed in our concepts, that, at best, they are to be treated as the unknowable causes of what appears in that realm. He challenges this conception on the ground that things in themselves 'collapse and become something in between form and lump, repulsive to look at', his criticism here being comparable to Berkeley's complaint that the Lockean conception of substance is 'repugnant'. Thus, and in response to Kant's insistence that 'representation does not produce its object as far as *existence* is concerned',[6] Hegel complains 'the fact that things merely *are* is of no help to them. Time catches up with *what is,* and so what is will soon be *what is not* as well'.[7] A rather picturesque way, perhaps, of insisting, à la Wittgenstein, that a nothing in this context would do as well as a something about which nothing can be said.

Concepts and intuitions

Thus far, Hegel has ignored the non-dualistic strand in Kant's position. This rather one-sided interpretation is continued into his discussion of Kant's conception of the categories of thought. Thus, we are told that:

(E)ven the objectivity of thinking in Kant's sense is itself again only subjective in its form, because, according to Kant, thoughts, although they are universal and necessary determinations, are still *only our* thoughts, and are cut off from what the thing is *in itself* by an impassable gulf. On the contrary, the true objectivity of thinking consists in this: that thoughts are not merely our thoughts, but at the same time the *in itself* of things and of whatever else is objective.[8]

Hegel is complaining that Kant's categories, although they are held to provide the universal and necessary determinations of appearances, remain subjective in the sense that they are cut off from things in themselves by 'an impassable gulf'. This result, as he sees it, is simply a consequence of Kant's contention that appearances are to be distinguished from things in themselves. Hegel's way of giving expression to this 'subjectivity' of thinking is to say that, for Kant, thoughts 'are still *only our* thoughts', that the categories belong 'only to us'.

A dualistic interpretation is presupposed also in Hegel's criticisms of Kant's conception of the matter of experience. Hegel is willing to concede with his predecessor that there is a given element to experience. Thus, he tells us that a system of idealism cannot be based on the idea that nothing comes from without,[9] and in the context of discussing Locke's philosophical position, he argues as follows:

(a)s to the question in point we must in the first place say that it is true that man commences with experience if he desires to arrive at thought ... . Consciousness thus undoubtedly obtains all conceptions and Notions from experience and in experience; the only question is what we understand by experience.[10]

It is the question of what we understand by experience that serves as the starting point for Hegel's criticisms of Kant in this context. For Hegel argues that Kant is working with a faulty conception of experience, a conception which, he believes, is really just an expression of the subjective idealism he is compelled to advance. We can begin to appreciate Hegel's criticisms by examining his attitude to Kant's claim that the categories need to be 'filled out' by the matter of experience. Hegel agrees that the categories, taken by themselves, are empty. Thus, he claims that we must be able to advance by their means to things in themselves. As I have noted, however, Kant has a difficulty accepting this latter claim. For although he tells us – not entirely consistently – that the categories have an unlimited field, he makes it quite clear that they have determinate application and use only in experience, whose other component is the faculty of intuition. It is this other component which, for Kant, delivers the *matter* of experience. As Hegel sees it, Kant is forced to conclude that this experiential matter is equally subjective. He is forced into this conclusion, he claims, because the appearances constituted by the joint production of concepts and intuitions are 'nothing but a species of my representation', and are to be distinguished from things in themselves. Hegel sums up the resultant position as follows, beginning with a description which corresponds to his own preferred viewpoint:

Now although the categories (e.g. unity, cause and effect, etc.) pertain to thinking as such, it does not at all follow from this that they must therefore be something subjective of ours, and not also determinations of ob-jects themselves. But according to Kant's view, this is what is supposed to be the case, and his philosophy is *subjective idealism,* inasmuch as the Ego (the knowing subject) furnishes both the *form* and the *material* of knowing – the former as *thinking* and the latter as *sensing* subject.[11]

And in his *Lectures on the History of Philosophy,* he claims that, for Kant:

(t)he whole of knowledge remains within subjectivity, and on the other side there is the thing-in-*itself* as external.[12]

Notwithstanding Hegel's criticisms of Kant in this context – criticisms which find support in one reading of the *Critique* – he applauds Kant for seeing that the joint product of sensibility and understanding is required if we are to have experience and knowledge of objects. Hegel's way of expressing this point is to say that '(t)here is thus here present a perceptive understanding or an understanding perception'. He continues, however:

(b)ut Kant does not see this, he does not bring these thoughts together: he does not grasp the fact that he has here brought both sides of knowledge into one, and has thereby expressed their implicitude. Knowledge itself is in fact the unity and truth of both moments; but with Kant the thinking understanding and sensuousness are both something particular, and they are only united in an external, superficial way, just as a piece of wood and a leg might be bound together by a cord.[13]

Given Hegel's willingness to concede that experience involves our being affected from without, it would be odd to suppose that his criticisms of Kant's conception of the relation between concepts and intuitions involves a denial of the idea that there is a given element to experience. Furthermore, since he accepts that Kant's imposition of a distinction between these two sources of knowledge constitutes a huge advance upon previous philosophical positions, he cannot be wanting to conflate these two sources. As he puts it, '(o)ur finding both these elements in experience demonstrates indeed that a correct analysis has been made'.[14]

Hegel's main bone of contention is that Kant conceives of concepts and intuitions as 'both something particular', as 'united in an external, superficial way'. The further accusation is that he does so even whilst advancing a claim which compels him to deny that this could be so, namely, that thoughts without content are empty, intuitions without concepts are blind. Why is Kant compelled to argue in this manner? According to Hegel's diagnosis, the explanation is to be found in his commitment to a realm of things in themselves which is set apart from the appearances yielded by the joint product of sensibility and understanding. Thus, having applauded Kant for claiming that experience requires both sensibility and understanding, he tells us that his mistake is to:

> (connect) with this the statement that experience grasps phenomena only, and that by means of the knowledge which we obtain through experience we do not know things as they are in themselves, but only as they are in the form of laws of perception and sensuousness.[15]

Hegel is suggesting here that Kant's conception of the data of experience as externally related to thought stems from his assumption that there is a non-conceptual realm of things in themselves which serves as its unknowable cause. The reason – which seems perfectly plausible – is that once the realm of things in themselves is in place, our capacity for receptivity is re-interpreted so as to become that by virtue of which we are affected by this realm.[16] Yet it is a consequence of accepting this account that the data of experience precisely can be understood in abstraction from the concepts by means of which it is rendered accessible to us.

It is at this stage that we can appreciate the force of Hegel's complaint that the spectre of subjective idealism looms large. For if it is accepted that the data of experience is caused by an unknowable realm of things in themselves, there must surely be an acknowledgment of the difficulties which accompany any attempt to explain how we could be affected in this manner. And once this explanatory difficulty is conceded, there is no guarantee that reference to the given element of experience will afford one the right to allow that the objects we conceptualize are independent of our minds.[17] All of this is familiar from the previous chapter.

A methodological objection

Hegel's criticisms of Kant are consolidated into a methodological objection to his approach. For although he agrees that the forms of thinking must be subject to scrutiny if we are to attain knowledge and truth,[18] he believes that there is something flawed and even incoherent about the way in which Kant sets about this task. This objection is developed in his *Phenomenology of Spirit*. Here, for example, is what he says in the opening section of the introduction:

> It is a natural assumption that in philosophy, before we start to deal with its proper subject-matter, viz. the actual cognition of what truly is, one must first of all come to an understanding about cognition, which is regarded either as the *instrument* by which we are to get hold of the Absolute[19], or as the *medium* through which one discovers it.

This assumption, he continues, leads eventually to the conclusion that:

> (t)he whole project of securing for consciousness through cognition what exists in itself is absurd, and that there is a boundary between cognition and the Absolute that completely separates them.[20]

Hegel does not mention Kant by name here, but it is clear that he is the object of his attack. As he sees it, Kant's approach contains two related difficulties. First, it does not concern itself with the proper subject matter of philosophy, namely, 'the actual cognition of what truly is', focusing as it does upon cognition in abstraction from 'what truly is'. Second, and Hegel takes this to be a consequence of Kant's indirect approach, it treats cognition as an instrument or a medium.

Hegel's first objection must be stated with care. As I have said, he has no difficulty with the idea that a philosopher should proceed via an investigation of cognition, where this is understood to involve an examination of the forms of thinking. What he objects to is the idea that the realm of cognition is to be understood in abstraction from 'what truly is'. As Hegel sees it, this idea finds expression in Kant's assumption that things in themselves are inaccessible to cognition – an assumption which is said to exclude the possibility of our attaining genuine knowledge. Second, and I shall return to this point below, Hegel believes that it is a consequence of Kant's commitment to this faulty conception of cognition that his thinking fails to yield *philosophical* knowledge. It is with this latter point in mind that we can appreciate the force of his complaint that Kant fails to meet the true aim of philosophy.

The idea that Kant treats cognition as an instrument or medium by means of which to gain access to things is a reference to the two 'fundamental sources of mind' which, for Kant, must be operative if we are to have experience and knowledge of things. Considered as an instrument, cognition is the capacity to think the objects of experience; considered as a medium, it is the capacity to be affected by them. I have noted that Hegel is happy to allow that understanding and sensibility must be operative if there is to be experience and knowledge of objects. And, to the extent that instruments and mediums can be adequate to the task of grasping things as they really are, there is nothing objectionable to conceiving of the joint operations of mind in these terms. On the face of it then, there is something odd about Hegel's claim later on in this passage that 'the use of an instrument on a thing certainly does not let it be what it is for itself, but rather sets out to shape and to alter it'.

Hegel's real objection emerges in a later paragraph when, after having described the 'fear of error' which goes hand in hand with the Kantian conception of cognition, he makes the following point:

> Should we not be concerned as to whether this fear of error is not just the error itself? Indeed, this fear takes something – a great deal in fact – for granted as truth … . To be specific, it takes for granted certain ideas about cognition as an *instrument* and as a *medium* … . Above all, it presupposes that the Absolute stands on one side and cognition on the other, independent and separated from it, and yet is something real; or in other words, it presupposes that cognition which, since it is excluded from the Absolute, is surely outside of the truth as well, is nevertheless true, an assumption whereby what calls itself the fear of error reveals itself rather as the fear of truth. [21]

It is clear from what Hegel says here that his difficulty with the idea that cognition is an instrument and medium stems from the further assumption that things in themselves are excluded from cognition. For once this assumption is in place, it follows that the joint operations of cognition have to yield something other than those things. At this point, the fear of error is inevitable, and one is forced to conclude, as Nietzsche did, that 'the adequate expression of an object in a subject is a contradictory impossibility'.[22] It is to be noted, however, that Hegel is not here telling us that the Kantian framework is false. All that he is questioning is the idea that it be taken for granted as true.

In order to appreciate the force of Hegel's criticisms, we need to understand his attitude towards scepticism – an attitude which finds expression in his 1802 essay 'The Relation of Skepticism to Philosophy' and in his discussion of ancient scepticism in the *Lectures on the History of Philosophy*.[23] Hegel takes scepticism very seriously. However, it is the scepticism of the ancients which, he believes, is of true philosophical significance. By contrast, he has little time for the sceptical arguments of more modern philosophers such as Descartes and Hume. Ancient scepticism involves the method of equipollence which is the method of setting in opposition equally good arguments on both sides of any given issue so as to produce an equal balance of justification for them. The upshot of engaging in this method is that one is led to suspend one's belief with respect to the relevant issue so that dogmatism is avoided.[24] From Hegel's point of view this method has two advantages. First, it does not involve the acceptance of any belief or assumption which might itself be a target for scepticism; second, it gains application to any kind of belief, regardless of its content, and is therefore quite general in scope.

I shall return to the significance of this sceptical method for Hegel's manner of proceeding. For the moment, though, let me consider the difficulties he finds with more modern approaches to scepticism. Modern scepticism proceeds, not by the method of equipollence, but rather by taking for granted one set of beliefs or propositions so as to demonstrate that it is unjustified to move from this first set to that of another which, by the non-sceptic's lights, is held to be equally unproblematic. A typical and familiar example here is the move from propositions about sense-experience to those concerning physical objects.[25] As Hegel sees it, this procedure, resting as it does upon the assumption that there are certain beliefs which are immune from sceptical doubt – in this case, beliefs concerning sense-experience – is both unjustified and dogmatic.

Hegel's criticisms here can be related to the particular grievance he has towards Kant's idea that cognition is to be viewed as an instrument or medium. For his main objection is that Kant is not justified in assuming that things in themselves are to be excluded from cognition. The point is expressed as follows in *The Relation of Skepticism to Philosophy:*

> According to this newest scepticism the human faculty of cognition is a thing which has concepts, and because it has nothing more than concepts it cannot go out to the things which are outside it. It cannot find out about them or explore them ... for the two things are ... 'different in kind'.[26]

At this point it would be open to the Kantian to object that Hegel has failed to appreciate the reasons for insisting that our cognitive capacities are limited, namely, the problem of the antinomies and the failure of metaphysics generally. According to this objection then, Kant is not simply assuming that the dualistic framework is to be taken as the default, rather, he has *argued* for this conclusion. From Hegel's point of view these arguments gain their force only to the extent that we accept the dualistic framework with which he takes issue, in which case there is a point to his criticism that Kant is making an unwarranted assumption. Nevertheless, nothing that has been said on Hegel's behalf shows that it is wrong to suppose that concepts and reality are to be dualistically opposed. Obviously then, something more needs to be done if it is to be demonstrated that the alternative non-dualistic framework is the correct one.

Given Hegel's wish to avoid importing unwarranted assumptions into his inquiry, it is crucial that he proceeds in a manner which sidesteps this difficulty. Thus, and in response to the requirement that nothing be taken for granted, he is going to proceed by examining on their own terms positions which presuppose the dualistic framework with which he takes issue, his aim being to show that they cannot withstand intellectual scrutiny. This approach is intended also to give expression to the respect he accords to the sceptical method of equipollence. For the point of rejecting in this manner viewpoints which stand opposed to his own is to show that there is not, after all, an equal balance of justification for the relevant positions, and that his own preferred viewpoint wins out.

The *Phenomenology of Spirit*: some introductory remarks

The opening chapters of the *Phenomenology of Spirit* offer a clear illustration of Hegel's approach as it applies to the problem of the concept/reality relation. In particular, we find Hegel examining a variety of positions exemplified by various philosophical figures both past and present – positions which, in their different ways, entail a breakdown of the subject–object relation. Hegel refers to the positions in question as forms of consciousness. 'Form of consciousness' is his general term for any knowledge-claim making practice. There can be knowledge claims which are not object-directed – ones, for example, which concern the relation between subjects. Nor is there any requirement that they be understood as philosophical accounts. By contrast, the knowledge claims in the opening chapters *are* object-directed and they are best viewed as particular philosophical accounts of object-directed consciousness.

The order of the forms of consciousness discussed by Hegel is not entirely arbitrary, the constraint coming from the fact that each new form purports to incorporate and to solve the problems inherent in the previous one.[27] It turns out, however, that the putative solution offered by the new form of consciousness raises difficulties of its own – difficulties whose acknowledgment generates yet another form which is shown on examination to be equally problematic. In this way the succession is invested with a retrospective necessity, this being the sense in which Hegel calls the *Phenomenology* a 'recollection'.

The most significant feature of the illustrated forms of consciousness is that they presuppose a common philosophical framework – one which is comparable to that which defines the syndrome. It is this framework which dictates the shape of the solutions thrown up by one form of consciousness to another, and which is held to guarantee their ultimate demise. Hegel's positive aim is to use this diagnosis as a starting-point from which to define an alternative framework by means of which to comprehend the subject–object relation, and in this way to give more adequate expression to the insights motivating the positions under attack.

Sense-certainty

The first chapter of the *Phenomenology* is entitled 'Sense-certainty: or the "this" and "meaning",' and the account of object-directed consciousness it provides is described by Hegel as 'knowledge of the immediate or what is'[28]. He offers the following characterization:

> Our approach to the object must also be *immediate* or *receptive;* we must alter nothing in the object as it presents itself. In *ap*prehending it, we must refrain from trying to *com*prehend it. [29]

The position described here rests upon the assumption that reality can be apprehended with no conceptual mediation – that non-conceptual apprehension is sufficient to account for experience of an object. Such an assumption was particularly prevalent in German Philosophy in 1806, furnishing Hegel with a contingent historical reason for beginning his inquiry at this point.[30] More significant for my purposes, however, is the relevance this position has for an understanding and assessment of Kant. I have argued already that Kant takes a rather ambivalent attitude to the issue of whether there can be non-conceptual apprehension – apprehension without comprehension, as Hegel puts it. His official position has it that determinate experience requires the joint operations of sensibility and understanding – a claim which, from Hegel's point of view, constitutes a huge leap forward. Nevertheless, we have seen that there is a reading of Kant according to which there is a non-conceptual order of things that stands dualistically opposed to the realm revealed in our concepts. And once this reading is in place, it looks as if we are compelled to suppose on his behalf that sensibility is that by virtue of which this non-conceptual realm affects us.

It should be clear from what I have said already on Hegel's behalf that he takes this dualistic picture to be inherently problematic. In particular, he believes that its acceptance leaves us with no way of explaining how we can be affected by things in themselves, and hence no way of lending substance to the idea that thought is constrained from without. It is his aim here to expand upon this negative line of thought.

He begins by pre-empting what is perhaps the most natural reaction to the initial description we have been given of object-directed consciousness, namely, that it provides an exemplary instance of the relation in which we stand to an object when we are conscious of it.[31] Thus, he claims that the subject–object relation described by Sense-certainty appears to constitute the 'richest kind of knowledge'.[32] It does so because it purports to provide an unmediated access to the object such that 'nothing is altered in the object as it presents itself':[33]

> Sense-certainty appears to be the truest knowledge; for it has not as yet omitted anything from the object, but has the object before it in its perfect entirety.[34]

This line of thought has provided what many philosophers have taken to be the death blow to any position which denies that acquaintance in this sense is the fundamental epistemic relation in terms of which to explain our capacity to experience objects. For, so the argument goes, it is only by allowing that the object exists in its perfect entirety before the subject that one can make sense of the idea that it is genuinely independent of the subject, and that the subject is appreciating it for what it really is. The further claim is that a position like Sense-certainty is the only way of accommodating these constraints.[35]

The evidence I have taken from Hegel so far suggests that he is happy with the idea that we have direct acquaintance with objects. For he tells us that a system of idealism cannot be based on the supposition that nothing comes to us from without, and is anxious to distance himself from the Kantian version of this claim on the ground that it implies that our relation to things is indirect. We must consider then whether this theme finds expression in the *Phenomenology,* and if so, how it bears upon the conclusions he reaches in the present chapter.

Having described the considerations which motivate philosophers to insist that our relation to objects is direct and unmediated, Hegel argues as follows:

> This very certainty proves itself to be the most abstract and poorest truth. All that it says about what it knows is just that it is; and its truth contains nothing but the sheer being of the thing.[36]

Hegel is claiming that what appears to be a paradigm epistemic relation – a paradigm in the sense that the relevant object is presented to the subject in such a way that 'nothing is altered in the object as it presents itself' – turns out to be entirely vacuous. It is for this reason that the certainty in question turns out to be 'the most abstract and poorest truth'. What is less clear is why this certainty is vacuous, and what Hegel means when he tells us that its truth contains nothing but the sheer being of the thing.

I have mentioned already that the Sense-certainty theorist is committed to claiming that non-conceptual apprehension is sufficient to guarantee experience of a determinate object. I have noted also that, on one reading, Kant's commitment to a realm of things in themselves leads him to conceive of sensibility as that by virtue of which we are affected by this realm. Hegel's attitude to this move is to question its coherence on various grounds, one of which is that the realm in question is indeterminate in content. As such, it is difficult to see how it can perform

its intended aim of providing a genuine constraint upon thought. It is with this latter objection in mind that we can appreciate his complaint that Sense-certainty is
vacuous, that its truth contains nothing but the sheer being of the thing.

Hegel purports to vindicate these criticisms by taking the theory of Sense-certainty on its own terms so as to determine whether it involves a conception of the
subject–object relation which can be said to constitute the richest kind of knowledge.[37] To this end, he begins by asking how we are to conceive of the object with
which the subject is immediately acquainted according to this theory. Now in line
with the requirement that the acquaintance in question is non-conceptual, it is
ruled out that one can specify *what* the object in question is. Thus, Hegel grants
the theorist what would appear to be the only kind of apparatus available to him if
he is to secure such a reference. That is to say, he allows that the theorist can refer
to the relevant object using the expressions 'this', 'here', and 'now'.[38]
Accordingly, Hegel's original question is transformed into that of how we are to
conceive of the *this-here-now* which, for the Sense-certainty theorist, is the determinate object of immediate apprehension.

Hegel's aim is to show that the Sense-certainty theorist is unable to secure reference to the object of his acquaintance. The difficulty he has in mind can best be
appreciated if it is remembered that the theorist's use of the relevant demonstra-
tive resources is intended to give expression to an apprehension of an object that
involves no conceptual component. Thus, he is unable to conceptualize the object
of his acquaintance, to say what it is. He cannot, for example, intend this object as
opposed to another which happens to be in the vicinity, and he cannot specify
which aspect of the object serves as the focus of his interest. At most then, he is
confined to allowing that the object of his acquaintance is all or none of the many
contenders which would lend determinacy to the use of 'this-here-now'. Hegel's
way of expressing this point is to say that the universal is the true content of
Sense-certainty, where the force of the term 'universal' is intended to capture the
sense in which the 'this-here-now' is indeterminate in scope. The difficulty is
described as follows:

> 'Here' is, e.g., the tree. If I turn round, this truth has vanished and is converted
> into its opposite: 'No tree is here, but a house instead'. 'Here' itself does not
> vanish; on the contrary, it abides constant in the vanishing of the house, and the
> tree, etc., and is indifferently house or tree .... *Pure Being* remains, therefore,
> as the essence of this sense-certainty, since sense-certainty has demonstrated in
> its own self that the truth of its object is the universal.[39]

Thus far, Hegel has sought to demonstrate that one initially plausible way of
accounting for a subject's experience of an object is unsuccessful. According to
this position, the subject stands to the object in a relation of non-conceptual
apprehension. Hegel has argued that acquaintance in this sense is insufficient to
establish reference to a determinate object, and that the putative knowledge is
indeterminate in content. Hence, the force of 'non-conceptual' in this context is
intended to rule out the possibility of saying *what* the relevant object is.

Perception

In the second chapter of the *Phenomenology* – 'Perception: Or the Thing and the Deception' – Hegel considers a response which promises to sidestep the difficulties inherent in the Sense-certainty theorist's position so as to render determinate the object of acquaintance. The chapter is not an easy read, and its theme can best be appreciated by considering the way in which Berkeley responds to Locke's conception of substance, for the position in question encapsulates the idea that the things we perceive are collections of sensible qualities.

It will be remembered that one motive behind such a position is to avoid the idea that substance is to be set apart from the things we perceive – things like cats and men, for example. For conceived as such, it is a something to which we can give no determinate content, and which can be of little use in comprehending the nature of these things. If, however, this new position is taken at face value, then we are forced to concede that the qualities which figure in the relevant collections do not belong to anything. I noted in Chapter 1 that there are metaphysical difficulties with such a position. In particular, it assumes without justification that there can be qualities without a bearer, and that these qualities can serve as the basis from which to construct the idea of a thing. Of equal significance, however, is the fact that it involves a commitment to the conception of substance which figures in the target position, namely, that according to which substance is to be set apart from the things we perceive.

Hegel's criticisms of Perception can be understood in a similar light,[40] for his main point is going to be that although it is intended to be an improvement upon Sense-certainty, promising as it does to lend determinacy to the object of experience, it fails ultimately to achieve its intended goal. It fails to do so, Hegel will argue, because it presupposes the very framework which frustrates the Sense-certainty theorist's attempts to render determinate the object of his acquaintance. That is to say, it rests upon the assumption that things in themselves are to be set apart from the things we perceive. Against both of these proposals, Hegel is going to claim that the qualities we experience can be rendered determinate only by reference to the idea of a thing to which they belong. He is committed to claiming therefore that the experience of the Perception theorist is indeterminate in content, and that he, no less than his predecessor, is unable to given an account of *what* he is experiencing.

Hegel begins by claiming that the Perception theorist takes what is present to him as universal, and although the force of this claim remains vague at this stage, it is clearly intended to call to mind his conclusion that 'the universal is the true content of sense-certainty'. Now this conclusion serves to spell the downfall of Sense-certainty, for Hegel's point is that the Sense-certainty theorist is confined to using terms like 'this' and 'here', terms which, in so far as they are indifferent to particular objects and places, cannot be used to secure reference to a determinate object. Thus, the sense in which the universal is the true content of Sense-certainty is the sense in which its content is indeterminate.

Hegel is going to conclude that Perception must suffer a similar fate. Initially, though, we are told that the Perception theorist is in a position to rectify this difficulty, that he has the resources for rendering determinate his use of such terms. He can do so, according to the present suggestion, by making reference to the qualities of a thing. Hegel's way of putting this point is to say that Perception contains 'difference or manifoldness, within its own essence',[41] that the 'This is ... established as *not* This', that the 'sense-element is still present, but not in the way it was supposed to be in immediate certainty'.[42] According to the Perception theorist then, the object with which one is acquainted is rendered determinate by virtue of the fact that one apprehends its qualities. At this point, of course, we arrive at a second sense in which this theorist can be said to take what is present to him as universal. For qualities are universal in the sense that they gain application to a range of particulars. Hegel describes the resultant position as follows:

> This salt is a simple Here, and at the same time manifold; it is white and *also* tart, *also* cubical in shape, of a specific gravity, etc. All these many properties are in a single simple 'Here', in which, therefore, they interpenetrate; none has a different Here from the others, but each is everywhere, in the same Here in which the others are. And, at the same time, without being separated by different Heres, they do not affect each other in this interpenetration.[43]

Thus far, Hegel has given us a preliminary characterization of Perception as involving the claim that the qualities of a thing are in a single simple 'Here' in which they 'interpenetrate'. He proceeds now to subject this proposal to more detailed scrutiny. To begin with, he considers how we are to view the qualities which interpenetrate in this single simple 'Here'. It is an implication of this position, he tells us, that these qualities are 'strictly indifferent to each other', that they are 'simply and solely self-related'. This idea relates back to his previous claim that the qualities in question 'do not affect each other in their interpenetration', but it is more properly understood to follow from the claim that the thing is nothing but a 'community' of such qualities. Hegel claims, however, that if we accept this conception of a thing, then it will not be possible to pick out these qualities and distinguish them one from another.[44] It is held to follow from this limitation that the relevant qualities are not, after all, determinate.

Why should it be thought to follow from the community conception of a thing that the relevant qualities cannot be picked out and distinguished from one another? One obvious reason is that there is nothing to which the qualities can be said to belong – something which allows them to be related and distinguished. This will be Hegel's eventual response. For the moment though, given his wish to avoid begging important questions, he accepts that one can re-introduce the idea of a bearer of qualities only at the cost of buying the difficulties which spell the downfall of Sense-certainty. Thus, he considers how one might try to lend determinacy to the relevant qualities in the absence of any reference to the idea of a thing to which they belong.

According to the solution Hegel proposes, we are to conceive of a thing, not as a community of qualities, but rather, as a 'broken up One'. This, we are told, provides us with a way of 'breaking up the continuity' to which we are confined on the 'community' conception of a thing so as to allow that the qualities in question can be differentiated from one another. It appears then that the sense in which the relevant qualities are broken up is the sense in which they can be picked out for what they are and distinguished from other qualities to which they are related. At this stage, however, Hegel foresees a difficulty, namely, that we have provided a way of distinguishing the relevant qualities only at the cost of being unable to relate them at all. As he puts it, the object has become 'a universal *common medium* in which many properties are present as sensuous *universalities,* each existing on their own account, and, as *determinate,* excluding the others'.[45] He concludes that:

> (w)hat I perceive as the simple and the True is also not a universal medium, but the *single property* by itself which, however, as such, is neither a property nor a determinate being; for now it is neither in a One nor connected with others. Only when it belongs to a One is it a property, and only in relation to others is it determinate ... it remains merely *sensuous being* in general, since it no longer possesses the character of negativity; and the consciousness which takes its object to be a sensuous being is only 'my' meaning, i.e. it has ceased altogether to perceive and has withdrawn into itself. But sensuous being and *my* meaning themselves pass over to perception: I am thrown back to the beginning and drawn once again into the same cycle which supersedes itself in each moment and as a whole.[46]

Hegel is making several claims here. First, the relevant broken up qualities are not genuine qualities. Second, they reduce to a single putative quality. Third, this single putative quality is indeterminate. The first claim – that the broken up qualities are not genuine qualities – is justified on the seemingly indisputable ground that qualities belong to things. As he puts it, 'only when it belongs to a One is it a property'. Presumably, it would be possible for a proponent of the position according to which a thing is 'a broken up One' in this sense to accept that the putative qualities do not belong to anything. Perhaps he could accept also that the use of the term 'property' or 'quality' in this context is quite misplaced. He could deny, however, that this precludes the possibility of our being able to pick out and to distinguish them.

   Now given that the Perception theorist is unable to make appeal to the fact that the qualities to be identified are qualities of a thing – the blue of this table, for example – his only recourse is to secure the required identification by making reference to the quality alone. That is to say, he must make reference to *this blue* and do so in such a way that this blue can be picked out and distinguished from other blues, other colours, and other qualities. It is at this stage that we can begin to appreciate the problem that Hegel has in mind, for qualities, being general, are indifferent to any particular. It follows therefore that the Perception theorist is faced with the task of identifying a particular instant of, say, blue, even whilst acknowledging that the materials at his disposal are incompatible with meeting such an aim.

The problem can be made to look merely apparent. For one might say that this identificatory exercise can be effected by making reference to the qualitative appearance which is exhibited by the particular instance of blue the theorist has in mind. The difficulty, however, is that reference to this qualitative appearance is simply another way of referring to the quality blue – a quality which, taken in itself, is indifferent to any particular instant thereof. On the face of it then, the Perception theorist is confronted here with a version of the problem which frustrated his predecessor, namely, that the putative things to which he is aiming to refer – in this case, free-floating qualities – cannot be pinned down to a particular object.

The Perception theorist could try to overcome this difficulty by claiming that it is, after all, possible to make reference to a particular instant of the property *blue*. One could do so, according to this line of thought, by appealing to the spatial location of the relevant quality – *this* blue is *here* as opposed to *there*. The quite obvious difficulty with this response, however, is that, in the absence of any reference to the things which occupy these different locations, we shall have simply added to the original problem by re-introducing the difficulties of Sense-certainty. For there is no way of rendering determinate the relevant uses of 'here' and 'there'.

It is to the difficulties of Sense-certainty that we are returned with the Perception theorist's final court of appeal. According to this response, we must abandon the idea that the 'broken up One' is a set of broken up *qualities*. Rather, the claim is that we are concerned with 'sensuous being in general' where this is intended to imply that the putative qualities with which a subject is acquainted are really just distinct sensory episodes. This is what Hegel is getting at when he says that we are left with the single property itself which is neither a property nor a determinate being. Again, however, this response is a capitulation, for as Hegel's previous arguments have shown, there is no way of rendering *this* determinate. We have not advanced.

Force and understanding

It is the task of Chapter 3 – 'Force and the Understanding: Appearance and the Super-sensible World' – to pave the way towards Hegel's alternative account of how we can have experience of determinate objects. According to this alternative, we are to abandon the assumption that consciousness is confined to a pure apprehension of its object, so as to allow that consciousness *does something* 'in taking what is given'. That is to say, it *comprehends* the object by conceptualizing it.

Hegel's claim that it is the activity of consciousness that allows one to discern objects is intended to call to mind the Kantian idea that the concept of a thing is presupposed in experience. His way of giving expression to this requirement is to say that this concept is an 'unconditioned universal'.[47] The use of the term 'unconditioned' captures the sense in which the concept of a thing is not derived from or conditioned by the data of experience as that data is understood by the theorist of Sense-certainty or Perception. Rather, it is presupposed in this data in just the way that it is on the Kantian way of thinking. The point then is that it is our capacity to conceptualize things which allows us to have determinate experience of them, there being no implication that this capacity is grounded in the kind of experience which is operative at the level of Sense-certainty or Perception.

It is more difficult to work out what Hegel is getting at when he refers to concepts as universals in this context. The term 'universal' is familiar from Chapters 1 and 2 of the *Phenomenology,* where it has two senses. According to the first sense, it refers to the qualities of a thing – qualities which, being general in their application, can be applied to any number of things, and which, in themselves, are insufficient to capture particularity. Now there need be no implication that universals in this sense are exhaustive of the materials available to experience, and no implication therefore that our use of quality terms – 'blue', 'white', etc. – precludes the possibility of our identifying a qualitied thing hereby – a blue thing, for example. As employed by the Perception theorist, however, such terms cannot be used to this end. For he believes that experience is limited to the apprehension of universals.

It is with this latter point in mind that we can appreciate the second, more pejorative use of the term 'universal'. For this second usage is intended to capture the kind of indeterminacy and emptiness to which we are confined if we accept the guiding assumptions of Sense-certainty and Perception. The assumptions in question are that universals are indifferent to particulars, and, more contentiously, that they are exhaustive of the materials available to experience. Understood with this interpretation in mind, the term 'universal' is expanded to refer not merely to the 'indifferent' qualities of Perception, but also to the indeterminate 'thises' of Sense-certainty.

In order to appreciate how these different senses of the term 'universal' contribute to an understanding of Hegel's claim that concepts are universals, we need to clarify his use of the term 'concept'. As in the case of Kant, Hegel's interest in concepts is an interest in the capacity we have to have determinate experience of things. Thus, when he describes experience as conceptual, the idea is that conceptual experience is determinate experience, where determinate experience is experience where it is determinate *what* is being experienced. Hence, conceptual experience is not universal in the second sense defined above. His further claim is that experience of determinate qualities requires that those qualities be understood in thing-involving terms. When this condition is satisfied the relevant experience can be said to involve universals in the first sense defined above, but universals thus conceived are not exhaustive of its content. To return then to the position of the Perception theorist, Hegel is telling us that experience, as understood by this theorist, is non-conceptual in the first sense, for it is indeterminate, and it is indeterminate because it does not involve the concept of a thing. By contrast, the Perception theorist would claim that experience of qualities is determinate and hence conceptual in the sense just described. He would deny, however, that conceptual experience in this sense must be thing-involving.

It is still not entirely clear why Hegel refers to concepts as universals. Perhaps the most likely explanation comes when we remember that, on the dualistic way of thinking, concepts are distorting instruments which shield us from things themselves. It is an implication of this position then that the relation between things as conceptualized and things in themselves can be modelled on that which exists between universal and particular, and hence that concepts *qua* that which lend determinacy to things are to be viewed on the model of qualities. The difference, of course, is that unlike the qualities which come to us from without, these 'qualities' are held to have their source in the mind and are that by virtue of which the sensible qualities of things are unified.

Given the criticisms Hegel has levelled against this dualistic picture it would be odd to suppose that his use of the term 'universal' in this context involves a similar commitment. The alternative is to suppose that he is borrowing Kant's terminology with the aim of providing further clarification of a position with which he is eventually going to take issue. Certainly, this interpretation finds support in his ensuing line of thought. For having made reference to the concepts of the understanding, he sets out to oppose what might be thought of as a quite natural way of supplementing the position just outlined – a supplementation which, I have argued, finds some expression in Kant. According to this way of thinking, things in themselves provide the ultimate ground for the things we perceive, and they are located in an unknowable non-conceptual realm.

Hegel commences his examination of this position by making reference to the notion of force as a possible contender for that which grounds the things we perceive.[48] Force in this sense is intended to capture the sense in which the things we perceive are *there anyway,* and it serves also to represent the below-the-surface activity of a thing which explains the appearances it exhibits. Thus, the notion of a *ground* in this context has two related roles: first, it is that by virtue of which we avoid phenomenalism; second, it is that by virtue of which we comprehend the nature of a thing. Both of these conceptions are operative in the arguments of Hegel's predecessors. The first finds expression in Locke's claim that the idea of substance is an inextricable component in our ideas of things and in Berkeley's immaterialist variant upon this position; the second is operative in Locke's use of the notion of real essence. Of more obvious relevance to Hegel's line of thought, however, is the idea mentioned in my discussion of Kant that the intrinsic properties of things are to be understood in causal/dispositional terms. For the point of postulating these powers or forces is to capture the sense in which the things we perceive are independent of mind and have a nature which is open to scientific investigation.

Hegel is happy to concede this much. Thus, it would be misleading to suppose that he is committed to rejecting the notion of force *per se.* At this stage, however, his aim is to clarify some of the implications of this way of talking about things, and to illustrate how the notion of force has been used to lend support to the position he seeks to reject. According to this position, the relevant below-the-surface activity of a thing is inaccessible to the realm revealed in our concepts. Thus, to the extent that this activity is identified with what the thing in question really *is,* it is an implication of this position that things in themselves are inaccessible to us. We have seen that there is more than a remnant of this line of thought in Locke, Berkeley, and Kant. For Locke suggests at times that the real essence of the thing is unknowable, Berkeley runs a similar line with respect to the activity of God, and Kant – although happy to concede that the scientist has no need for properties other than powers – implies that there is something further to the thing, something which eludes the 'surface' scope of scientific inquiry and which serves as its unknowable and real essence.

The most important part of Hegel's argument occurs in the 'inverted world' section. In the lead-up to this section he has considered some of the difficulties which arise when the ground of what appears – force proper, as he calls it – is situated in a second inaccessible realm. The main difficulty, familiar from my criticisms of Locke's substratum, Berkeley's God, and Kant's thing in itself, is that this unknowable ground can be of no use in accounting for the nature of the things we perceive. It is unable to meet this aim because it is set apart from anything to which we could gain access at this level. Now once we accept this dualistic framework, it follows that there is nothing at the level of appearance to which we can appeal in order to satisfy the required explanatory aim. Furthermore, if it is assumed also that this unknowable ground is that by virtue of which appearances count as mind-independent things, we are forced to conclude that the appearances to which we have access are not appearances of things. Thus, our confinement to this level is incompatible not merely with the possibility of attaining knowledge of things, but also with that of making contact with the things we are seeking to comprehend. The problem is familiar from the first two chapters of the *Phenomenology,* and it is familiar also from the opening chapters of this essay.

Hegel begins by introducing the notion of a super-sensible world. We have been told already that force is the ground of the perceived thing. The suggestion to be examined now is that this ground, considered as its inner reality, is to be located in a super-sensible world. Hegel objects that this super-sensible world is '*empty*', 'a *pure beyond*', a mode of the inner being of things which 'finds ready acceptance by those who say that the inner being of things is unknowable'.[49] He also refers to it as a 'tranquil kingdom of laws, the immediate copy of the perceived world'.[50] The idea that it is a tranquil kingdom of laws calls to mind Plato's realm of unchanging forms.[51] Presumably we are to suppose that Plato's position carries a commitment to a world which is super-sensible in the required sense. Furthermore, in so far as this world lacks a 'principle of change and alteration' it is unable to account for the things we perceive.[52] In this respect, it is a *pure beyond* which is an 'inversion' of the world of appearance.[53]

Thus far, the super-sensible world is an inverted copy of the sensible world – one which is useless to the task of providing a ground for the things we perceive. In the next stage of his argument, Hegel considers how one might be moved to respond to this difficulty by postulating a super-sensible world which is exactly the same as the world of appearance. The line of thought is as follows. First, one assumes the framework presupposed in the first option – a framework which enforces a dualistic distinction between the things we perceive and their 'super-sensible' ground. Second, one grants the difficulty it throws up, namely, that the ground in question has nothing in common with the things we perceive. Third, one tries to rectify this difficulty by inverting the original inversion so as to allow that the super-sensible world is a non-inverted copy of the sensible world.[54] The result is a super-sensible reproduction of the sensible world.

The obvious difficulty with this second proposal is that a reproduction of the things we perceive can be of no assistance in supplying the required ground, for we have simply provided more of the very thing which stands in need of explanation, namely, the ungrounded appearances to which we are confined if it is assumed that their ground has to reside in a second super-sensible world. The problem with both of these proposals then is that they are articulated from within a framework which assumes a dualism of thing and appearance, the upshot being that we are forced either to ground the appearances in something to which they could bear no relation, or to leave them groundless. The alternative is to drop the offending framework so as to allow that the ground of the things we perceive is no longer dualistically opposed to them. It is at this point that the explanatory dilemma is broken, for we are now in a position to grant that the things we perceive are independent of our minds, there being no implication that their natures are in principle inaccessible to us. Hegel's rather picturesque way of describing this solution is to say that appearances are grounded in an 'inner difference' as opposed to a 'different sustaining element'.

Absolute idealism

The position I have reached on Hegel's behalf promises to do justice to the idea that we are capable of exercising conceptions of mind-independent things. The difficulty, however, is that he makes further claims which are suggestive of a quite different picture. He claims, for example, that consciousness recognizes itself in the reflected object, that it has grasped the Concept of the unconditioned as Concept.[55] Elsewhere, he tells us that the Concept produces reality from its own resources,[56] and that all is mind. Taken at face value, Hegel's claims here seem expressive of just the kind of idealism which has served as the target of his arguments, implying as they do that thinking something makes it so, and that something's being so requires that it be thought to be so.[57] Yet he is adamant that the brand of idealism towards which he is gesturing – absolute idealism – is to be distinguished from its inferior subjective versions.

When Hegel claims that the Concept produces reality from its own resources, he refers to 'the demonstrated absoluteness of the Concept relatively to the material of experience and, more exactly, to the categories and concepts of reflection'. He then adds that its absoluteness consists in the fact that 'this material as it appears apart from and prior to the Concept has no truth; this it has solely in its ideality or its identity with the Concept'. The idea that the material of experience has no truth when taken in abstraction from the Concept calls to mind the Kantian claim that intuitions without concepts are blind. It is reminiscent also of Hegel's dismissal of the idea that this material is related to thought in an 'external' and 'superficial way' – a theme which re-emerges in the opening chapters of the *Phenomenology*. Working on the basis of such claims, then, it seems plausible to suppose that he is simply wishing to press the point that determinate experience requires the contribution of concepts. The further claim that the Concept has absoluteness not merely relative to the material of experience but also to the categories can be seen as a continuation of Hegel's anti-Kantian diatribe. For he can be understood as wishing to reject the idea that the understanding is purely discursive – meaning by this that it operates on non-conceptual material – so as to replace it with a conception which is compatible with the idea that the things which constrain our thinking are accessible to thought. On this way of thinking then, the point is that we must reject the conception of concepts which comes with a commitment to a non-conceptual order of things in themselves.

Thus far, we have an interpretation of Hegel's position which is compatible with the idea that the things we conceptualize are independent of mind. What is less clear is how we are to comprehend the force of his claim that the Concept produces reality from its own resources. For the implication here is that he is concerned with a conception of thought which is not constrained from without – a conception which has more in common with that of Kant's divine intellect. Hegel refers to the idea of a non-sensuous or intellectual intuition in *Faith and Knowledge* in the context of discussing Kant's aesthetic theory. This is what he says:

> Kant himself recognised in the beautiful an intuition other than the sensuous. He characterised the substratum of nature as intelligible, recognised it to be rational and identical with all Reason, and knew that the cognition in which concept and intuition are separated was subjective, finite cognition, a [merely] phenomenal cognition. Nonetheless, there the matter must rest; we must absolutely not go beyond finite cognition. Although the cognitive faculty is capable of [thinking] the Idea and the rational, it simply must not employ it as a cognitive standard.[58]

The objection that Kant's conception of cognition is subjective is familiar, as is the recommendation that it be transcended. The further claim Hegel is making here is that its subjectivity consists in the separation it enforces between concept and intuition. I have noted already that Hegel's criticisms of Kant's conception of the relation between concept and intuition stems from the implication it carries that intuition is wholly independent of thought, and that it provides for a more direct contact with things in themselves. And according to my realist interpretation, Hegel is wishing to insist, as does Kant himself, that the given element of perception is rendered determinate only to the extent that it is conceptualized in thing-involving terms. The further crucial claim is that there is no additional non-conceptual realm which could serve to undermine its objective status.

If we accept this interpretation, then we are furnished with a quite obvious sense in which Hegel is committed to denying that cognition is subjective and finite, namely the sense in which it is to be opposed to something which eludes cognition. Understood along these lines, a non-sensuous intuition is one that affords access to things in themselves. Furthermore, it seems clear from the above quotation that we are concerned with a mode of cognition which functions as a cognitive standard for us as opposed to being something unique to the mind of God. It is with this point in mind that we can appreciate the pejorative tone in which Hegel berates Kant for refusing to allow that 'finite' cognition can be transcended.

Thus far, there is no implication that Hegel's conception of an intellectual intuition is intended to be a placeholder for the cognitive activity of God. Yet the problem remains of how we are to reconcile this interpretation with his further claim that the Concept produces reality out of its own resources – a claim which suggests that we precisely *are* concerned with something approximating to Kant's notion of a divine intellect. One way of reconciling this claim with the realist position under present consideration is to allow that Hegel is wishing to lend emphasis to the fact that we are capable of exercising conceptions of mind-independent things. The claim then is that the Concept produces *a conception* of reality from its own resources, the concept in this context being a placeholder for our conceptual capacities. Certainly, this interpretation promises to make sense of those places in the text where Hegel proclaims that all is mind. For the idea now is that we are to interpret 'mind' from the point of view of content so as to allow that there is nothing in reality which is not a possible content of thought. To put it in terms which will be introduced in the following chapter – that every fact is the content of a possible thought. This position promises to lend substance to Hegel's insistence that the superior form of cognition with which he is concerned is a form to which *we* can aspire. Furthermore, it could appear unrealistic only to one who rejects the flexibility of mind which is such an important ingredient of Hegel's position – a flexibility which, he believes, is compromised the moment we submit to the 'finite' thinking of Kant by insisting that there is a non-conceptual order of things which must forever remain elusive to us.

It is undeniable, of course, that Hegel, no less than Berkeley and Kant, has an interest in the question of God. Indeed, he goes so far as to say that the subject-matter of both religion and philosophy is 'God and nothing but God and the self-unfolding of God'. Bearing this point in mind, one might object that the above interpretation is in danger of sidestepping this interest. One might object also that once this theological theme is brought to the fore, we are compelled to rethink Hegel's conception of thought and to concede the possibility that Kant's notion of an intellectual intuition is not as irrelevant to his position as my previous arguments suggest.

Kant's interest in the question of God raises difficulties because it is unclear that any remnant of dualism in his position can be written off by allowing that it is indicative of his interest in the problem of the relation between God and the world. On the contrary, it is a dualism which has quite explicit implications for an understanding of the status of the things we perceive, implying as it does that they are mere appearances which are to be set apart from things in themselves. In this respect, it is left unclear how we are to comprehend the relation between, on the one hand, God and the thing in itself, and, on the other hand, the thing in itself and the thing perceived.

It seems clear from what I have said on Hegel's behalf that there is no remnant of dualism in his position as far as the relation between thing in itself and thing perceived is concerned, the thing in itself in this context being that which guarantees that the things we perceive are independent of our minds. On the contrary, he is adamant that it can satisfy this ontological role only if comprehended from within a non-dualistic framework. It is with this point in mind that we can appreciate his rejection of the idea that things in themselves lie in an inaccessible non-conceptual realm. The question we must raise now, however, is how we are to comprehend his interpretation of the ground of what appears when that ground is understood in theological terms, and whether the resultant position has any implications for an understanding of the nature of the things we perceive.

We have seen that, for both Berkeley and Kant, there is a real sense in which God is to be treated as the unknowable substratum of the world – something which is to be set apart from anything of which we could have determinate experience or thought. In Berkeley, this position finds expression in his commitment to the idea that God is 'not so much as aimed at' when we perceive things, and although he is at pains to avoid this sceptical position – by allowing that God is revealed in the ideas He produces in us – there remains a problematic gap between God and the realm of ideas. Once this gap is in place, of course, the claim that God is that by virtue of which the things we perceive can be said to be independent of our minds leads all too quickly to a phenomenalist position with respect to these things. Kant claims in similar vein that God is beyond our comprehension, and, like Berkeley before him, is haunted by the spectre of phenomenalism.

I have argued that one can uphold a dualistic conception of the God/world relation whilst rejecting phenomenalism with respect to the things we perceive. One can do so by making a clear distinction between the thing in itself considered as that which guarantees that the things we perceive are independent of our minds and the thing in itself considered as the divine ground of the world – the world in this context being inclusive of the mind-independent things we perceive. Such a position would no doubt be anathema to Berkeley given his anti-materialist resistance to the very idea of there being such a distinction. By contrast, if we concentrate upon the non-dualistic strand in Kant's position – that which grants him the right to allow that we are capable of exercising conceptions of mind-independent things – there is no obvious bar to combining such a position with one which denies the possibility of our gaining knowledge of the divine ground which has ultimate ontological responsibility for the things we perceive.

The interesting thing about Hegel is that he is not prepared to make this move. In particular, he is adamant that the criticisms he has levelled towards the offending conception of the thing in itself – the conception according to which it is to be dualistically opposed to anything of which we could have determinate experience and thought – apply in equal measure when it is treated as a placeholder for God. As he puts it in his *Encyclopaedia Logic* in the context of attacking Kant's position:

> The *thing-in-itself* (and here 'thing' embraces God, or the spirit, as well) expresses the ob-ject, inasmuch as *abstraction* is made of all that it is for consciousness, of all determinations of feeling, as well of all determinate

thoughts about it. It is easy to see what is left, namely, what is *completely abstract,* or totally *empty,* and determined only as what is 'beyond'; the *negative* of representation, of feeling, of determinate thinking, etc. ... We must be quite surprised, therefore, to read so often that one does not know what the *thing-in-itself* is; for nothing is easier to know than this.[59]

There is an obvious motive for denying that God is to be dualistically opposed to anything of which we could have determinate experience or thought if He is intended to be that by virtue of which we avoid phenomenalism with respect to the things we perceive. And as I have said, there is evidence in both Berkeley and Kant – more explicitly so in the case of Berkeley – that God is indeed intended to perform this metaphysical role. Furthermore, I have suggested that one way of articulating this position from within a non-dualistic framework is to identify God with the things we perceive. The upshot, however, is that we are left with a position in which the theological vocabulary is rendered superfluous, its only point from Berkeley's perspective being to guarantee that these things are causally active in a manner which is compatible with their being accessible to us. Presumably this is the position which corresponds to the non-dualistic reading of Kant's conception of the things we perceive – a reading which, I have said, is compatible with a further commitment to a dualistic conception of God. Hegel, by contrast, although he is happy to allow that the things we perceive are independent of our minds, and that God is to be distinguished from these things, denies that the distinction between God and the world is to be viewed in dualistic terms.[60] The implication here is that there may well be a version of the syndrome working in this theological context too.

It is beyond the scope of my enquiry to provide a detailed account of Hegel's conception of God, but I shall be saying something in the conclusion about its relation to a line of thought which has had some influence in recent theology. For present purposes, it suffices simply to say something about the relevance his position could have to the problems at issue. Now once we allow that there is a distinction between God and the world – the world in this context comprising the qualified things we perceive – there is no need to introduce God as a way of guaranteeing that these things are independent of our minds. On this way of thinking then, the question of God is dislodged from the pivotal position it assumes in Berkeley's scheme of things, and is delegated to the philosophy of religion. Such a position is compatible with allowing that God has a role to play in creating objects and the environment they are in – in this respect He need not be entirely irrelevant to the nature and existence of things. The point, however, is that there is no immediate move to the involvement of God in the way that He needs to be involved in a position like that of Berkeley, this for the reason that a clear distinction is maintained between the God/world relation and the substance/quality relation, there being no implication that the latter requires to be analysed in terms of the former.

Conclusion

Let me leave these theological matters on one side now, and use the conclusions I have reached to summarize the conditions which must be met if one is to succeed in putting to rest the spectre of universal scepticism. According to Jonathan Lear, we shall have succeeded in making good this aim only to the extent that an explicit reference to our ways of thinking is superfluous. As he puts it, the 'we' must disappear.[61] Stroud claims in similar vein that 'we must not be able to isolate our ways of thinking, or our simply thinking certain things to be so, in a way that leaves it an open question whether, in general, things are that way'.[62]

It is a virtue of Berkeley's approach that he seeks to avoid a sceptical position of this kind, doing so by defining an alternative which promises to close the question which remains open so long as it is assumed that things in themselves are inaccessible to cognition. Ultimately, however, his alternative fails to deliver the required goods, re-introducing as it does a version of the offending sceptical framework. The further difficulty is that we are left with a highly problematic conception of a thing – one which is a by-product of the dualism which remains at the heart of his position and which generates a further sense in which the 'we' must remain a perpetual presence, namely, the sense in which he is under pressure to conclude that, in perceiving things, we are 'confin'd barely to our own ideas'.

If we accept a dualistic interpretation of Kant's position – one which likewise imposes an insurmountable distinction between cognition and things – then we face a similar set of difficulties. On this interpretation then, Kant's transcendental idealism fails to establish the objective validity of our representations, and, as such, offers little more than a variation upon the kind of position which Berkeley finds in Locke and which I have found in Berkeley and Nietzsche. By contrast, if we focus upon the non-dualistic strand in his arguments – that which affords him the right to allow that we can exercise conceptions of mind-independent things – then we can resist this sceptical conclusion as far as the things we perceive are concerned. The implication, however, is that there is a further dimension of reality which transcends our capacity to know, namely, the dimension to which we refer as 'God'. It is arguable, of course, that this sceptical implication is perfectly in order, there being good grounds for supposing that God is elusive to cognition in a way that things are not. The problem in Kant, however, is that it remains unclear whether an acknowledgement of this limitation is intended to undermine the objective validity of our representations of things – this unclarity stemming from his tendency to treat the thing in itself, considered as something which guarantees the mind-independence of the things we perceive – in terms which suggest that it is to be identified with God.

The position I have recommended on Hegel's behalf promises to put to rest this residual tension. First, his rejection of the dualism between cognition and things suggests that he is in a position to allow that we can exercise conceptions of mind-independent things. Second, his apparent willingness to concede that there is a distinction between God and the world affords him the resources to resist the idea that God has to be involved in our ideas of things in the way that Berkeley must suppose if he is to avoid phenomenalism. Thus, even if Hegel were to agree with Kant that God must remain elusive to thought, there would be no immediate move to the conclusion that things in themselves must suffer a similar sceptical fate.

Hegel's position promises to close the question of whether things really are as we take them to be given his rejection of the idea that things in themselves are in principle inaccessible to us. Nevertheless, if he is to give due weight to our fallibility, he must allow for the possibility of there being ignorance and error with respect to things – a possibility which implies that in the course of our investigations it often will be an open question whether things really are as we take them to be. The crucial point, however, is that this healthy sceptical attitude – an attitude which finds expression in Locke's reference to the shortcomings of science – does not imply that these questions cannot be closed in particular cases. In this way, it is allowed that the 'we' can remain a presence when we are seeking to comprehend the nature of things. It is denied, however, that its presence is perpetual. Finally, because this conclusion has been arrived at by a method that promises to avoid importing unwarranted assumptions into the inquiry, it presents itself as a genuine candidate for philosophical knowledge.

I shall be examining Hegel's conception of philosophical progress and the truth to which it aspires in the final chapter. First, though, I want to consider the implications of my findings for an understanding of the truths to which our non-philosophical thoughts aspire – the truths which, from Nietzsche's point of view, constitute an impossible ideal.

5   Truth

Nietzsche again

I have argued that we cannot distinguish concepts and reality in the manner demanded by the framework under attack. Thus, we must deny that reality is that which no concept can capture, and, hence, that the things we conceptualize are to be set apart from things in themselves. The alternative is to suppose that things are rendered accessible only to the extent that they are conceptualized, and that there is no further non-conceptual realm which serves to undermine their objective status. I have left it open that a dualistic model may be applicable to the relation in which we stand to God – that there is an ineliminable gap between what we take Him to be and what He really is – whilst giving due weight to the possibility that the syndrome may be operative in this context too. Regardless of where we stand with respect to this theological issue, however, there are no implications for an understanding of the status of the things we conceptualize, it being essential that we distinguish the question of the relation in which we stand to things and that of the relation in which we stand to God.

For Nietzsche, the idea that things in themselves are inaccessible to our concepts goes hand in hand with a commitment to a conception of truth which is said to be 'pure'. Pure truth, and the conception of reality it implies, is held to be incomprehensible to us, and because its attainment requires that we transcend the limitations of thought, it follows that truth in this sense cannot be a property of our thoughts. We have seen that Nietzsche takes a rather ambivalent attitude to this conception of truth. On the one hand, he claims that it is an unintelligible notion, the implication being that we should reject both it and the conception of reality it implies. On the other hand, he believes that if we do reject it, then we shall no longer be able to make sense of the idea that our thoughts are constrained from without, and hence, that there is something in the world in virtue of which they are true. It is for this reason that he takes issue with what he takes to be the only alternative to this account of truth. For this alternative 'anthropomorphic' conception succeeds in closing the gap between thought and reality, but only at the cost of eliminating the very reality which seems necessary if we are to make sense of the idea that we can engage in thought with mind-independent things.

According to my diagnosis, Nietzsche's error is to suppose that a rejection of the idea that things in themselves are inaccessible to thought is tantamount to a rejection of things in themselves *per se*. The further crucial claim was that this error lends expression to the metaphysical framework which underpins the conception of reality he wishes to call into question, the upshot being that he remains in the grip of the syndrome. The alternative, I suggested, is to allow that things in themselves *are* accessible to thought, and hence that an account of truth can accommodate the required worldly constraint whilst avoiding the metaphysical difficulties of the position with which Nietzsche takes issue.

Bradley on truth

The idea that our thoughts are constrained from without, that there is something in the world in virtue of which they are true, takes us fairly rapidly to the correspondence theory of truth. For one natural way of glossing this idea is to claim that that which confers truth upon our thoughts is that to which they must *correspond* if they are to be true. Such a claim does not immediately yield the difficulties which were bothering Nietzsche. However, once articulated from within a framework which imposes an insurmountable distinction between concepts and reality, it leads without much ado to the conclusion that that to which a thought must correspond if it is to be true is inaccessible to thought.[1]

Such an interpretation can be read into some of the things F.H. Bradley says about the correspondence theory of truth.[2] Bradley accepts with Nietzsche that the answer one gives to the question of how we are to conceive of the nature of truth must provide the resources for explaining how we gain knowledge of it. Furthermore, he believes that it is no response to these difficulties to accept the kind of 'anthropomorphic' alternative which Nietzsche himself found to be so problematic. As he sees it, this alternative, no less than the theory it is intended to replace, involves defining truth by reference to something external to it. In the case of the correspondence theory – referred to by Bradley as the 'copy theory' – it is the reality a true thought is held to copy; in the case of the anthropomorphic alternative – referred to here as the 'pragmatic theory' – it is the end it is supposed to realize. Thus, in his 1907 paper 'On Truth and Copying', which presents the clearest exposition of his objections to the correspondence theory, Bradley tells us that its error consists in:

> (t)he division of truth from knowledge and of knowledge from reality. The moment that truth, knowledge, and reality are taken as separate, there is no way in which consistently they can come or be forced together.[3]

He claims also that:

> (w)e must not use words that have no positive sense, and, with this, all reality that falls outside experience and knowledge is, to my mind, excluded.[4]

Thus far, Bradley's objections to the correspondence theory are best understood as being applicable to the version which imposes an insurmountable distinction between the contents of our thoughts and that which confers truth upon them. They do not, however, exclude the possibility of there being a version which is divorced from this metaphysical framework. Nevertheless, Bradley rehearses a further objection to the theory – one which, he tells us, is that upon which it 'goes to wreck in principle and at once'.[5] We are to assume then that this 'fatal objection' is sufficient to undermine all versions thereof. It is stated as follows:

> Truth has to copy facts, but on the other side the facts to be copied show already in their nature the work of truth-making. The merely given facts are, in other words, the imaginary creatures of false theory. They are manufactured by a mind which abstracts one aspect of the concrete known whole, and sets this abstracted aspect out by itself as a real thing.[6]

And:

> The given facts in other words are not the whole of reality, while truth cannot be understood except in reference to this whole.[7]

It is not obvious how we are to take these remarks about abstraction, and their true import will become evident only when we have examined the conception of truth which Bradley proposes as an alternative to the correspondence theory. At first sight though, it looks as if he is claiming that it is a condition upon the attainment of truth that one possess the whole truth, where possessing the whole truth requires that one embrace 'the whole of reality'. It follows therefore that the correspondence theory, in so far as it is pitched at the level of the putative truths which are identified by reference to individual facts, involves an abstraction which is inimical to the project of attaining truth properly so-called.

I shall return to the correspondence theory in due course. For the moment though, let me expand upon the alternative conception of truth which comes with Bradley's claim that it be understood only by reference to the whole of reality. He introduces this alternative as follows:

> The division of reality from knowledge and of knowledge from truth must in any form be abandoned. And the only way of exit from the maze is to accept the remaining alternative. Our only hope lies in taking courage to embrace the result that reality is not outside truth. The identity of truth, knowledge and reality, whatever difficulty that may bring, must be taken as necessary and fundamental. Or at least we have been driven to choose between this and nothing.[8]

The claim that reality is not outside truth, when taken in conjunction with the idea that the correspondence theory involves the postulation of a gap between thought and reality, suggests that Bradley's alternative is intended to close this gap. Thus understood, the claim is that reality *is* accessible to thought, and that our thoughts are capable of being true in the sense that their contents are revelatory of the way things are. One reason for being sceptical about this interpretation is that it is not obvious that this proposal has to be inherently problematic. Yet according to Bradley's present remarks, we are concerned with an alternative which it takes courage to embrace, but that we must do so 'whatever difficulty that may bring'. More telling, however, is his commitment elsewhere to the idea that thought and reality *are* incommensurable – a commitment which rules out an interpretation of this kind.

Bradley on thought and reality

In order to understand Bradley's metaphysical position we need to look at some of the arguments advanced in his 1883 *Principles of Logic*. His concern in this work is with the nature of judgement, in particular, the question of how we are to account for the unity of a judgement – what it is that holds its parts together. He rejects the assumption that the elements of a judgement are to be viewed in the psychological terms assumed by the British empiricists.[9] In this respect, he is agreeing with Frege that logic must be distinguished from psychology.[10] Second, he denies that these elements are separate entities which require to be cemented together by some further entity.[11] Thus, to take a judgement like 'the cat is on the desk', he is denying that the judgement is composed of three separate elements – 'cat', 'desk' and 'on' – which are then to be combined together. According to his alternative, the elements of a judgement are abstractions from the whole of which they are a part, and can be understood only in terms of this more primitive whole. To put it in more familiar Fregean terms, an element of a judgement can be understood only in the context of the judgement of which it forms a part. There is no requirement then to suppose that the elements of a judgement are separate building blocks, and no need to postulate a separate relation – a relation like 'on' for example – to bring together these elements. To return to our example, when I judge that the cat is on the desk it is not that there is a relation of 'on-ness' in addition to the cat and the desk. Rather, I see that the cat is on the desk and judge accordingly. Another way of making the point is to say that the elements of a judgement are internally related, the force of 'internal' being to rule out the idea that the relevant relation is a separately existing entity.[12]

Bradley's position seems perfectly acceptable, and it promises to put to rest the difficulties which accompany Russell's multiple relation theory of judgement.[13] What is less clear, however, is how it is intended to relate to his metaphysical concerns, and in particular, the role it has in generating the idea that thought and reality are incommensurable. Russell implies that the connection is rather obvious, claiming that:

> The question of relations is one of the most important that arises in philosophy, as most other issues turn on it: monism and pluralism; the question whether anything is true except the whole of truth, or wholly real except the whole of reality; idealism and realism, in some of their forms; perhaps the

whole existence of philosophy as a subject distinct from science and possessing a method of its own.[14]

And Bradley himself, in Chapter III of his 1897 *Appearance and Reality*
–'Relation and Quality' – draws a conclusion which suggests that Russell is right
on target here. As he puts it:

> The reader who has followed and has grasped the principle of this chapter,
> will have little need to spend his time on those which succeed it. He will have
> seen that our experience, where relational, is not true; and he will have con-
> demned, almost without a hearing, the great mass of phenomena ...

The difficulty is that it is hard to find anything within this chapter which warrants
a condemnation of the great mass of phenomena. To be sure, Bradley offers arguments in support of the conclusion that relations are unreal. Yet these arguments
show, at most, that we must dispense with the position according to which relations exist as separate entities, and in this respect offer further support to the
criticisms advanced in *Principles of Logic.* They do not, however, imply that our
experience, where relational, is not true.

Something more interesting emerges if we look at the later chapters of
Appearance and Reality. For one of the themes here is that judgements – the uni-
ties with which he is concerned in *Principles of Logic* – are defective. They are
defective – so the argument goes – because they abstract from the reality they
purport to represent. Bradley is suggesting then that not only is it an error to
abstract a part of a judgement and to treat it as an entity in its own right, but that
it is an error also to abstract a part of reality and to treat it as an entity in its own
right. The assumption here is that reality is a unity in much the way that judgements are said to be a unity in the earlier work on logic.

Bradley sums up his metaphysical position in Chapter XV. He begins by claiming that he is going to state the main essence of thought and to justify its
distinction from actual existence.[15] He adds that it is only by misunderstanding
that we find difficulty in the idea that thought is something less than reality. He
then tells us that a real thing has two aspects. These aspects are inseparable, and
they correspond respectively to the 'what' of the thing – its content – and the
'this' of the thing – its existence. The comparison with Kant's conception of the
relation between concept and intuition should be obvious, and Bradley expresses
in his own words the requirement that these aspects be understood only as
abstractions from a more primitive whole.

Having made this point, he claims that 'thought seems essentially to consist in
their division', and he justifies this claim on the ground that:

> thought is clearly, to some extent at least, ideal. Without an idea there is no
> thinking, and an idea implies the separation of content from existence. It is a
> 'what' which, so far as it is a mere idea, clearly *is* not, and if it also *were,*
> could, so far, not be called ideal.[16]

Bradley's argument for the claim that thought is ideal is that thinking involves ideas. But what does he mean by 'idea'? If 'idea' is taken as an act of thinking, then the claim is that thought is ideal in the sense that thinking is something that we do, and is to be distinguished from what it is we think about. However, this does not seem to be what Bradley has in mind, for he tells us that an idea is a 'what', the implication being that he is concerned with the content of an idea. Hence, his claim is that the content of an idea is ideal, and that this content is to be distinguished from the 'that' of the thing it involves.

Bradley proceeds to spell out what he means by considering the nature of judgement. In judgement, he tells us, we qualify a subject – a 'that' – with a predicate – a 'what'. To use his example, we judge that this horse is a mammal. In this way, judgement is 'essentially the reunion of two sides, "what" and "that", provisionally estranged'. He claims, however, that 'it is the alienation of these aspects in which thought's ideality consists'.[17] He then argues as follows:

> Reflect upon any judgement as long as you please, operate upon the subject of it to any extent which you desire, but then (when you have finished) make an actual judgement. And when that is made, see if you do not discover, beyond the content of your thought, a subject of which it is true, and which it does not comprehend. You will find that the object of thought in the end must be ideal, and that there is no idea which, as such, contains its own existence.[18]

It is not easy to understand what Bradley is getting at here. We can agree that the subject of a judgement is what the judgement is of or about, and that in this sense we are concerned with a subject of which the judgement is true. We can agree also that this subject may have aspects which are not captured by the relevant judgement, and that there will be cases where there is nothing in reality to which our judgement corresponds. What does not follow is that things themselves are elusive to thought, nor that a judgement involving a particular aspect of a thing is incapable of telling us how that thing really is. Bradley, however, insists on making a distinction between the object of thought, which, we are to assume, is the object as captured at the level of content, and the 'that' of the actual subject which, he tells us, is not 'a mere idea'.

At this stage, it would be natural to suppose that Bradley is committed to a version of the Kantian claim that things in themselves must remain elusive to thought. Yet he remains steadfast in his opposition to Kant's metaphysical framework – his understanding of this framework corresponding to the dualistic interpretation we have examined. As he puts it:

> (t)o think of anything which can exist quite outside of thought I agree is impossible. If thought is one element in a whole, you cannot argue from this ground that the remainder of such a whole must stand apart and independent. From this ground, in short, you can make no inference to a Thing-in-itself. And there is no impossibility in thought's existing as an element, and no self-contradiction in its own judgement that it is less than the universe.[19]

Bradley is denying that the 'that' which remains elusive to thought is to be viewed as the Kantian thing in itself, where conceiving of it as such implies that it stands apart from and independent of thought. Rather, his claim is that thought exists as one element of a whole, there being an aspect of this whole which remains elusive to thought. It is in this sense that, in qualifying reality, 'thought consents to a partial negation', and it is in this sense that truth, in so far as its aim is to 'qualify existence ideally', 'shows a dissection' and can never be 'equivalent to its subject'.[20]

It would be difficult to deny that thought exists as an element in a more inclusive whole – that, as Bradley puts it, it is less than the universe. It would be difficult to deny also that there is more to reality than what is made thought's object, and that the judgements we make involve the 'differentiation of a complex whole'.[21] What remains unclear, however, is how these points are intended to contribute to his argument, and in particular, how they relate to what Bradley has said already about the 'that' which remains elusive to thought.

One problem is that Bradley's previous remarks suggest that the elusive 'that' is to be viewed as an individual thing as opposed to the universe as a whole. The example he gives of a judgement concerning a horse is an obvious case in point, as is his claim that a real thing has two aspects – the 'that' and the 'what'. Furthermore, in the context of spelling out the conception of truth he takes to be implied by his position, he tells us that the crucial question 'is whether, if you thought it and understood it, there would be no difference left between your thought and the thing'.[22] All of this suggests that Bradley is not simply making the innocuous point that the judgements we make can be focused upon individual things as opposed to the universe as a whole, but rather that such judgements elude the true nature of these things.

One reason for questioning this interpretation comes with an acknowledgement of Bradley's commitment to the idea that individuation is the constructive work of mind[23] – a commitment which rules out the possibility of claiming on his behalf that thought could fail to capture individual things. However, even if we are forced back to the conclusion that Bradley *is,* after all, wishing to claim that the 'that' which eludes thought is reality considered as an all-inclusive whole, we are still left with the question of how we are to understand his position. The interpretation I have suggested already is relatively innocuous, implying as it does simply that there is more to reality than any particular thing which can be made the object of thought. Bradley, however, would appear to be making a much stronger claim, for he tells us that 'the content of the subject strives, we may say, unsuccessfully towards an all-inclusive whole',[24] and that 'if the object were made perfect, it would forthwith *become* reality, but would cease forthwith to be an object'.[25]

Bradley seems to be suggesting that the true nature of a thing is attained only when that thing is no longer an individual – that in order to be what it really is, the thing in question must merge with the reality of which it forms a part. The further implication is that this merging must remain elusive to thought. Certainly, this interpretation allows us to make sense of Bradley's tendency to oscillate between treating the elusive 'that' as a thing and as the universe as a whole – an oscillation which might be thought to bear comparison with the ambiguity which attaches to Kant's conception of the thing in itself. Nevertheless, it raises the following questions. First, what are Bradley's arguments for accepting this metaphysical position? Second, how, if at all, is it to be distinguished from Kant's scheme of things?

We have seen that Bradley's arguments about relations are insufficient to warrant the conclusion that reality itself is non-relational. Rather, they show merely that we must reject the position according to which relations exist as separate entities. It should be clear also that the remarks he makes in Chapter XV about the abstractive nature of judgements are equally incapable of delivering this conclusion. On the contrary, they imply simply that there is more to reality than that which is made thought's object, and could be interpreted in stronger terms only on the prior assumption that we accept Bradley's metaphysical position – a position which implies that to reach a true mode of apprehension 'predicate and subject, and subject and object, and in short, the whole relational form must be merged'.[26]

As I have said, Bradley is adamant that there is a distinction to be drawn between his conception of reality and the Kantian conception thereof. In particular, he tells us that the reality he postulates does not stand 'apart from and independent of thought', and that thought is to be viewed as an element of this more inclusive whole. Once it is acknowledged on his behalf, however, that individuation – and more generally, the 'whole relational form' – is to be cast aside if we are to gain a true apprehension of reality, then it follows that the reality which remains elusive to thought has rather a lot in common with Kant's conception thereof. In particular, it is to be set apart from anything to which we could gain access at the level of thought, it cannot account for individuality, yet it is intended somehow to serve as a place-holder for the real essence of a thing. Indeed, it does not seem absurd to suppose that, as in the case of Kant, there is a theological dimension to Bradley's remarks that the reality he has in mind is the reality to which we would have access if we were to attain a God's eye view upon things. Again, however, there is no obvious sense in which the acknowledgement of such a dimension should compromise our capacity to think truly about things, yet from what we have seen this is precisely what Bradley is wanting to conclude.

There is a further element in Bradley's position which might be thought to distinguish it from that of Kant, namely, that he is prepared to allow that there is another way in which we can engage with reality. We can do so by means of our capacity for *feeling,* feeling being that which grants us a kind of non-conceptual access to reality. Bearing this point in mind then, it could be argued that, from Bradley's point of view, Kant's mistake was to suppose that because the thing in itself is inaccessible to thought it is entirely inaccessible to us. This complaint rests upon the assumption that Kant is committed to a dualistic conception of the relation between appearance and reality – an assumption which, I have noted, is presupposed throughout Bradley's argument. Furthermore, once this interpretation is in place, there is a sense in which Kant, too, can grant that there is a non-conceptual way of making contact with reality, namely, by virtue of our capacity for receptivity. Of course, Kant is adamant that any such access would be indeterminate in content – a concession which undermines the idea that we are concerned with a genuine mode of access here. Crucially, however, Bradley himself makes a similar point, claiming that the kind of experience which is delivered by 'mere feeling' or 'immediate presentation' is 'most imperfect and unstable, and its inconsistencies lead us at once to transcend it'. He concludes that 'we hardly possess it as more than that which we are in the act of losing it'.[27]

Truth again

Having set up his metaphysical position, Bradley hypothesizes that the dualism inherent in thought has been transcended, so that truth can be understood in the manner dictated by the requirement that truth and reality be identified. As he puts it: 'let us assume that existence is no longer different from truth, and let us see where this takes us. It takes us to thought's suicide'.[28] This assumption takes us to thought's suicide, he tells us, because thought is relational and discursive, and as such, cannot contain 'immediate presentation' or 'feeling' which latter constitute a 'side of existence beyond thought'. He concludes that '(i)f truth and fact are to be one, then in some such way thought must reach its consummation'.

The position seems to be that there is an ineliminable difference between the things we think about and things in themselves, although, as noted previously, it would be more accurate to say that the distinction in question obtains between things thought about and reality considered as an integrated whole. As Bradley sees it, this difference is definitive of thought, it is exhibited whenever judgement occurs, and can be overcome only by means of a mode of apprehension which no longer involves the making of judgements. It follows therefore that judgement is inimical to truth – at least, this follows on the assumption that truth is to be identified with reality – and that truth becomes accessible only to the extent that the limitations of thought have been transcended. The implication, however, is that the resultant mode of apprehension is not really an apprehension properly so-called, nor is it an apprehension of an object. For in so far as it involves a merging of the subject/object relation, there is no subject to do the apprehending and no object to be apprehended. Again, there is a quite obvious sense in which Bradley is gesturing towards Kant's conception of a divine intellect – his requirement that the subject/object relation be conflated suggesting likewise a mode of cognition which does not involve being affected from without.

It should be clear that there are significant similarities to be drawn between Bradley's 'identity theory' of truth, and Nietzsche's paradigm of 'pure' truth. In particular, both positions rest upon the assumption that thought and reality are incommensurable, the upshot being that truth cannot be a property of thought. Bradley's position yields this conclusion with the idea that truth requires identification with reality, the further claim being that this identification demands thought's suicide. Nietzsche's position is at times articulated in a similar vein, when, for example, he tells us that pure truth is to be identified with the thing in itself. The more obvious point of comparison, however, is that version of the correspondence theory according to which a true thought must correspond to something which is inaccessible to thought, namely, reality in itself.

Of course, there are important differences between their respective positions. In particular, Bradley denies that the reality with which truth is to be identified is to be modelled on the Kantian thing in itself. Rather, it is an all-inclusive whole of which thought is but an element. Nevertheless, to the extent that an apprehension of this whole demands a merging of the relations which are definitive of thought – that between subject and object, and subject and predicate – it follows that reality thus conceived is transcendent of both thought and individuality. It is not absurd to conclude therefore that we have been left what is really just a terminological variant upon Nietzsche's conception of 'pure' truth – a variant which seems equally ill-equipped to satisfy Bradley's demand that truth and reality be identified with knowledge.[29]

If there is a significant comparison to be made between these putatively distinct conceptions of truth, then how are we to account for Bradley's apparent desire to reject a correspondence theory of the kind implied by Nietzsche's position? One of Bradley's objections to this theory is that it involves the imposition of a distinction between truth and reality and, according to my initial gloss, he is making a similar epistemological point to that which is to be found in Nietzsche's negative arguments. It was left unclear how this epistemological objection was to be related to Bradley's further claim that the error of the correspondence theory resides in its postulation of facts which are 'manufactured by the mind'.

The idea that the correspondence theory involves the imposition of a distinction between truth and reality, when wedded to Bradley's understanding of the requirement that these terms be identified, suggests that a distinction occurs whenever there is judgement or thought. The existence of this distinction is said to exclude the possibility of truth properly so-called, and it can be eliminated, he believes, only when judgement or thought has been transcended. If this interpretation is correct, then we can begin to appreciate how Bradley's objection to the correspondence theory – that it imposes a distinction between truth and reality – relates to his further criticism that it involves reference to facts which are 'manufactured by the mind'. For working on the assumption that the facts in question are identified by reference to the contents of true thoughts, Bradley is claiming that it is the essential reference to thought which confounds the theory.

It follows therefore that there is a crucial difference between Bradley's and Nietzsche's criticisms of the correspondence theory, and this is so despite the fact that they both believe that the theory involves the imposition of an unwarranted distinction between thought and reality. For whereas Nietzsche believes that the theory flounders because it fails to explain how our thoughts can be true, and in this sense involves an unwarranted distinction between thought and reality, Bradley holds that its main difficulty stems from the fact that it fails to transcend thought. Thus, Bradley's way of eliminating the distinction between thought and reality is to embrace a theory of truth which entails that thought or judgement cannot be true. Nietzsche, by contrast, eliminates the distinction in the other direction, so that reality is rejected in favour of thought. The upshot is that we retain what is missing from Bradley's picture, but at the cost of being unable to accommodate the idea that a true thought is constrained by the way things are.

The identity theory of truth: an alternative interpretation

I shall be saying something about the holistic constraints which are motivating Bradley's line of thought in the final section. For the moment though I want to examine a version of the identity theory which promises to accommodate the idea that our thoughts can be true. Understood from this alternative perspective, the claim is that the content of a thought can be revelatory of the way things are, and when it is so, the relation between true thought and fact is one of identity. Some recent philosophers have taken up and developed an identity theory of this kind.[30] Furthermore, they have been drawn towards it because of a desire to resist the implication that that which confers truth upon our thoughts is to be located in a realm which is inaccessible to thought. Hence, the position is targeted at the metaphysical framework undermined by Hegel, one whose acceptance leads to the kind of correspondence theory with which Nietzsche takes issue.[31]

The focus upon thoughts as opposed to sentences or statements suggests that the fundamental bearers of the properties of truth and falsity are not to be viewed as linguistic items. Rather, it is the contents of these sentences or statements that are at issue – what they are used to say and the objects of particular acts of saying. There are two reasons for respecting this point in the present context. First, it lends emphasis to the metaphysical aim of one who accepts this conception of truth, namely, that he takes the important issue to be the question of how we are to understand the relation between thought and reality, and seeks to undermine the idea that reality is inaccessible to thought. Second, it would be misleading in the extreme to characterize the positive outcome of this position as involving the claim that language and reality are to be identified.

The idea that this version of the identity theory provides a corrective to the view according to which reality is to be located on the far side of thought is important, and its acknowledgement allows us to clear up any misunderstanding which might be thought to accompany the claim – accepted by a philosopher of this persuasion – that facts confer truth upon our thoughts, that they make our thoughts true. Perhaps the most obvious way of misunderstanding this claim is by taking it to involve a commitment to the metaphysical picture under attack, a picture according to which facts are worldly entities which are distinct from the contents of true thoughts. By contrast, if we reject this framework, it becomes possible to allow that when one comes to identify the fact which confers truth upon a thought, one can do no more than state the content of that thought. So, for example, the thought that things are wheeling and revolving is made true by the fact that things are wheeling and revolving. Thus, when it is claimed that this fact makes the thought true, there is no implication that it has to be *distinct* from the content of the relevant thought, that the act of bestowing truth upon the thought is tantamount to grafting some extra property onto its content. Rather, the thought in question already contains, at the level of its content, the property which is required to make it true, namely, that it is identified with a fact. To put it in an even more compelling manner, talk of the facts is just another way of giving expression to what is true – facts are truths.[32]

Even if we concede that facts are identified only by reference to the contents of true thoughts, this does not preclude our saying that there is something in the world in virtue of which our thoughts are true. For as I have said, it is built into this version of the identity theory that, in thinking, we are capable of engaging with mind-independent things. It is the way these things are which provides the measure by means of which to assess our thoughts about them, and it is when we get things right that the relevant thoughts can be said to be expressive of the facts. To be sure, there is going to be the possibility of error, in which case, the putative facts we take ourselves to be expressing are not genuine. The important point to grasp, however, is that this concession to our fallibility does not imply that when we *are* thinking truly, the relevant facts are external to the contents of our thoughts. To suppose that this does follow is to commit an error which is similar to that which is operative when it is denied that the content of a veridical perception can be comprehended in externalist terms on the ground that there are putative perceptions which demand an internalist interpretation.[33]

The position then is that truth can be a property of thought, and when it is, there is a relation of identity between the content of the relevant thought and the fact which makes it true. There are some issues surrounding the question of whether we should be talking about relations in this context, and I shall return to them below. For the moment though, let me assume that this way of talking is harmless enough, and consider whether identity is the correct relation in terms of which to meet the required metaphysical constraint. One reason for resisting this conclusion is that, just as it is possible to define a version of the identity theory which avoids the offending metaphysical framework, so, too, it does not seem absurd to suppose that a similar move can be made with respect to the correspondence theory. On this way of thinking then, the claim that a true thought corresponds to a fact does not have to carry the implication that the relevant fact is irreducibly external to the relevant thought's content. Rather, we can allow that it is identified only by reference to that content.

G.E. Moore, in his early writings, implies that that no such modification is possible. Take, for example, the following extract:

> A truth differs in no respect from the reality to which it was supposed merely to correspond: e.g. the truth that I exist differs in no respect from the corresponding reality – my existence.[34]

Moore's claim here – that a truth differs in no respect from the reality to which it was supposed merely to correspond – is intended to undermine the use of the correspondence theory in this context. For it suggests that, according to this theory, there has to be a *difference* between a truth and the reality to which it must correspond if it is to count as such – that corresponding facts are distinct from the contents of true thoughts. The further implication is that it is only by means of an identity theory that we shall be able to remedy this defect so as to allow that 'a truth differs in no respect from the reality to which it was supposed merely to correspond'. Moore's example, however, would seem to demonstrate, rather, that the correspondence theory *can* be used to such an end, for he tells us that the truth that I exist differs in no respect from the corresponding reality – my existence, yet the use of the notion of correspondence here is quite compatible with the identity claim he is seeking to advance by its means. That is to say, the claim that the truth that I exist differs in no respect from the *corresponding* reality does not imply that there has to be an ineliminable difference between the relevant truth and the corresponding reality. On the contrary, the point is that the relation between them is one of identity.

We can conclude then that the terms 'identity' and 'correspondence' can be used interchangeably in the context of articulating a conception of truth which resists the offending metaphysical framework. According to this way of thinking, it is denied that true thought and fact are distinct entities and claimed, rather, that the fact to which a true thought corresponds can be identified only by reference to the content of that thought.[35]

An explanatory dilemma?

The idea that true thought and fact cannot be identified in independent terms has led some philosophers to reject the idea that there can be a genuine relation between these two terms, the usual target here being the correspondence theory of truth.[36] Certainly, we must resist the idea that true thought and fact can be specified in independent terms if we are to avoid the implication that facts have a distinct mode of existence which is inaccessible to the contents of our thoughts. What is unclear, however, is that this negative demand precludes the possibility of allowing that there is a genuine relation between these terms.

We can get a clearer understanding of why philosophers have wished to resist such a conclusion by considering one of the motives for insisting that there *is* a relation between true thought and fact. According to this line of thought, an adequate account of truth must be genuinely explanatory, and we can meet this aim only by specifying what the truth of a thought consists in – a specification which demands that we make reference to materials which go beyond the content of the relevant thought. On this way of thinking then, reference to corresponding facts affords an independent explanatory grasp upon the problem of what it is for a thought to be true. It allows us to say what the truth of a thought consists in. The further implications are that truth consists in a *relation* between true thought and fact, and that the second term of this relation can be specified in thought-independent terms.

The 'pure' conception of truth to which Nietzsche objects would satisfy the required explanatory aim, for according to such a position, a true thought can be said to stand in a relation of correspondence to the facts, and this relation can be specified in thought-independent terms given that the facts are independent of anything we could access at the level of content. Now if we accept, as I believe we must, that facts cannot be conceived of in this manner, then it follows that the truth of a thought cannot consist in a relation of this kind. The questions we must press though are why one might be attracted to a position which makes this demand, whether its rejection implies that the truth of a thought cannot consist in a relation of any kind, and what follows for an assessment of the explanatory pretensions of the identity theory under present consideration?[37]

As I have said, one motive for insisting upon a correspondence theory according to which facts are independent of the contents of true thoughts is that it promises to provide us with an independent explanatory grasp upon the concept of truth. The assumption here is that an account of truth is genuinely explanatory only if it involves an explanation which satisfies a requirement of non-circularity. It does so, on the present way of thinking, with the claim that the truth of a thought consists in the relation it stands to something which is not a possible thought-content, namely, the fact which makes it true.

Why should it be thought that an explanatory account of truth must proceed in these terms? Perhaps the line of reasoning is as follows: if we are going to succeed in saying what it is for a thought to be true, then it is imperative that we produce an explanation which is non-vacuous – one which does not simply provide a repetition of the very thing which stands in need of explanation. We can satisfy this aim, so the argument goes, by making reference to some property possessed by a true thought, a property the possession of which guarantees that, in ascribing it, we have closed our original question. The further claim is that the property of standing in a relation of correspondence to a fact can deliver the required explanatory goods provided that the relevant fact exists beyond the content of the true thought.

The line of thought here should be familiar from my discussion in Chapter 4 of a similar dilemma which might be thought to occur in the context of explaining what it is that grounds the things we perceive – a dilemma which is brought to the fore in Hegel's discussion of inverted worlds. For in this case, too, it can look as if we are faced with two mutually exclusive options, neither of which can satisfy the required explanatory aim. According to the first option – the vacuous one – we seek to ground the things we perceive by reference to a further realm which turns out to be identical to the one which requires to be grounded. The result is that the things we perceive remain groundless, and the putative explanation we have offered involves simply a repetition of the thing which stands to be explained. The second option, by contrast, involves the postulation of a genuine ground, and in this respect promises to avoid the non-explanation to which we are confined on the first way of thinking. The difficulty, however, is that the ground in question cannot be intelligibly related to the things which require grounding, and, as such, is equally useless to the task of explaining what needs to be explained. The alternative, as Hegel sees it, is to abandon the framework which is common to these two alternatives – a framework according to which ground and appearance are to be dualistically opposed. In this way, we accept with a proponent of the first position that a dualistically opposed ground is no ground at all, whilst challenging his conception of the materials to which we are confined once this dualistically opposed ground has been rejected.

Let me relate this line of thought to the case of truth. We begin with the question of how we are to explain what the truth of a thought consists in. This starting point leads to two options, neither of which seems placed to explain what needs to be explained. The first option, focused as it is upon the content of the true thought, appears to provide nothing more than a repetition of the thing which demands explanation, and, as such, is no more helpful than the claim that a thought is true when it is true. The second option, by contrast, promises to break this explanatory bind, moving as it does beyond the content of the true thought. The difficulty, however, is that it involves the postulation of some further property – standing in a relation of correspondence to an extra-conceptual fact, say – which cannot be related to the content of the relevant thought and which is equally ill-equipped therefore to explain what its truth consists in. Either way, we have failed to explain what it is for a thought to be true.

According to my diagnosis of the previous example, the dilemma arises because the putative explanations presuppose a dualism of appearance and ground – a dualism whose acceptance implies that the things we perceive are to be grounded, if at all, in something to which they can bear no intelligible relation. And given what I have said about the case of truth, it seems plausible to suppose that there is a comparable dualism at work here, namely, that which obtains between the content of the true thought and the fact which makes it true. Presumably then, we are to break the explanatory dilemma by rejecting the assumption that true thought and fact are to be dualistically opposed, so as to allow, rather, that the facts are identified only by reference to the contents of true thoughts.

It is important to see why this move doesn't simply take us back to the option which made it so tempting to introduce a realm of extra-conceptual facts in the first place. For the difficulty with the first option was not simply that it confines us to the level of a thought's content, but, rather, that it rests upon the assumption that what we have at the level of content is insufficient to explain what it is for a thought to be true. And, of course, this criticism is right on target as long as we insist upon locating the facts in a realm which is inaccessible to thought. By contrast, if we drop the dualism of true thought and fact, then this objection loses its force. It loses its force because we now have at our disposal the facts insisted upon by a proponent of the second position, the difference being that they are now accessible to thought. It follows that their postulation precisely can explain what it is for a thought to be true. A thought is true, on this way of thinking, when its content can be identified with a fact. (The point can be expressed equally well, of course, by reference to the notion of correspondence.)

The requirement of non-circularity has been dropped on this alternative explanatory approach. However, this move should worry us only on the assumption that non-circular explanations are the only philosophically acceptable ones, and it is unclear that this assumption should be granted.[38] Certainly, it is an implication of my argument that we must reject this assumption in the contexts under discussion lest we succumb to the syndrome. As for those who would insist that circularity has to be a vice, I have two responses to make. First, this criticism would have some force if the presence of circularity led inevitably to the kind of non-explanation to which we are confined if we insist upon a dualistic framework, but there is no reason for accepting that such a framework is exhaustive of the available options. Second, on the alternative non-dualistic framework, circularity in an explanation is just another way of ensuring that we are getting to grips with the phenomenon to be explained as opposed to dissecting it in the manner preferred by one who is in the grip of the syndrome. The conclusions of the previous chapters should testify to that.

It should be clear from what I have said that there is no difficulty in allowing that there is a relation between true thought and fact, the relation in question being one of identity. For the point of making such a claim in the present context is to resist the implication that true thought and fact are distinct entities so as to allow, rather, that the facts are identified only by reference to the contents of true thoughts. To be sure, one could object to such a position by insisting that talk of there being a relation between true thought and fact loses its point if we abandon the explanatory pretensions of one who insists that these terms have to be set apart. As I hope to have shown, however, there are no good grounds for taking this objection seriously, and, given the difficulties which are generated by the dualistic option, every reason for supposing that the position under present consideration offers the best available hope of saying something genuinely explanatory about the concept of truth.

Hegel on truth

I want now to consider where Hegel stands with respect to the kind of identity theory I have recommended. One might object that such a line of enquiry has to be misconceived, doing so on the ground that Hegel's theory of truth outstrips the epistemological concerns which have been my focus here, and can be appreciated only by taking account of the broader context of his thinking. Certainly, Hegel's conception of the problem of truth seems at odds with that of the contemporary analytic philosophers I have mentioned here. Indeed, it has been argued that it has little in common with that of Bradley.[39] Nevertheless, there are several reasons for thinking that this line of enquiry is not entirely misplaced. First, even if it is acknowledged that much of Hegel's discussion of truth exceeds the scope of my epistemological concerns, there is still the question of the extent to which he would be prepared to accept the conclusions I have reached in this epistemological context. Second, it has been argued – convincingly, I think – that there are certain resonant similarities between Hegel's conception of truth and that of Bradley.[40] Given the criticisms I have levelled towards Bradley's version of the identity theory of truth, then, it is important that I clarify the nature of this putative connection. Finally, and I shall expand upon this thought in the following chapter, Hegel's theory of truth is relevant to an understanding of his overall philosophical approach – an approach which, I have argued, is best understood in methodological terms. It is in these methodological terms that we can best appreciate the broader context of Hegel's thinking, and it is this broader context which, if not in letter but in spirit, has provided the inspiration for my understanding and assessment of the syndrome.

Let me begin with the question of where Hegel stands with respect to the claim that there is an identity between the content of a true thought and the fact which makes it true. Given that it is one of his aims to deny that things are inaccessible to thought and to allow, rather, that cognition can provide a route to truth, it is plausible to suppose that he would be sympathetic to such a position. Certainly, it is possible to read its expression into some of the things he says. Take, for example, his remark that 'truth means that objectivity corresponds with the Concept' – a remark which he follows up by denying that he is concerned with the question of whether 'external things correspond with my representations'.[41] We shall see that the true import of his remarks here can be appreciated only by acknowledging the broader perspective of his thinking about truth. For the moment though, we can note that there is an interpretation of them which squares with the epistemological concerns I have rehearsed on his behalf. According to this interpretation, Hegel is taking issue with the kind of position which has it that a true thought must stand in a relation of correspondence to something which is external to thought, where 'external' is taken to be equivalent to 'inaccessible'. Understood from this perspective, the point of saying that truth means that objectivity corresponds with the concept is to deny that an adequate conception of truth requires that thought be transcended.[42]

This interpretation finds support in the following remarks, taken from the second volume of the *Lectures on the History of Philosophy,* where Hegel discusses the conception according to which truth consists in the harmony of object and consciousness. This 'celebrated definition', he tells us:

> (i)s not to be understood as indicating that consciousness had a conception, and that on the *other side* stood an object, which had to harmonize one with the other.

This for the reason that:

> (w)hat consciousness can compare is nothing more than its conception, and – not the object, but – its conception again. It is not, as is ordinarily represented, that an object here impresses itself upon wax, that a *third* something compares the form of the object and of the wax, and finding them to be similar, judges that the impress must have been correct, and the concept and the thing have harmonized.[43]

Finally, in the opening sections of the *Phenomenology,* we find Hegel casting aspersion upon the assumption that cognition is excluded from things in themselves – an assumption which, he tells us, forces the conclusion that cognition is 'outside of the truth'. He refers disparagingly to those who are compelled to introduce 'some other kind of truth', doing so on the ground that 'this kind of talk which goes back and forth only leads to a hazy distinction between an absolute truth and some other kind of truth'.[44] The relevance of this complaint to an assessment of Nietzsche's position should be obvious.

All of this is familiar from the previous chapter. It is to be noted, however, that in the *Phenomenology* Hegel's use of the term 'correspondence' involves an important ambiguity.[45] According to the first more familiar sense, he is referring to the kind of correspondence assumed by one who locates facts on the far side of thought. According to the second sense – which is of relevance to the procedure he follows in the opening chapters of the *Phenomenology* – correspondence is a placeholder for logical consistency. It is with this sense in mind that we can best appreciate his claim that 'consciousness finds that its knowledge does not correspond to its object', where this implies that there is an inconsistency between a particular conception of object-directed consciousness and how it really is. Hegel's strategy in these opening chapters then is to employ the second sense of 'correspondence' in the context of demonstrating the inadequacy of a particular position. Thus, to take the example of Sense-certainty, he demonstrates that the object of consciousness cannot be viewed in non-conceptual terms. The further implication is that we must reject that version of the correspondence theory which has it that a true thought must correspond to something inaccessible to thought.

Thus far, I have argued that Hegel's position is compatible with the idea that there is an identity between true thought and fact. One difficulty with this line of argument is that there is some evidence to suppose that it would be more appropriate to compare Hegel's version of the identity theory with that of Bradley. Yet according to the conclusion I have reached, Bradley believes that truth requires 'thought's suicide'. Assuming that this comparison is justified then, it looks as if my interpretation of Hegel has to be flawed.

One piece of evidence for such a comparison comes from Bradley himself in the preface to the first edition of his *Principles of Logic*. For he tells us that:

> I have no wish to conceal how much I owe to his [Hegel's] writings; but I will leave it to those who can judge better than myself, to fix the limits within which I have followed him.[46]

Thomas Baldwin cites this passage in a paper on the identity theory of truth, claiming that:

> On the issue of the identity theory, I think, we can definitely say that Bradley 'followed' Hegel, at least to the extent of developing a line of thought that is present in Hegel's *Logic* (1975, part 1). This is not the place to explore Hegel's position, but it will suffice for now to cite one characteristic passage. 'Truth in the deeper sense', Hegel writes, 'consists in the identity between objectivity and the notion' (p. 276).[47]

Robert Stern has objected to Baldwin's line of thought here, doing so on the ground that the identity theory is a theory of propositional truth, and that Hegel is concerned, rather, with what Stern refers to as *material* truth, material truth being ascribable to things rather than to propositions. In support of this interpretation, he cites the full passage from which Baldwin's quotation is taken:

> Truth is understood first to mean that I *know* how something *is*. But this is truth only in relation to consciousness; it is formal truth, mere correctness. In

contrast with this, truth in the deeper sense means that objectivity is identical with the Concept. It is this deeper sense of truth which is at issue when we speak, for instance, of a 'true' state or a 'true' work of art. These objects are 'true' when they are what they *ought* to be, i.e. when their reality corresponds to their concept. Interpreted in this way, the 'untrue' is the same as what is sometimes also called the 'bad'. A bad man is one who is 'untrue', i.e. one who does not behave in accord with his concept or his destination.[48]

He then adds the following extract taken from the same work:

Certainly, when we raise it [the question of the truth of thought-determinations], we must know what is to be understood by 'truth'. In the ordinary way, what we call 'truth' is the agreement of an object with our representation of it. We are then presupposing an object to which our representation is supposed to conform.

In the philosophical sense, on the contrary, 'truth', expressed abstractly and in general, means the agreement of a content with itself. This is therefore a meaning of 'truth' quite different from the one mentioned above. Besides, the deeper (philosophical) meaning of 'truth' is also partly found in ordinary linguistic usage already. We speak, for instance, of a 'true' friend, and by that we understand one whose way of acting conforms with the concept of friendship; and in the same way we speak also of a 'true' work of art. To say of something that it is 'untrue' is as much as to say that it is bad, that it involves an inner inadequacy.[49]

Bradley's claim that his theory of truth has its origins in Hegel's philosophical vision is not decisive. For it remains open that he has misunderstood the true import of Hegel's position. And as I have said, it is Stern's contention that this is precisely what has happened, a conclusion he justifies on the ground that Hegel's theory of truth, unlike that of Bradley, is not a theory of propositional truth. One difficulty with Stern's line of thought is that there are good grounds for thinking that Bradley himself is unconcerned with propositional truth. Such, at least, is the implication of his claim that truth requires 'thought's suicide'. On the other hand, there is little evidence to suggest that the alternative conception which arises in the light of this 'suicide' bears any resemblance to that rehearsed by Hegel in the above extracts.

Certainly, Hegel's remarks imply that an identity theory according to which truth is a property of thought is not, properly speaking, a theory of *truth*. For, as he puts it, such a theory is concerned simply with truth 'in relation to consciousness' – a kind of truth, which, he tells us, is to be understood as formal truth or *correctness*. This theme emerges also in the continuation of a previous extract I quoted when discussing Hegel's rejection of the dualistic framework which accompanies a certain version of the correspondence theory. Thus, having denied that truth means that external things correspond with my representations, he claims that 'representations of this kind are just *correct* representations held by *me* as *this* [individual]', and that 'In the Idea we are not dealing with this or that – be it representations or external things'. It is in the *Addition* to this section that we get the first extract cited by Stern above.

It seems clear that Hegel is wishing to make a distinction between, on the one hand, formal truth or correctness, and on the other hand, truth in the deeper or philosophical sense. Formal truth is at issue when we are concerned with 'the agreement of an object with our representation of it'. Truth in the deeper sense, by contrast, 'means the agreement of a content with itself'. This second meaning of truth is held to be quite different from the first, and Hegel tells us that it is prefigured in ordinary linguistic usage when we talk of a true friend or a true work of art. He claims also that truth in the deeper sense is the proper concern of logical thinking, and that it is the business of logical thinking to consider how far the thought-determinations are capable of grasping what is true. By contrast, 'the question of the truth of the thought-determinations does not arise in ordinary consciousness'.[50]

The idea that truth can be ascribed to things as well as thoughts is tied up with Hegel's interest in the question of the extent to which an object can be said to conform to its concept, where 'concept' in this context is a placeholder for essence or nature. The claim then is that a 'true' object is as it ought to be, and an 'untrue' object is, as Hegel puts it, 'self-discordant'. 'Object' in this context admits of a relatively broad reading, encompassing as it does the 'objects' of the various positions with which he takes issue in the *Phenomenology*. Thus, when Hegel tells us that consciousness finds that its knowledge does not correspond to its object, he is claiming that the relevant position fails to meet its intended aim – it is not as it ought to be, it involves an inconsistency. Second, however, there is evidence to suggest that, for Hegel, any finite object is bound to contradict itself to the extent that it is abstracted from the whole of which it is a part. It is an implication of this way of thinking then that only the Absolute or what he refers to as 'the Idea' is true in the deeper sense.

This second theme implies that Hegel's conception of truth has something in common with Bradley's. On the other hand, it is possible also to see it as a continuation of the theme which pervades Hegel's arguments in the opening chapters of the *Phenomenology*. Thus understood, Hegel is simply wishing to transcend the partial truths – or 'untruths' as he refers to them – which find expression in the positions with which he takes issue so as to define an alternative standpoint which combines their respective insights whilst avoiding their more problematic features. The point of referring to these positions as finite then would be to insist that they are inadequate as they stand and can be rendered adequate only to the extent that they are made to incorporate the insights of the positions against which they are initially defined. I shall return to this theme below.

An attempt at reconciliation

Thus far, I have provided a preliminary account of the various distinctions with which Hegel is operating in his theory of truth. Let me turn now to the question of how, if at all, they are to be reconciled. It would be difficult to deny that the term 'truth' is used in a variety of ways in ordinary discourse, and that it can be applied both to thoughts and judgements and to things. Furthermore, it does not seem absurd to suppose that the various senses of 'true' – true thoughts, true works of art, true friends, true emotions – have something in common, something which warrants the use of the same term in these seemingly disparate contexts. One such common element is to be found in the etymology of the term 'true' – an etymology which derives from the Old English *treowe,* meaning loyalty and fidelity, and *treow* and *treo* which is the root of the word 'tree' and suggests reliability and uprightness.

Hegel, however, would appear to be questioning the idea that there is a common element to these various uses of 'true', at least in so far as these uses suggest that it is appropriate to talk of there being true thoughts or judgements. For according to his line of thought, this latter use of the term is shallow and non-philosophical. The further implication is that truth in the deeper philosophical sense is better revealed by locutions such as that of 'true' friend or 'true' work of art. It is not immediately obvious why Hegel should be denying that truth, properly so-called, can be a property of thought. For as we have seen, it is his explicit and repeated contention that thought is that by virtue of which things themselves are made manifest to us – as he puts it in the *Logic,* it is that by virtue of which 'the *true* nature of the object comes into consciousness'.[51] However, Hegel's point is not that thought *per se* is inimical to truth. Rather, his idea is that the true thoughts with which a theorist of truth is typically concerned – thoughts which, as he puts it, concern this or that – are not of any philosophical significance. There would appear to be two related reasons why Hegel seeks to downgrade the status of these putative truths: first, he believes that they are different in kind from philosophical truths; second, they do not succeed in comprehending the whole of things. The first point finds expression in the following extract, taken again from the preface of the *Phenomenology:*

> *Dogmatism* as a way of thinking, whether in ordinary knowing or in the study of philosophy, is nothing else but the opinion that the True consists in a proposition which is a fixed result, or which is immediately known. To such questions as, 'When was Caesar born?' or 'How many feet were there in the stadium?', etc. a clear-cut answer ought to be given, just as it is definitely true that the square on the hypotenuse is equal to the sum of the squares on the other two sides of a right-angled triangle. But the nature of so-called truth of that kind is different from the nature of philosophical truths.[52]

One of the points Hegel is making here can be related to a complaint he makes on the previous page that 'truth is not a minted coin that can be given and pocketed ready made'. For he seems to be suggesting that it is wrong to suppose that philosophical truth is something which can be handed to one on a plate – that it consists in a 'fixed result' that can be passed from person to person, and is a candidate for immediate knowledge. The implication here is that the putative truths with which a theorist of truth is typically concerned – truths like 'there were twenty feet in the stadium' – precisely can be handed to one on a plate as fixed results, and that there is nothing wrong in conceiving them as such.

We can agree that philosophical truths are of a different order to the truths with which we are concerned when we are, say, counting feet in stadiums. We can agree also that facts about feet in stadiums can be handed around on a plate in a manner which would be quite out of place with philosophical truths. All that follows from these observations, however, is that a distinction is to be made between *what* is true in each case – in the respective examples under consideration, something pertaining to stadiums and something pertaining to philosophy. What does not follow is that 'truth' itself has a different meaning in each context.

As I have noted, however, Hegel has another reason for downgrading putative truths of the former kind, namely, that they do not succeed in embracing the whole of things. Hence he tells us in the preface to the *Phenomenology of Spirit* that '(t)he True is the whole',[53] it is 'actual only as system'. The idea that the true is the whole returns us to Bradley's position. Bradley, it will be remembered, concludes that truth cannot be a property of thought – that truth requires thought's suicide. He does so on the ground that thought imposes distinctions upon reality which abstract from the whole which must be captured if truth properly so-called is to be attained. The assumption here is that truth can be predicated only of reality as a whole, and that the putative truths which concern aspects of that whole are, at best, only partially true. The further implication in Bradley is that truth, i.e. the whole truth, is unattainable to us.

For reasons I have mentioned already, Hegel must deny that truth – even truth in Bradley's sense – requires thought's suicide. On the contrary, given the stress he places upon the flexibility of thought – a flexibility which, he believes, grants us the right to grasp the divine realm which, for Kant, must remain a closed book – it seems reasonable to conclude on his behalf that we are in principle capable of aspiring to the kind of truth which Bradley has in mind. How though are we to interpret the idea that truth embraces the whole once it is denied that its attainment requires thought's suicide?

Hegel seems to be implying that the claim that the true is the whole is to be restricted to a special category of truth, and the category with which he is concerned is that of philosophical truth. He claims also that truth in this sense is not to be viewed as a 'fixed result', that it is comparable to that which is involved when we talk of a true friend or a true work of art, and that untruth in this sense involves an inner inadequacy. Now I have conceded on his behalf that there is a difference between philosophical truth and the more mundane truths which are at issue when we are concerned with, say, the number of feet in a stadium. Furthermore, it seemed plausible to suppose that this difference helps to explain why it is that truths of the latter kind can be conveyed as 'fixed results' in a way that philosophical truths cannot. This point needs to be articulated with care, however, for there does seem to be a sense in which there *can* be fixed results in philosophy, when, for example, a conclusion is drawn and agreed upon in some context or other. To be sure, we can agree with Hegel that these conclusions are often quite difficult to come by – in this respect they are not obvious candidates for immediate knowledge, nor does it seem appropriate to hand them round on a plate in the way that one might hand round empirical truths. However, there is nothing absurd to the suggestion that philosophical truths can be presented as fixed results, and further, that they can be presented thus without introducing the 'dogmatism' that Hegel is so anxious to avoid.

One might argue that there is something deeper for philosophy to identify than the putative truths which present themselves as fixed results, and that it is this deeper something which serves as the focus of Hegel's concern with philosophical truth. It is plausible to suppose also that this focus gives a point to his claim that the true is the whole. I shall be providing a more thoroughgoing examination of Hegel's conception of philosophical truth in the following chapter. In particular, I shall relate this conception to the claims of other philosophers whose thinking can be said to bear the mark of the Hegelian dialectic, and determine how it might be situated with respect to my own diagnostic approach. At this stage, and as a precursor to the line I shall be pursuing, it suffices to note that there is a very obvious sense in which it is appropriate to claim on Hegel's behalf that, in a philosophical context, the true is the whole. For as I have stressed, it is integral to his way of proceeding that he defines a philosophical standpoint which captures the insights of positions which, on a non-Hegelian way of thinking, might be thought to be mutually exclusive. Furthermore, to the extent that the relevant positive outcome may itself be a candidate for further philosophical debate, there need be no implication that the position at which we have arrived is a permanently fixed result. Finally, it becomes possible also to give a sense to the claim that truth in philosophy requires that thought be transcended. However, this claim is no longer to be read as an invitation to shed the fetters of thought in favour of the boundless heights of a Bradleyan Absolute. Rather, the point is simply to guarantee that one transcends those modes of thinking whose inner inadequacies – or 'untruths' as Hegel would put it – preclude one from achieving an adequate conception of things.[54]

6   Philosophy and dialectic

The syndrome again

Let me return to the suggestion that philosophy should be seeking to transcend those modes of thinking whose limitations preclude one from achieving an adequate conception of things. Certainly, it has been intrinsic to the approach I have followed that some such aim be fulfilled. For I have sought to expose the distortions which find expression in certain ways of conceiving of the relation between, on the one hand, things in themselves and, on the other hand, ideas or concepts. The distortions in question stem from the metaphysical framework presupposed by the positions under attack – a framework which involves the imposition of an insurmountable distinction between things in themselves and the realm revealed in our ideas or concepts. It is a consequence of accepting this framework that one is compelled to oscillate between the equally unsatisfactory and mutually exclusive alternatives it yields. According to these alternatives, things in themselves must be either ever inaccessible to the realm which is revealed in our concepts or reduced to materials which do not themselves add up to genuine things.

The idea that philosophers have displayed a tendency to oscillate from one untenable position to another has been taken up and discussed by some recent figures. Here, for example, is John McDowell in his *Mind and World* giving us a description of the tendency to oscillate between two equally problematic philosophical alternatives when attempting to explain the relation between sense experience and conceptual thought:

> (W)e are prone to fall into an intolerable oscillation: in one phase we are drawn to a coherentism that cannot make sense of the bearing of thought on objective reality, and in the other phase we recoil into an appeal to the Given, which turns out to be useless.[1]

There is an ambiguity in McDowell's description here, which I shall mention and put aside. Is McDowell suggesting that individuals are prone to the oscillation, or is it, rather, that there is an oscillation over time within our intellectual community? Given the conclusions I have reached previously, it seems plausible to suppose that oscillations of both of these kinds are possible, and hence that

McDowell's talk of 'we' can be understood to refer both to individual philosophers and to the community as a whole. In the former case, the claim is that no stable individual view emerges; in the latter, that there is no stable communal view.

Hilary Putnam has coined the expression 'recoil phenomenon'[2] to describe such oscillations, and Steve Gerrard argues with some plausibility that its diagnosis forms the negative part of Wittgenstein's approach to philosophy. Gerrard describes this recoil phenomenon as involving:

> an oscillation between two extreme positions, with each camp reacting to the untenable part of the other, resulting, finally, in two untenable positions. The current recoil ricochets across both analytic and Continental philosophy. On one side are those who deny objectivity in all fields in all ways; there are only incommensurable narratives. On the other side are those who attempt to secure objectivity, but do so at the cost of clothing it in metaphysical mystery. The first side (justifiably) points out the illusions in the second's metaphysics, and then recoils to anarchy. The second (justifiably) shows the inherent contradictions in the anarchist's position, and then recoils to building more epicycles in its metaphysical castle.[3]

The suggestion then – which finds ample support in my previous conclusions – is that there is a virulent syndrome at work in philosophy. This syndrome is and has been manifested in a tendency to oscillate between two equally untenable positions and it is to be found at all levels of philosophical inquiry both past and present. The philosophers who have sought to identify this syndrome have wished also to support their negative arguments with a positive proposal that promises to rectify the difficulties faced when one occupies either of the positions which figure as the endpoints of this oscillation. The positive proposal – which again bears comparison with my diagnostic approach – is described in various related ways. Steve Gerrard suggests that it involves 'argu(ing) against both sides',[4] McDowell suggests that we must find a way of 'dismounting from the seesaw'[5].

McDowell's conception of the relation between sense-experience and thought has much in common with the neo-Hegelian stance I have sought to recommend. Thus, he claims that the oscillation with which he is concerned – between coherentism and the myth of the Given – occurs when the integral relation between concepts and the data of experience is rejected in favour of a position which prioritizes either one of these terms to the exclusion of the other. The result is that we are left with two possible options, neither of which can account for our capacity to engage in object-directed thought. According to the first (coherentist) option, we give priority to concepts at the expense of the given of experience. This results in a 'frictionless spinning in the void' – a description which warrants comparison with Hegel's talk, in a similar context, of being spun around in a 'whirling pool', and which is a picturesque way of giving expression to the Kantian claim that thoughts without content are empty. Alternatively, and this is the option which involves the myth of the Given, we give priority to experience at the expense of thought. However, this leads to a position which promises to provide the requisite link with reality but at the cost of rendering that reality inaccessible to us – intuitions without concepts are blind. Both of these problems should be familiar from previous chapters.

The solution is familiar too, for as should be clear from what I have said already, McDowell accepts – with Hegel and Kant – that concepts and intuitions are necessarily integrated, and hence that experience is conceptual. Once we accept that experience is conceptual, he argues, we no longer have to suppose that experience stands opposed to thought in the manner demanded by either of the positions under attack. Rather, it becomes possible to allow that thought can be integrated with the material delivered by the senses. The result is that we can accommodate the idea that thought is constrained by experience, and we can allow also that the experience in question plays a justificatory role in the beliefs we form about reality. The promise then is that we shall be in a position to abandon the myth of the given whilst also retaining the insight which is responsible for generating this myth in the first place, namely, that thought is constrained by things given in experience.

So far, I have provided examples of the negative and positive aspects of what appears to be a particular approach to philosophical problems. The negative arguments involve the identification of an oscillation, recoil or seesawing between two equally problematic positions, both of which contain insights yet neither of which can accommodate all those insights given the further assumptions to which they are committed. In the examples I considered in previous chapters, the recoil in question obtains between different accounts of the relations between substance and quality or thing in itself and our concepts – accounts which, in their different ways, assume that the terms of these relations are to be dualistically opposed. The positive position seeks to rectify the difficulties in the relevant opposing positions by somehow bringing together their respective insights. McDowell refers to this positive move as a dismounting of the seesaw. Gerrard suggests that it involves arguing against both sides.

If it is plausible to identify a recurring pattern in these treatments of philosophical problems, then there are several questions to be raised. First, are we really concerned with a particular approach to philosophical problems, and if so, does it impose a real constraint upon the shape of philosophical problems and their solutions? Second, if we are concerned with a particular philosophical approach, then how extensive is its application? That is to ask, can it be employed at all levels of philosophical inquiry, or is it applicable as a solution to merely a subclass of philosophical problems? The idea that 'seesaw dismounting' can (and should) occur at all levels of philosophical inquiry, when coupled with the further idea that it constitutes a particular philosophical approach, suggests that philosophical thinking, as such, has a certain determinate structure. On the other hand, it may turn out that we are not really concerned with a particular philosophical approach at all, and that 'seesaw dismounting' is just a fancy way of describing what goes on all the time when we identify errors and endeavour to avoid them. Obviously, if this latter interpretation is forced upon us, then the idea that philosophical thinking has a determinate structure will be much less exciting in its implications.

One way of determining the extent of this approach is by considering whether there is any principled way of unifying the assumptions which are responsible for the relevant oscillations. Of course, it may turn out that there is no particular feature common to the assumptions in question, in which case we shall be forced back to the conclusion that getting stuck on seesaws is simply a matter of making mistakes. Alternatively, if the assumptions that give rise to the oscillations admit of a more specific interpretation, then it may be justified to conclude that we are concerned with a more particular way of getting things right and wrong.

Third, how should we understand the positive aspect of the approach that emerges once the relevant 'seesaw' is dismounted? The idea that 'seesaw dismounting' is really just a placeholder for getting things right suggests that the positive outcome of this approach should be such as to yield answers to questions which remain elusive at the negative stage. That is to say, we should be in a position to explain what needs to be explained by avoiding assumptions that preclude such an enterprise. McDowell, we shall see, has a rather different understanding of the positive outcome, suggesting that a dismounting of the seesaw leads to a disappearance of the questions that set in motion the relevant oscillations. The idea that philosophical questions can and should be made to disappear implies that the culmination of this approach spells the end of much philosophical activity. It remains to be seen just how far this line of thought can to be pursued, and in particular, whether there is a limit upon the kind of question that can be 'exorcised' in this manner.

Schematizing the syndrome

Let me return to Gerrard's characterization of the recoil phenomenon. Gerrard argues that the recoil we are seeking to avoid involves an oscillation between two positions – call them A and B – each of which contains something problematic. Presumably then, in arguing against both A and B we are rejecting the untenable aspect of these respective positions. The implication, however, is that A and B also contain features that are worth preserving. Thus, the claim that we are arguing against both is not intended to imply that these positions are to be rejected wholesale. What does their untenable part consist in then? It is at this stage that McDowell's seesaw metaphor can be put to work. For this metaphor suggests that when we are 'on the seesaw' A and B are viewed as mutually exclusive but also exhaustive – that we must choose either one or the other but that we cannot choose both. A dismounting of the seesaw, then, should lead to a position which synthesizes the good features of A and B and excludes their bad features precisely because A and B are no longer exhaustive of the options. This suggests that one of the bad things about these respective positions is that they contain something which suggests that they are exhaustive of the options. Rather, they each contain some but only some of the truth. It would appear then that there is an important sense in which a dismounting of the seesaw involves arguing *for* both, but in a way that no longer involves the incoherence to which we would be committed if we were still wedded to the seesaw.

There are two ways of schematizing the approach:

Model 1

According to this model, options A and B can be represented as follows:

$$A = D + E$$
$$B = G + F$$

We are assuming that D+E is incompatible with G+F, and that both of these options are unacceptable. However, there is no common assumption at work here that stands in need of rejection. Rather, there are two distinct assumptions – D and G – which must be rejected in order to arrive at position C (= not-D and not-G and E and F).

Model 2

According to this model, options A and B can be represented as follows:

$$A = D + E$$
$$B = D + F$$

Now if we assume D, then D+E is inconsistent with D+F; but both D+E and D+F are unacceptable. So according to this method, (i) we detect D as a common assumption, (ii) we reject D, and (iii) we arrive at C = not-D + E + F.

If the first model contains what is being suggested, then viewing philosophical problems in accordance with it does not impose any particular structure upon philosophical thinking. Rather, it serves simply to illustrate the way in which faulty philosophical positions can emerge and be corrected with the rejection of one or more of the assumptions they involve. Furthermore, it is no requirement that the relevant assumptions be common to the positions under consideration. Rather, it is enough that they each contain some philosophical error and some philosophical insight. This also suggests that there is nothing explanatory within the model as to why A and B should have appeared to exhaust the possibilities, that is, of why the oscillation should have occurred. Finally, it can be noted that such a model is entirely appropriate to the kind of erroneous thinking that can occur in any area of discourse, whether we are talking about scientific reasoning, politics, or how best to achieve one's goals. In this respect, it is a model that is highly general both in its philosophical and non-philosophical application. We need, therefore, to concentrate on Model 2.

Further, if we are considering models of philosophical problem solving, there is an element common to both models which is worth noting, namely, that they represent the position to be resolved as requiring two incompatible views. On the face of it, however, there is no reason why the oscillation in question must be between just two positions. To be sure, the examples I have focused upon lend some substance to this assumption. It seems plausible to suppose though that there can be philosophical puzzles which naturally generate, say, three responses between which we oscillate, and hence that the duality of initial views is merely a simplifying assumption.

The second model imposes a more specific structure upon philosophical thinking, for it conceives of the resolution of a philosophical problem as involving the rejection of an assumption that is common to two opposing and problematic positions. This further restriction, however, is open to various interpretations. According to the first and least demanding interpretation, the model is simply a further example of a perfectly general phenomenon, the only difference being that the respective positions A and B happen to involve a common assumption. Yet the fact that these positions have this much in common is not in itself of any general philosophical significance. It merely happens to be a structure found in certain areas. There will, in all areas of debate, be times when two competing views – standard or otherwise – happen to share a problematic assumption that stands in need of rejection, in favour of a third view.

Something more significant emerges if it is held that all philosophical thinking must conform to the structure exhibited by this second model – that it is in the nature of philosophical problems to have this structure. On the face of it, it is difficult to see how this stronger interpretation could be defended, unless it is assumed that there is some kind of underlying force imposing its form upon the emergence of philosophical problems and their solutions. For the moment, we can note that there are no immediately compelling reasons for adopting this line of thought, although it is not absurd to suppose that some of Hegel's headier proclamations are expressive of such a commitment.

Identifying some assumptions

The question I want to raise now is whether there are further similarities to be discerned between the positions under criticism – similarities which go beyond those of general structure, and which provide a deeper unity to the relevant approaches. According to my diagnosis of the positions discussed in previous chapters, it is a commitment to a dualism of thing and idea which generates the relevant oscillations, and which is common to the disputants in question. With Locke and Berkeley, this commitment finds expression in the imposition of an insurmountable distinction between substance itself and the things we perceive, which latter are held to be collections of sensible qualities. With Nietzsche and Kant, by contrast, the distinction in question is held to obtain between things in themselves and the realm revealed in our concepts. In all of these cases, however, it is assumed that things in themselves are inaccessible to us, and there is evidence to suggest that the things we perceive, *qua* things, involve the constructive work of mind.

One could argue that it is not particularly helpful to claim that the positions in question stem from an underlying dualistic framework, if the aim is to give them a unity which goes beyond that of general structure. For, so the objection goes, talk of dualistic frameworks is just another way of describing the relevant oscillations. One way of responding to this objection is to deny that we are compelled to remain at the level of general structure, that, on the contrary, we are in a position now to pursue a more specific line of enquiry. We can do so by focusing upon the particular kinds of dualism which are operative in the relevant oscillations.

Such a response is perfectly reasonable. However, it does raise the question of how we are to conceive of this more specific line of enquiry. According to one way of thinking, the aim is to focus upon a particular kind of oscillation and to identify something responsible for it, something which explains its pervasive hold. Now I spent some time considering the question of why Locke and Berkeley remain wedded to a dualism of substance and quality. One such answer, I suggested, is to be found in some of the grammatical confusions surrounding the concept of substance – confusions which lead one to suppose that the true substance is something whose revelation demands the removal of the qualities of the relevant thing. A confusion of this kind, of course, is propagated further with the assumption that the substance is a substratum and that, as such, it is a separable entity – something which *supports* the things we perceive.

There are no doubt analogous grammatical confusions lurking in the arguments of Nietzsche and Kant, and which, likewise, help to account for the distinction they impose between things in themselves and concepts. Confusions surrounding the term 'concept' provide an obvious case in point, in particular, those which lead one to suppose that concepts are *applied* to reality, where this is intended to imply the kind of form/matter model to which Kant is susceptible. Furthermore, it is not absurd to suppose that there are similar misconceptions operative when it is insisted that there can be no appearance without something that appears. Kant, for example, refers to the thing in itself as the substratum of appearances – a mode of expression which readily invites the applicability of the 'support' metaphor, and the conclusion that things in themselves are distinct from that which appears.

My protagonists are influenced also by more ideologically based considerations. One such consideration – evidence for which can be found in the arguments of Locke and Berkeley – is that the things we perceive cannot involve material substance, and that they are to be viewed, rather, as collections of sensible qualities. Berkeley's justification for this negative claim is that there is no way of making sense of the idea that material things could causally effect us. We have seen that there are analogous ideological considerations to be identified in the positions of Nietzsche and Kant – ones which lead them to insist that things in themselves have to be inaccessible to the realm revealed in our concepts. Again, the justification for this conclusion is that there can be no causal interaction between these two realms – a conclusion which gains some plausibility when taken in conjunction with Kant's tendency to treat the thing in itself as a place-holder for God, but which becomes more difficult to accept when it is intended to be that by virtue of which the things we perceive can be said to be independent of our minds.

At this point, we are faced with the questions of how we are to comprehend the status of these grammatical and ideological explanations, whether one of them is more basic than the other, or, alternatively, whether a more fundamental ground requires to be identified. Someone of a Wittgensteinian persuasion would argue that grammatical explanations are fundamental. He would do so on the ground that all philosophical confusions are grammatical in form – confusions which arise from our perennial tendency to be bewitched by language. The difficulty with this line of thought, however, is that it depends for its cogency upon the prior correctness of the claim that all philosophical errors are grammatical in form, and, even on a broad understanding of the meaning of 'grammatical', it is unconvincing to suppose that this is so.

Are we to conclude then that the so-called ideological explanations are more basic? And, if so, does it follow that our explanations can terminate at *this* point? One reason for thinking that this ideological level is not basic enough is that the claim that our protagonists maintain a dualism of substance and quality or thing and concept is surely just another way of describing the metaphysical framework which stands to be explained. To be sure, we can add to this explanation by making reference to the beliefs they have about causation – beliefs which are intended to provide some kind of justification for imposing the relevant dualism. That is to say, the idea that things in themselves are to be dualistically opposed to the realm revealed in our concepts is justified on the ground that there can be no causal interaction between these two realms. The difficulty, however, is that this justificatory ground is itself just a further expression of the dualism which stands in need of explanation – a ground which would be challenged by one who is prepared to allow that we can conceptualize things in themselves.

McDowell is prepared to go deeper at this point, and he spends some time considering what is responsible for the oscillations with which he is concerned, his main focus being the epistemological problem of how thought can have a bearing upon reality. To this end he suggests that the culprit is naturalism. Naturalism, as he understands it, is the position according to which nature is identified with 'what natural science aims to make comprehensible', namely, 'the realm of law', and this identification threatens 'to empty it of meaning', 'to leave it disenchanted'.[6] However, once nature is disenchanted in this manner, he continues, it becomes impossible to see how thought – and more generally, mind itself – can be part of the natural world. For thought – in so far as it involves the meaningful relations that constitute the 'space of reasons' – exhibits a mode of intelligibility that remains elusive to nature *qua* realm of natural law. Thus, once mind and nature are dualistically opposed in the manner demanded by this picture, there is no way of explaining how it is that thought can be integrated with the material delivered by the senses so as to have a bearing upon the natural world.

It is at this stage, McDowell argues, that the oscillation between coherentism and the myth of the given takes hold as each side clings persistently to one side of the mind/nature divide, ruling out any hope of the reconciliation which is required in order to meet the task at hand. The difficulty does not stop here, however, for it is a further consequence of accepting this mind/nature dualism that we are unable to solve the ontological problem of how to comprehend our nature as thinking things. McDowell identifies a corresponding oscillation in this context also.

According to the first option, the mind is to be 'reconstructed' from purely naturalistic materials. McDowell refers to this position as 'bald naturalism',[7] and he rejects it on the ground that the materials are inadequate by definition. According to the second option, by contrast, we deny that mind can be 'reconstructed' in this manner, and seek instead to locate it in some non-natural 'platonic' realm. McDowell refers to this position as 'rampant platonism'.[8] However, this second option is equally problematic because it leaves us with no way of explaining how minds can be part of the natural order.

How are we to assess these remarks about naturalism? And can they be of any use in solving the problem at issue, namely, that of whether it is possible to delimit the syndrome by showing that it involves a particular kind of philosophical error? We have seen that the kind of naturalism under attack is reductive naturalism – a position which is given a specific scientific interpretation in so far as it is tied to the idea that it is exhausted by the descriptions of it in terms employed in the statement of laws of nature. One point to make is that whatever the merits of this picture as a model for much recent philosophy, it can hardly figure as a model for pre-Enlightenment philosophical debate and its oscillations.[9] Nor is it applicable to philosophical debates where a scientific conception of nature can have no grip. Second, even when this model applies (if anywhere) we must not overestimate its explanatoriness. It is easy to get the impression that where it applies we have an explanation for the offending pattern of argument. The explanation is, however, merely partial, at best. Thus, we can explain why we oscillate between A and B; it is because we assume D. However, why do we assume D? The grip of D is itself unexplained.

I shall return to this worry in due course. First though, let me consider the extent to which McDowell's model can be put to use in the context of comprehending the positions I have examined. Now provided that we focus upon the sceptical strand in Locke's position, it seems plausible to suppose that he is committed to a conception of the material world which excludes the possibility of thought. We can suppose also that the material world, thus understood, is the proper province of science, for it is this realm which is said to incorporate the real essences of things. Are we to conclude then that a commitment to reductive naturalism can figure in an explanation of why Locke is compelled to accept a dualism of substance and the things we perceive, that it is a naturalism of this kind which can explain why he is compelled at times to deny that the material realm can be revealed in our ideas? One reason for being wary about the adequacy of this diagnosis is that even if we accept that a commitment to reductive naturalism can be cited in an explanation of why Locke accepts a dualism of substance and the things we perceive, it cannot be denied that there are other considerations which are motivating his line of thought.

A further difficulty arises when we look more closely at the relation between reductionism and scientism in Locke's scheme of things. From what I have said, it looks as if the reductive side of Locke's story comes in at the level of the things we perceive – the level of ideas, as he would call it. Furthermore, this brand of reductionism is not exclusive of thought. It is exclusive, rather, of material substance. In this respect it is a position which has something in common with the coherentist option described by McDowell, implying as it does that mind-independent reality must remain elusive to thought. Now we might argue that, to the extent that material substance remains elusive to thought on this framework, Locke is under pressure to conclude that the scientist works at the level of ideas. However, it would be misleading to say that this brand of reductionism is explained by reference to a bias he has towards science. On the contrary, it looks as if the order of explanation is reversed. That is to say, it is Locke's exclusion of substance from the realm of ideas which explains why he might be moved to conclude that the scientist is compelled to work within this realm. Finally, if we are going to introduce the concept of platonism into the discussion, it seems more appropriate to do so in connection with Locke's postulation of an unknowable substance. For this unknowable something cannot be intelligibly related to the realm which is revealed in our ideas, and provided that we identify this latter realm with nature – doing so on the ground that it comprises the things we are seeking to comprehend – it is a something which can be described as 'non-natural'.

We have seen that Locke is under equal pressure to deny that the scientist is confined to the realm of ideas. Berkeley, by contrast, can accept rather less ambivalently that the scientist *is* concerned with the realm of ideas, for he rejects the realm of the material, and claims quite explicitly that the things we perceive are nothing but collections of ideas. He also makes it clear that the realm of ideas is to be understood as the realm of nature, and in doing so, makes reference to the laws of nature.[10] Nevertheless, there is no obvious sense in which, simply by claiming that the scientist is concerned with the realm of ideas, Berkeley commits himself to a specifically scientific outlook. Nor can it be said that the realm of nature, thus conceived, is to be opposed to that of thought. As in the case of Locke, however, it is at the level of ideas that reductionism enters into the picture – a reductionism which likewise leaves us with a coherentist position, implying as it does that, in perceiving things, we are confined 'barely to our own ideas'.

There is, of course, a sense in which Berkeley *is* committed to divorcing nature from thought, nature in this context being the realm to which the materialist is committed. Furthermore, he makes it quite clear that nature thus understood is thoroughly disenchanted, his way of giving expression to this criticism being to say that a materialist position estranges us from God – a claim which is intended to imply that the estrangement in question is inclusive of all those features we possess *qua* thinking beings. The position then is that nature – as understood by the materialist – is inert and unthinking, and that a materialist framework can account neither for the causal activity we take to be operative in the things we perceive nor for our status as thinking things.

Now if Berkeley were in a position to provide a viable alternative to this materialist framework, then we could claim that the nature he is divorcing from thought deserves to be rejected. And as I have said, this line of argument would have a point if the material realm had to be understood in the terms he assumes. I have claimed, however, that this conception is by no means mandatory, and further, that the immaterialist alternative he proposes is fraught with difficulty, resting as it does upon a theological framework which is just as problematic as the materialist standpoint it is intended to replace. Indeed, it is with this latter criticism in mind that we can appreciate McDowell's second point, namely, that a 'platonist' option becomes a compelling alternative to materialism/naturalism so long as one remains within the offending dualistic framework – platonism in the present Berkeleyan context finding expression in the idea that nature can be 're-enchanted' only by bringing God into the equation.

Kant, like Berkeley, holds that the scientist is concerned with the realm of ideas, that this realm constitutes the natural world, and that it is the proper province of scientific investigation. Furthermore, provided that we attend to the dualistic reading, we can say that reductionism enters into the picture at this level – a reductionism which likewise throws up a coherentist position, implying as it does that there is no sense to be made of the idea that thought can have a bearing upon mind-independent reality. Second, Kant accepts a version of Berkeley's claim that a materialist outlook has the effect of disenchanting the world. For he makes it clear that nature is to be understood in deterministic causal terms, the implication being that we must look elsewhere if we are to capture those features which set us apart from the natural order. It follows that there is indeed a sense in which Kant is committed to a conception of the natural world which has a bias towards a scientific outlook. Again, however, it is a naturalism which remains inclusive of thought, and which is exclusive, rather, of those aspects of reality which, he believes, cannot be treated in naturalistic terms.

We can conclude that scientific reductionism is simply a particular and temporary expression of a more general drive towards reductionism, that it is operative to some extent in the positions under consideration, but that they also involve reductionisms for which the charge of scientism would be quite inappropriate. Now reductionism in this broad sense serves as one side of the oscillating seesaw. The other side is the position that McDowell labels 'rampant platonism' – a position which stands in for some form of ontological dualism. Thus, to return to my examples, we have an oscillation between a reductive account of the things we perceive, and a platonist alternative which has it that things in themselves are to be located in some unknowable other-worldly realm.

What is the relation between platonism and reductionism? Are we concerned here with an assumption that is common to both sides of the seesaw, or is there some further error responsible for generating the platonist option? The fact that platonism stands opposed to reductionism suggests that the assumption generating the platonist's position has to be different from that which underlies reductionism. So, reductionism, in that sense, has to be dislodged from its pivotal explanatory position. On the other hand, if it is right to say that a commitment to reductionism, in some sense, is responsible for the seesaw in its entirety, then it looks as if the error we are seeking to identify must be common to both sides.

The platonist's starting point is that the things for which he proposes an account cannot be comprehended in the relevant reductive terms. In the example under consideration, it is denied that the objects of perception can be viewed in terms which make no reference to the idea of a thing, and that the idea of a thing is a construction of consciousness. Having made these negative claims, the platonist then proceeds to locate things in an 'other-worldly' realm. It is other-worldly in the sense that it is set against the world which is revealed in our concepts. Now this positive move rests upon the assumption that the reductionist, in his various guises, has the monopoly on the world which is available to thought and experience. For it is only by accepting this assumption that one is forced to move in the direction of platonism when seeking to comprehend those phenomena that cannot be accommodated in the relevant reductive terms. Thus, even though the platonist rejects reductionism in one important sense, he is committed nonetheless to the reductionist's conception of the realm which is revealed in our concepts. It is for this reason that he is compelled to postulate a second world in terms of which to situate the phenomena which remain elusive to the reductionist. It may seem that the assumption that is common to both sides of this seesaw is an underlying dualism of worlds, but, of course, the reductionist, in so far as he fails to acknowledge the second world, cannot see things this way. However, what is now common is an understanding of the reductive side of things, and both the platonist's and the reductionist's positions serve merely as a response to this common conception. We are returned then to the conclusion that the second model, described previously, serves as an appropriate formalization of the approach in so far as it traces the relevant error back to an assumption which is common to both sides of the dispute.

One question to be raised is whether it would be appropriate to reintroduce the concept of naturalism in the context of comprehending this more general drive towards reductionism, doing so with the proviso that it be understood in terms which go beyond the scientific bias preferred by McDowell. One advantage of making this move is that there would be a more definite point to claiming that a specific kind of error is at issue. The error in question would be that of viewing the natural world in unduly restrictive terms – terms which are not necessarily motivated by exclusively scientific considerations, but which, for various reasons, omit phenomena which have a central place in our thought and experience. To be sure, it would be unnecessary to assume that there is a uniform error operative across all cases, except in so far as we are concerned with the error of viewing the natural world in unduly restrictive terms. In this respect, a variety of diagnoses would be applicable to the question of why the relevant restriction is accepted. As to the problem of where the diagnostic explanations should terminate, it seems plausible to suppose again that there is no one general and *a priori* answer to this question. Rather, we must content ourselves by proceeding case by case, using our philosophical acumen to determine whether it is necessary and, indeed, possible to pursue our investigations to a deeper level.

Finally, we can note that this drive towards a more fundamental explanatory ground may itself be symptomatic of the syndrome at issue. For as I have illustrated, those who remain in its grip have tended to assume that we are faced with two mutually exclusive and exhaustive options in our attempts to provide an adequate explanation of some phenomenon. The first option provides no explanation at all, producing as it does simply more of what stands to be explained. The second option, by contrast, involves the identification of an explanatory ground, one, however, which turns out to be equally incapable of completing the required work. The alternative, I have suggested, is to abandon the framework which forces this dilemma so as to allow instead that the phenomenon in question can be grounded in something which is of genuine explanatory worth. The upshot is that we arrive at an explanation which involves an element of circularity, but the circularity in question is to be distinguished from the vacuous kind which characterizes the first option described above, its presence guaranteeing that we remain with the phenomenon to be explained as opposed to shifting to a level which can have no bearing upon the problem at hand. Thus, we can agree that the explanations I have given for the syndrome are, in their different ways, expressive of the dualism which stands to be explained. The suggestion now, however, is that the presence of such circularity is compatible with allowing that the relevant explanations are genuinely informative.

The non-dualistic alternative

Once the syndrome has been put to rest, it becomes possible to incorporate the insights of the positions under attack whilst avoiding their difficulties. Thus, we reject the reductive position which seeks a 'reconstruction' of the things we conceptualize, and we reject the platonist alternative which responds to the failure of this reconstruction by postulating a second world in terms of which to accommodate things in themselves. And once we have acknowledged that neither position in the oscillation has to be occupied, the way is paved for a third alternative – one which, in this case, grants us the right to allow that we can exercise conceptions of mind-independent things. In this way, we retain the reductionist's insight that these things must be accommodated in terms which disallow the postulation of a second unknowable world, but we agree with the platonist that the reductionist's materials are inadequate to the task of completing the required aim. McDowell refers to the resultant position as a 'relaxed naturalism'[11] or a 'naturalized platonism',[12] his point being to capture the sense in which it succeeds in accommodating the phenomena which are eliminated from the world by the positions under attack.

Of course, we require a more detailed account of this third way, and I shall consider in a moment how the conclusions of previous chapters might be utilized to this end. First though, it is necessary to diffuse the objection that such a task cannot be completed. On the face of it, this objection is a straightforward case of question-begging, assuming as it does that the options thrown up by the offending dualistic framework are exhaustive of the available conceptual space. Furthermore, it is difficult to see how such an objector could substantiate this assumption other than by offering considerations which are simply further expressions of the offending framework – by insisting, for example, that the realm revealed in our concepts is to be defined in the terms dictated by the reductionist.

Let us allow then that there are no compelling arguments against the very idea of there being a third alternative, and, given the difficulties which are thrown up by the offending pattern of argument, every reason for taking it seriously. What though are we to say about the details of such an account? One potential difficulty is that it can look as if there is very little to say in this context. However, it is important to be clear about why this should be so. Perhaps the most obvious sense in which there is little to say is that we are no longer required to engage in the explanatory strategies which are forced upon one who remains in the grip of the syndrome. That is to say, there is no need for reductive explanations which are ruled out by definition given the nature of the available materials, nor is it necessary to respond to this failure by embracing some form of ontological dualism. Yet it would be absurd to conclude on this basis that there is an explanatory lack at the heart of such a position.

The conclusions I have reached in previous chapters provide ample illustration of what can be said at a more positive level. Thus, the position is that we are capable of exercising conceptions of mind-independent things, and that these things are *irreducibly* present in our experience of the world, where this is intended to imply that for creatures who possess the concept of a thing there will be experiences in which this concept is irreducibly present. Furthermore, because this conclusion is articulated from within the framework of a broader conception of the conceptual realm – a conception which grants us right to put forward this claim of irreducibility – there is no prima facie difficulty in explaining how this can be so. As to the question of whether this kind of explanatory strategy is satisfactory, there are two points to make. First, and as mentioned already, a proponent of this position can stress once more that the air of dissatisfaction stems from a residual and unjustified hankering after the kind of explanatory metaphysics which is demanded by one in the grip of the syndrome. Second, he can appeal to the conservative principle that we all think and talk in a way that gives credence to the position he endorses, and further, that his position makes sense of such thought and talk in a way that is unrivalled by any other available option.

The idea that explanatory metaphysics[13] must be abandoned in the quest for a satisfactory account of the things we conceptualize raises the question of how best we are to understand the status of this alternative position. Gerrard, as I have noted, suggests that a diagnosis of the 'recoil phenomenon' serves as the negative aspect of the later Wittgenstein's approach to philosophy, and much of what Wittgenstein says in more positive mode is traded upon and repeated by McDowell in his *Mind and World*. In particular, both Wittgenstein and McDowell emphasize that the approach they are adopting is not to be viewed as a way of solving philosophical problems. Rather, it is intended to dissolve or to exorcise them.[14] It is in this way that we abandon what McDowell refers to as 'constructive philosophy'.[15]

The idea that the positive position culminates in a dissolution of the relevant problems can be interpreted in two ways. According to the first interpretation, it involves an 'exorcism' of the questions which provide the focus for the positions under attack – for example, the question of how we are to comprehend the relation between concepts and reality. In favour of this interpretation, we can agree that it is futile to attempt to answer these questions whilst accepting assumptions which are incompatible with meeting such an aim. In this respect, the relevant questions are unanswerable when posed from within a framework that incorporates such assumptions. However, it is more difficult to accept that a rejection of these assumptions brings with it a disappearance of the questions for which they precluded any answer.

Such a conclusion can be made to sound a lot less absurd if we accept the Wittgensteinian view that philosophy is an inherently distortive activity which requires to be eradicated – that a good philosopher must bring about the downfall of his subject. The difficulty, however, is that although it is harmless enough to suppose that some ways of doing philosophy involve distortions – those which are beset by the syndrome, for example – it is implausible to insist that all philosophy be viewed in this light. Indeed, if we did impose this definitional requirement upon the activity of philosophy, all that would follow is that a range of problems and questions are thrown up which do not count as philosophical yet which demand nonetheless to be addressed at some highly general level of enquiry. The questions thrown up by the position under current consideration provide an obvious case in point, as does Wittgenstein's so-called therapeutic approach to philosophy.

On a weaker understanding of the positive approach, there is no implication that philosophical questions require to be exorcised. Rather, there is room for allowing that an abandonment of the assumptions that stood in the way of answering those questions leads to a framework by means of which they can be tackled anew. This weaker interpretation accords with some of the things said by McDowell, and it promises to make sense of the positive conclusions he himself wishes to advance. The general conclusion then is that it is important to recognize that the dialectical conception of philosophical debate is one thing, and the idea of the vanishing of philosophical questions another; the two ideas are independent. One can share the picture of seesaw dismounting that McDowell has, but suppose that the dismounting places oneself in a position to provide explanatory and informative claims. On the other hand, Wittgenstein would hold that there are no philosophical theories, but there is no ground for ascribing to him the same account of the origin of philosophical questions.

Hegel again

Hegel's dialectical method has been the target of various criticisms, and my Introduction gives an indication of some of its alleged sins. Hegel himself is an easy target for such criticisms, claiming, for example, that 'it is contradiction that moves the world',[16] and implying that the oppositions and conflicts he 'courts' are intrinsic to all phenomena, both natural and spiritual. It is unsurprising therefore that he has been accused of imposing upon reason (and philosophy) a necessity whose structure is dictated by the contradictions and conflicts which 'move the world'. And it is unsurprising that many have found it difficult to make sense of such claims.

It is not my purpose here to discuss and to develop these criticisms, for, as should be clear from my arguments, I believe that there is something of significance to be found in Hegel's approach. Furthermore, given the focus of the present chapter, it should come as no surprise that the area of significance I wish to focus upon concerns the extent to which it is appropriate to view his methodology in the terms dictated by McDowell's seesaw metaphor. That there is a significant connection to be made here should come as no surprise to those who are familiar with the preface of McDowell's *Mind and World,* for he tells us that his book is to be viewed as a prolegomenon to a reading of Hegel's *Phenomenology of Spirit.*[17] Furthermore, Hegel himself provides further compelling evidence in favour of a connection here, for he employs the seesaw metaphor in his *Science of Logic* when describing one way in which the dialectic finds expression:

> Dialectic is often no more than a subjective seesaw of arguments that sway back and forth, where basic import is lacking and the (resulting) nakedness is covered by the astuteness that gives birth to such argumentations.[18]

Hegel is concerned with the problems we confront when faced with two positions or arguments that are in conflict with each other, yet both of which seem equally compelling – positions like those with which he is concerned in the opening chapters of the *Phenomenology of Spirit.* This 'contradictory' way of seeing things, he believes, has a profound grip upon the way in which we reason, and it results in a scepticism whose 'invincibility' must be granted.[19] Nevertheless, he holds also that this seesawing – which reduces argument to a 'tug of war'[20] – is merely the 'negative result of the dialectic',[21] and that philosophy must go beyond this result even whilst acknowledging that this sceptical stage is an integral part of its progression. It is at this point that we pass beyond what Hegel refers to as the 'one-sided' determinations of the understanding, and move towards the 'affirmative' contained within their 'dissolution'.[22] As he puts it, we move beyond the mere logic of the understanding to speculative logic. The use of the term 'speculative' in this context is not intended to imply that we are concerned with something 'incomprehensible' and 'inaccessible to thought'. All that it implies – and this should be familiar from previous chapters – is that we have transcended the understanding, where 'understanding' is a placeholder for the limited, 'one-sided' modes of thinking characteristic of the positions under attack.[23] Thus, Hegel tells us that the speculative 'expressly contains the very antitheses at which the understanding stops short' and that it is 'the concrete unity of just those determinations that count as true for the understanding only in their separation and opposition'.

It is not difficult to see how these Hegelian reflections might be related to the approach I have followed, for much of what I have said encourages such a comparison. In particular, what Hegel refers to as the 'negative result of the dialectic' can be compared to the negative aspect of this approach in so far as it involves the identification of the oscillations which have stood in the way of an adequate conception of things. In this respect, Hegel's 'mere' logic of the understanding corresponds to the kind of thinking which is indicative of the syndrome.

The question of how we are to view the positive aspect of Hegel's approach is more difficult to answer. It is clear enough that Hegel is seeking to incorporate the insights of the positions under attack whilst avoiding their difficulties. And, to the extent that he dispenses with the framework responsible for these difficulties, he sidesteps the need to engage in the kind of explanatory strategy which is forced upon one who remains wedded to the oscillatory way of thinking. How though does he view the status of the position which is reached when the relevant one-sided determinations are superseded? Does he see this position as paving the way towards an exorcism of the relevant problems? And if so, what conclusions does he draw about philosophical activity in a more general sense?

Certainly, there is much in Hegel to suggest that the positive outcome of the dialectic is intended to pave the way to some kind of philosophical completion. Such at least is the implication of his use of expressions like 'absolute knowledge', 'final results', and 'the Calvary of absolute spirit'.[24] Furthermore, it is not difficult to read into these claims a conception of the dialectic which sees it as some kind of necessary force imposing its structure upon the shape of philosophical reasoning and leading it to its own destruction. On the other hand, there is equal evidence to suggest that the very idea of there being an end to philosophical activity – a stage at which final results are attained – is utterly alien to the spirit of Hegel's enquiry, and that he has a much more open-ended conception in mind.[25]

The idea that the dialectic involves an ongoing process accords with the further idea that it is really just a placeholder for the rational procedures which define the shape of philosophical arguments. Certainly, an emphasis in this latter direction helps to explain why some commentators prefer to deny that we can pin a determinate method upon Hegel's manner of philosophizing.[26] Nevertheless, if the comparison I have sought to develop is justified, then it may be that a more modest conception of the dialectic – along the lines just recommended – is compatible with the further idea that it admits of a more definite interpretation. For Hegel, no less than his more modern descendents, is aiming to reject and to transcend the various dualisms which have pervaded philosophical enquiry – in the examples I have considered, those which occur in the context of comprehending the relation between concepts and reality.

If we accept that Hegel's method involves an ongoing process, there is no need to insist that philosophical questions should terminate at the point at which progress has been reached with respect to the problem at issue. Rather, it is allowed that the relevant proposal is itself a source for continuing philosophical debate. It may be thought that if we accept this possibility we must accept also that talk of progress in this context is quite misplaced – that philosophy is an ongoing process along the road to nowhere. The conclusions I have reached in previous chapters should help to undermine the force of this objection. More relevant to the present chapter, however, is the idea that this objection may be an expression of an oscillatory way of thinking, assuming as it does that philosophy must either be a process without progress or one which spells its own destruction. Hegel would surely wish to allow that it can be both of these things – that it can be a process which makes progress, and that it does so by exposing and transcending flawed ways of thinking. Arguing along these lines, we can say that philosophy destroys not itself, but, rather, its flawed aspects, and, in doing so, remains a perpetual presence.

I raised the question of where Wittgenstein's philosophical stance is to be situated with respect to the more contemporary activity of seesaw dismounting. I suggested that elements of that stance are unjustified, in particular, the implication it carries that philosophy is a fundamentally distortive activity. Nevertheless, it does contain the important insight that philosophy *can* be distortive, when, for example, it remains in the grip of the syndrome. When Wittgenstein gives expression to the doubts he has about philosophy, he links this to the complaint that it leads us away from our ordinary ways of thinking about things. The implication here is that these ordinary ways of thinking are superior to those which arise in the wake of philosophical enquiry. McDowell appropriates this Wittgensteinian theme in his *Mind and World,* his aim being to vindicate the idea that mind stands in a direct (albeit fallible) relation to world, and to show how it might be 'intellectually respectable' to ignore the questions which are raised by the sceptic in this context. The hope then is that one might arrive at a position where it is possible to treat these questions as 'unreal in the way that common sense has always wanted to'.[27]

Now if we assume that philosophy is an essentially distortive activity, and that there is a conflict between the results it throws up and those of common sense, then it is clear that the latter should be given default priority. By contrast, if we deny that philosophy has to be understood in this pejorative sense, then we shall be in a position to acknowledge its significance and to allow that it is not bound to be in conflict with common sense. We can allow also that common sense may be flawed in important respects and that these flaws can be exposed and corrected by philosophical reflection.

Hegel would be sympathetic to these concessions, for, unlike Wittgenstein, he believes that common sense – what he refers to as 'natural' or 'ordinary' consciousness – is fundamentally oscillatory and stands to be corrected by philosophy. Here, for example, is what he says in his *Lectures on Fine Art:*

> Absolute truth proves that neither freedom by itself, as subjective, sundered from necessity, is absolutely a true thing nor, by parity of reasoning, is truthfulness to be ascribed to necessity isolated and taken by itself. The ordinary consciousness, on the other hand, cannot extricate itself from this opposition and either remains despairingly in contradiction or else casts it aside and helps itself in some other way. But philosophy enters into the heart of the self-contradictory characteristics, knows them in their essential nature, i.e. as in their one-sidedness not absolute but self-dissolving, and it sets them in the harmony and unity which is truth. To grasp this Concept of truth is the task of philosophy.[28]

And in the introduction to the *Phenomenology,* he talks of the way in which it will be shown that 'natural consciousness', which 'takes itself to be real knowledge' is deluded in this respect.[29] By contrast, 'in pressing forward to its true existence' – doing so by careful philosophical reflection – consciousness will come to grasp its own essence, arriving thereby at the standpoint of absolute knowledge.[30]

We can conclude that there are important differences between Wittgenstein and Hegel, both with respect to the question of how we are to transcend the dualisms which have pervaded philosophy, and of how we are to view the relation between common sense and philosophy. According to the Wittgensteinian approach – the approach favoured by McDowell – we make evident the metaphysical framework that imposes a forced choice between untenable options. Then, having made this framework explicit, we abandon the assumptions it involves so as to arrive at an alternative which returns us to our ordinary way of thinking. In the example under consideration, we are returned to a common sense realist position with respect to the relation in which we stand to things, having seen that philosophy led us astray in this context. The implication here is that common sense is superior to philosophy. For Hegel, by contrast, the dualism is characteristic of common sense. His approach then is to get 'ordinary consciousness' to engage in self-criticism, the upshot being that we are led into a variety of standpoints – 'forms of consciousness' – each of which turns out to be expressive of the offending dualism. By contrast, the standpoint of absolute knowledge – a standpoint which is arrived at by careful philosophical reflection – serves to overcome the dualism, the result being that the problems endemic to the positions under attack are put to rest.

Now it is surely a point in Hegel's favour that he allows that common sense can be flawed and that philosophy can rectify its deficiencies. Furthermore, given his belief that the deficiencies of common sense can be present in philosophy – when, for example, it is in the grip of the syndrome – he can agree with Wittgenstein that philosophy *can* be distortive. He must deny, however – and rightly so – that this deficiency cannot be rectified. One might object that the differences in their positions are not so great as my argument would suggest, not least because Wittgenstein himself must accept that there is some sense in which his mode of enquiry counts as philosophical. On this way of thinking then, it is crucial to both Hegel and Wittgenstein that we make a distinction between good philosophy and bad philosophy so as to allow that bad philosophy is oscillatory in the sense previously described. It is important also to make an analogous distinction with respect to common sense, for, although it is undeniable that common sense can be flawed, it is absurd to suppose that it is ineliminably so. Of course, we can concede that common sense is inadequately reflective, and that this deficiency is to be remedied by sound philosophical thought. However, it does not follow from an acknowledgement of this point that there is anything fundamentally wrong with common sense. All that follows is that it must be reflected upon philosophically, and that this reflection may reveal assumptions or presuppositions which cannot withstand intellectual scrutiny. According to this line of thought, then, it is not common sense *per se* which is inherently flawed. Rather, it is the particular shape it assumes when the syndrome takes hold.

It is unimportant that I resolve the question of whether Hegel would be prepared to concede these points, for regardless of where he stands, we have arrived at an approach to philosophy which offers the resources for identifying and diagnosing the difficulties which are inherent in certain views of phenomena and for paving the way towards an alternative which promises to put these difficulties to rest. Given the somewhat sympathetic reading of Hegel I have recommended, the implication is that this approach is to be found in his dialectical method, and that he both acknowledges and transcends the difficulties with which I have been concerned. However, I have allowed on his behalf that philosophy is an ongoing process – in this respect, there is no implication that the position at which he has arrived constitutes any kind of completion or closure with respect to the problems at issue. It is to be expected then that there may be elements of his position which stand in need of modification and even rejection – a concession which can be made without undermining the significance of his overall methodological stance. If my conclusions are justified, there is every reason for supposing that further examination of the issues he raises will yield important results for an understanding of the ways in which philosophers can go astray, and of the kind of progress to which they can justifiably aspire.

Conclusion

I have been concerned with the question of how we are to comprehend the relation between concepts and reality, and have sought to identify a syndrome whose presence leaves one with no way of providing a coherent account of this relation. I have argued that the syndrome is at work in the positions of Locke, Berkeley, Kant, and Nietzsche, that it leads them to endorse a highly problematic conception of a thing, and that it prevents their better insights from gaining adequate expression. I have claimed further that the positions they arrive at have important consequences for an understanding of the concept of truth, and that there is an analogue of the syndrome at work in this context too. The upshot is that we are forced to choose between a variety of equally unsatisfactory alternatives, all of which are metaphysically motivated to bad effect, and none of which can accommodate the sense in which we are capable of thinking truly about things. Nietzsche provides the clearest example of this oscillatory tendency, and Bradley offers an uncompromising illustration of what follows if we try to avoid this oscillation by sticking resolutely to one side of the offending divide – in this case, the side which has it that truth requires 'thought's suicide'.

My diagnosis and treatment of the syndrome has been inspired by Hegel's dialectical method – a method whose results, I have argued, serve to define the absolute knowledge to which he aspires. Applied to the problem of the concept/reality relation, it is a method which rectifies the deficiencies of the positions under attack by repairing the conceptual separations they exploit. The position at which we arrive promises to make sense of the idea that we can exercise conceptions of mind-independent things, and in this way provides a genuine corrective to the scepticism which is kept alive by the syndrome. The implication in all of this is that we now have the resources for defining a conception of truth which renders it an attainable ideal.

Various issues are thrown up by my inquiry overall. One issue concerns the accuracy of my history of an error, and it raises the question of whether I really do justice to the positions of my protagonists. In his essay 'On a Discovery' Kant complains that many historians of philosophy 'with all their intended praise, let the philosophers speak mere nonsense'. He goes on to say that '(t)hey cannot see beyond what the philosopher actually said, to what they really meant to say'. Taken to its extreme, this complaint is rectified only by allowing that there are no real disagreements in philosophy – that all philosophers have arrived at the correct position. The less extreme version is that one's chosen hero has arrived at the correct position, and that any false steps which he might have made in his argument are to be excused on the ground that he did not really intend them.

It is essential that we uphold a distinction between what a philosopher says and what he meant to say, for it is only by so doing that we can avoid the absurd conclusion that there are no disagreements in the history of philosophy. However, it is necessary to avoid the opposite error of treating the relevant philosophers as fools. One must allow, for example, that philosophers do not always express themselves clearly, and hence that one may have failed to appreciate the real import of their claims. One must be wary also of approaching them with a particular agenda in mind, say, an agenda which requires that they be treated as fools – the opposite error of one who refuses to see no wrong. Schopenhauer's attitude to Hegel is an obvious case in point.

It would be easy for someone to complain that I have taken a rather too sympathetic approach to Hegel – that I have played down the more problematic aspects of his position, and that it has suited my purposes to do so. Now I am prepared to accept that my interpretation will seem unduly sympathetic to some scholars, and further that Hegel's position contains elements that are rather more difficult to defend than those upon which I have chosen to focus. As I have stressed though, my interest in Hegel is primarily an interest in his methodological approach – an approach which, I hope to have shown, admits of a perfectly sober interpretation and which, if followed, allows us to appreciate the difference between what a philosopher says and what he should have said. Furthermore, it does so without implying that he is to be treated as a fool. On the contrary, it allows us to acknowledge the insights which lurk in the relevant positions – insights which, in the cases I have considered, are compromised by the presence of the syndrome.

An appreciation of this latter point has been essential to my own neo-Hegelian approach, and it should help to fend off the criticism that I have treated some of my protagonists as fools. I have said already that some will object to my treatment of Nietzsche, and to the extent that I have focused exclusively upon one of his early essays, there is a point to this objection. Nevertheless, I have stressed that there is a real question as to whether he ever succeeds in overthrowing the syndrome, and this is so even though his later works suggest that he was well aware of the kind of error with which I have been concerned. Criticisms notwithstanding, however, it is no implication of what I have said that he is talking nonsense, and I hope that it serves as an indication of the respect I accord him as a thinker that I have included him in this work.

I have treated Berkeley in a relatively sympathetic manner, one of my aims being to put to rest the idea that he is speaking nonsense. As a group of students once put it 'we have been taught that he is mad'. That this diagnosis is wide of the mark should be obvious from all that I have said, and what I have said should give pause to those who are willing to tarnish all idealists with a similar damning brush. These idealists really do mean what they say, and what they say needs to be taken very seriously if we are to avoid those versions of realism which leave us out of touch with the world.

The position I end up with offers a vindication of idealism – an idealism which has been shorn of some of the more problematic features it assumes at the hands of Berkeley and Kant. Thus understood, it is a position which any sensible realist should be prepared to accept. Details have been left unspecified – understandably so given that my concern has been to define the form of a solution to the problems set in motion by Locke and Berkeley. Nor can it be ruled out that some of the ingredients of the solution stand to be rejected and that their deficiencies will be brought to light by further investigation. I am therefore allowing that I do not always say what I should be saying, but hoping that this does not justify the conclusion that I am speaking nonsense!

The most important questions thrown up by my inquiry concern the syndrome. I have drawn some more general conclusions about its nature in Chapter 6, and I hope that my discussion in previous chapters has been sufficient to illustrate its presence in accounts of the concept/reality relation. One outstanding question is that of how we are to comprehend its scope – a question which I have left undeveloped. However, it is an implication of what I have said on Hegel's behalf that it may well have a more extensive scope, one possible context being in accounts of the God/world relation. The question of God has been of relevance to my discussion because of the central role God assumes in Berkeley's – and to a lesser but by no means irrelevant extent Kant's – understanding of the concept/reality relation. I have argued that this centrality is misconceived and that it is imperative that we maintain a distinction between the question of the relation in which we stand to things, and that of the relation in which we stand to God. As I have said, it is not absurd to suppose that such a conflation is responsible for generating the conclusion that truth is an unattainable ideal. In any case, this must, I think, be so if it is claimed also that God stands dualistically opposed to anything of which we could have determinate experience or thought.

Hegel is prepared to challenge this dualistic conception of God, and it is with this challenge in mind that we are returned to the possibility that there is a version of the syndrome at work in this theological context too. In particular, although Hegel is adamant that there is a distinction between God and the world – in this respect there is no requirement that God is needed to maintain a realist position with respect to the things we conceptualize – he rejects the Kantian assumption that God is to be relegated to an unknowable beyond. An examination of Hegel's conception of God belongs in a different inquiry, and I mention the matter here simply to lend credence to the possibility that the syndrome has infected other areas of philosophy, the relevance of this theological context being it that it promises to cast a more interesting light upon the idea – taken so seriously by Berkeley, Kant, and Hegel – that a metaphysics without God is a metaphysics in which something of great importance has been lost.

Berkeley gives voice to this complaint in the context of his attack upon the materialist standpoint. In particular, he tells us that materialism has the effect of 'estranging the minds of men' from God – a complaint which, when taken in conjunction with all of the difficulties his own position involves, suggests that it is an estrangement we would do well to court. Nevertheless, there is an insight lurking in what he says – a similar insight, perhaps, to that which has led some theologians[1] to object that we shall forsake all reference to God only at the cost of losing our grip upon a really important dimension of reality, the dimension that religious language, in its different and often picturesque ways, has endeavoured to capture. The further claims are that this dimension is at issue when we are concerned with the question of why there is a world at all, and – more contentiously one might think – that its acknowledgment allows us to make sense of that which sets us apart from the realm of unthinking things: for example, our capacity to act freely, to make moral distinctions, and to pose the very questions which are at issue here.

It would be easy enough to deflate the force of these claims. One could do so by insisting that the question of why there is a world at all is either a non-question, or an unanswerable one, or one which falls within the province of science. And although one can agree that there are facts about ourselves and the world which remain elusive to a crude materialistic framework, it is a further question whether their acknowledgement is sufficient to warrant the introduction of God into our ontology. Bearing this latter point in mind, one can sympathize with Berkeley's complaint that materialism may have an estranging effect, whilst denying that the estrangement in question can be remedied only by means of a theological detour.

These counter-responses are perfectly understandable. Indeed, they would have to be taken very seriously if reference to God were simply a matter of locating or not locating some unknowable supernatural entity. However, the interesting thing about the theologians I have mentioned is that, like Hegel, they are prepared to challenge the assumption that this dualistic conception of God is mandatory. They do so on the ground that it is a conception which is philosophically indefensible, and that it has no relevance to the question of the *reality* of God in any sense in which the Christian is interested. The complaint is reminiscent of Berkeley's criticisms of the Lockean conception of substance, and it is no accident that we find the theologian John Robinson asserting that he had reached the same sort of position which Berkeley had reached in his questioning of Locke's philosophy of substance.[2]

There are many questions to be raised about Robinson's position – questions which need not detain us here.[3] The important point to grasp is that if we are prepared to accept that a dualistic conception of God may not be the only available option – a concession which gets us to the stage where we can at least acknowledge that the meaning of 'God' is unclear – then we are forced to rethink the question of what is really at issue when we move in a theological direction. In particular, we have to ask whether anything important is lost if we forsake all reference to God, where this no longer has to amount to asking whether it matters if we give up on the idea of there being some supernatural entity set alongside the world we are trying to comprehend, the answer to which would seem to be a fairly obvious 'no'. Once we have reached this stage, the possibility opens up that there is a version of the syndrome at work in this context too, that its presence has led to a variety of positions which presuppose a dualistic conception of the God/world relation, and that its identification can lead to a more satisfactory understanding of what is really at issue when God is brought into the equation.

There is a further point of similarity between this theological case and my previous examples – one which is implicit in Berkeley's complaint that materialism has an alienating effect. For the theologians who have been tempted by this alternative way of thinking about the God/world relation have argued that the offending dualistic framework stems from a commitment to an exclusively scientific conception of the world. They have argued further that an acknowledgement of the difficulties which accompany this conception suggest that it may well be necessary to reintroduce God into the equation, doing so by rejecting the dualistic framework which is presupposed by one who shares this bias towards science.

As I have said, one of the difficulties with exploiting this explanatory model in a theological context is that although it seems plausible to suppose that an exclusively scientific outlook is in danger of estranging us from certain aspects of reality, it is a further question, Berkeley notwithstanding, whether this concession is sufficient to yield an alternative which vindicates the reality of God. By contrast, it seems much less contentious to suppose that a structurally similar move is available for some of the other phenomena which worry the theologians to which I have referred – the phenomenon of value, for example. It is understandable therefore that several recent philosophers – McDowell included – have focused upon this case, arguing that a commitment to a crude scientific framework has been instrumental in generating the oscillations which have occurred in this context too.[4] They have argued further that the form of a solution is to be found in a rethink of the boundaries of the natural world – a rethink which, in this case, involves a rejection of the assumption that we can secure the irreducibility of value only at the cost of locating it in a second supernatural world. Given what I have said on Kant's behalf it is not absurd to suppose that a rethink about nature would afford him the resources for providing a more satisfactory account of our capacity to engage in moral thought – in this case, a rethink which can make sense of the freedom this capacity requires, doing so without any recourse to the idea of a noumenal realm.

The idea that certain forms of reductionism lead us away from the phenomena we are seeking to comprehend is familiar from some of the criticisms which have been levelled at the programme of reductive analysis,[5] and there are interesting questions to be raised about the extent to which the syndrome can be said to be operative in this context too. One of the motives behind this programme is that it promises to provide informative and genuinely explanatory results about the concepts[6] we are seeking to comprehend, and, as far as those which occur in a metaphysical context are concerned, to guarantee that we avoid the non-explanations which become inevitable when we are tempted to lapse into speculative metaphysics. Thus, Ayer tells us that propositions about material things call for analysis because they 'encourage a belief in a physical world behind the world of phenomena,[7] and that belief in the existence of material things is on the same level as belief in invisible substrata.[8]

It is familiar from all that I have said that we must avoid any reference to a physical world behind the world of phenomena. It is familiar also that those who remain in the grip of the syndrome have responded to this negative demand by insisting that the concept of a thing be reconstructed from experiential materials which are not themselves thing-involving. It is with this demand in mind that we can appreciate Ayer's complaint that belief in the existence of material things is on the same level as belief in invisible substrata, and his positive claim that we must analyse the concept of a material thing in terms of 'sense-contents' – sense-contents in this context involving no reference to the idea of a thing.

A further point of similarity emerges when we look more carefully at the underlying presuppositions of this programme of analysis: in particular, the demand it carries that concepts be dissected into more basic components. For given the difficulties which accompany this demand when applied to the concept of a thing, it looks as if the dissection in question has the effect of enforcing a separation which cannot be effected – in this case a separation between the thing in itself and the materials to which we are confined at the level of experience. We are returned then to the idea that the reductive analyst is committed to separating concepts that belong together – an idea which, we have seen, constitutes the defining moment of the syndrome.

The philosophers who have taken issue with the programme of reductive analysis have recommended that we take a more holistic approach to the concepts we are seeking to comprehend. This amounts to resisting the programme of dismantlement favoured by the reductive analyst, so as to allow instead that the relevant concept is irreducible. The further claim is that the illumination we seek is to be found by making explicit the connections the concept has to other concepts.[9] As P.F. Strawson has put it, we are to connect the concept in question rather than to reduce it. Thus, to take the concept of a material thing, we deny that this concept can be resolved into more basic experiential components, and we deny also that it is to be set apart from anything to which we could gain access at the level of experience. And, once these negative requirements are in place, we can set about connecting it to other concepts with which it is inextricably involved – the concept of causation, for example. In this way, we are returned to the Newtonian idea – discussed in Chapter 3 – that the nature of a thing is to act upon other things. There is no longer any implication, however, that the acted upon things are confined to minds, nor that these causal properties must remain forever inaccessible.

It should be clear that there is a significant connection to be made between this 'connective' treatment of concepts and the approach I have recommended we adopt, for in both cases there is a reparation of the separations which are exploited by one who remains in the grip of the syndrome. Furthermore, there is no implication in either case that one has forsaken the right to engage in explanatory metaphysics. The point is simply that one has abandoned the explanatory strategies which are forced upon one who insists upon imposing the relevant separations, and is in a position now to say something genuinely informative about the concept in question. In this respect, an analyst of this persuasion is in a position to tackle the concepts which must remain the exclusive preserve of the speculative metaphysician so long as the offending framework is in place. Finally, the idea that this approach is holistic rather than foundationalist provides us with a further take upon the claim that the true is the whole – a take which is reminiscent of my own preferred interpretation. For according to this interpretation, we attain the 'whole' by repairing the conceptual separations exploited by one who is in the grip of the syndrome – a similar reparation, I am suggesting, to that which is operative in the activity of conceptual connection.

The issues I have raised in connection with the syndrome give an indication of a possible direction for further inquiry, both with respect to its scope and to the relevance it has for an understanding and assessment of some of the reductive programmes which have held sway in analytic philosophy. There is no implication, of course, that we have at our disposal any kind of *a priori* argument against the possibility of imposing a separation between concepts. Thus, it remains open that there will be contexts where concepts require to be separated, contexts where reductionism may well constitute the best available alternative. Equally, however, there will be cases where it is unclear what precisely one ought to be saying – cases where the boundaries of the relevant concept are too unclear to allow us to adjudicate on the question of whether a reduction is in order or not.

It is with an acknowledgement of these points that we are returned yet again to Hegel. For as I have said, it is a merit of his approach that it promises to avoid the importing of unwarranted assumptions into one's inquiry – assumptions which have the effect of prejudging the issue at hand. Working with this constraint in mind, the best we can do is to take a particular position on its own terms, try it out, and if it raises difficulties, consider whether there may not be an alternative way of giving expression to the insights it contains. The further implication in Hegel's approach is that an inquiry along these lines will put us in a position to get a clearer picture of what is at issue so far as those concepts with murky borders are concerned – the concept of God, for example. An optimistic picture, without a doubt, but a picture which can hold no solace for one who seeks instant edification or, as Hegel puts it, 'sky-rockets of inspiration'. It is fitting then that I close with a quotation which warns of the deceptions which await us in our pursuit of truth – deceptions to which we shall succumb only at the cost of shielding philosophy from the goal where 'it can lay aside *love* of knowing and be *actual* knowing':[10]

> The commonest way in which we deceive ourselves or others about understanding is by assuming something as familiar, and accepting it on that account; with all its pros and cons, such knowing never gets anywhere, and it knows not why. Subject and object, God, Nature, Understanding, sensibility, and so on, are uncritically taken for granted as familiar, established as valid, and made into fixed points for starting and stopping. While these remain unmoved, the knowing activity goes back and forth between them, thus moving only on their surface.[11]

Notes

Introduction

1 1954, III, 6.
2 As Erich Heller (1984, p. 57) has put it, 'the logically self-evident does not need the rhetorical support of the accents of prophecy'.
3 See Clark (1990) for a detailed study of this issue.
4 See, for example, Allison (1983), Langton (1998), Robinson (1994).
5 Several recent philosophers have argued that epistemological issues are central to Hegel. See, for example, Forster (1998), Maker (1994), Rockmore (1997), Westphal (1989).
6 Horstmann (1999) provides a helpful discussion of some of the issues which arise in connection with Hegel's philosophical legacy.
7 1969, vol. 1, p. 429.
8 1994.
9 1994.

1 A philosophical syndrome

1 All references to Berkeley will be to *A Treatise Concerning the Principles of Human Knowledge* unless otherwise stated. The numbers refer to the sections. 17.
2 All references to Locke will be to the *Essay* unless otherwise stated. II.XIII.17–18.
3 II.XIII.19.
4 II.XIII.20.
5 Locke, 1894, p. 234.
6 W IV, p. 448.
7 1894.
8 II.XII.6.
9 II.XXIII.6.
10 1829, p. 375 cf. II.XIII.20.
11 II.XXIII.4.
12 III.III.15.
13 Ibid.
14 III.VI.2.
15 III.VI.6.
16 Ibid.
17 III.III.17.
18 III.VI.6.
19 III.VI.7.
20 III.VI.9.
21 III.VI.9.

22 III.VI.25.
23 III.VI.49.
24 III.VI.26.
25 IV.III.16.
26 IV.III.13.
27 IV.III.28.
28 IV.III.29.
29 Both Locke and Berkeley are careless with their use of the term 'idea'. In the present context, however, Locke is referring to the things the ideas are of – in this case, the sensible qualities of things.
30 III.VI.2.
31 III.VI.28.
32 IV.IV.8.
33 IV.XI.9.
34 III.VI.9.
35 Maurice Mandelbaum (1964) suggests that we treat the notion of a substratum as the real essence of the thing in question. He claims also that the idea of a substratum, thus construed, is a 'surrogate for what in the object is material and exists independently of us', and that it is 'the atomic constitution of objects, not "pure substance in general", which cause the ideas of them we actually have' (p. 39). These claims admit of a perfectly innocent reading which is consistent with the idea that our relation to things is direct. However, once the causal claim is read in conjunction with the Lockean idea that the *being* of substance is inaccessible to thought, it is easy to see how one might conclude that our ideas of things are effects of some unknowable cause.
36 1993, p. 517.
37 1979, p. 71.
38 1993, p. 606.
39 III.VI.9.
40 1979, p. 77.
41 Ibid.
42 It is to be noted that the materialism in question does not involve a commitment to the idea that there are only material things. Rather, the claim is that there are material things and immaterial minds. It is the claim that there are material things which serves as the object of Berkeley's attack.
43 3.
44 This position is announced emphatically in the opening section of *Principles*. In what follows, I am going to refer to Berkeley's position as the claim that things are groupings of sensible qualities. As he puts it at 7, 'that therefore wherein colour, figure and the like qualities exist, must perceive them; hence it is clear there can be no unthinking substance or *substratum* of those ideas.' These qualities are referred to as ideas then because they are sustained in existence by mind.
45 89.
46 26, 29.
47 This line of thought finds expression in his discussion in the *Third Dialogue* of whether two people can be said to perceive the same thing (p. 80).
48 See, for example, 37.
49 See, for example, 57, 148–9.
50 Berkeley does not spell out in any detail how we are to understand this alternative conception of cognition, but see 89, 137–42 and the *Third Dialogue* for some marginally helpful comments. It will be a task of subsequent chapters to spell out how this conception of cognition is taken up and developed by his idealist successors.
51 See *Third Dialogue*, p. 65.
52 64–66.
53 28–30, 33.

54 28.
55 See, for example, 89.
56 145.
57 103.
58 105.
59 106.
60 65.
61 147.
62 148.

2 Concepts and reality: Nietzsche

1 Much of Nietzsche's Kantian influence derives from his interest in Schopenhauer's work, in particular, *The World as Will and Representation*.
2 Pp. 82–3. All references will be to Nietzsche's essay 'On Truth and Lies in a Nonmoral Sense' unless otherwise stated.
3 1968, s. 586.
4 Clark argues that this innocuous interpretation fits much of what Nietzsche says, as she puts it, '"Perspectivism" is the claim that all knowledge is perspectival' (1990, p. 127). 'The perspectival character of knowledge places no limit whatsoever on our cognitive capacities. That seeing is perspectival in the sense I have emphasized – that we cannot see things from no perspective … places no limit on what we can see because there is no look things have from no perspective' (ibid, p. 134). Clark argues, however, that the perspectivism of Nietzsche's earlier writings is to be interpreted in more radical terms, implying as it does that human knowledge distorts reality.
5 This interpretation is similar to the one recommended by Clark, although she grants that we have to look to Nietzsche's later writings to find such a position.
6 This interpretation fits with Danto's claim that, for Nietzsche, no one interpretation is better than any other – that 'we cannot speak of a true perspective, but only of the perspective that prevails' (1965, p. 77). Danto's interpretation is a peculiar hybrid of those I have outlined so far. He accepts that perspectivism involves a rejection of the thing in itself. As noted, however, this rejection need not imply that our capacity for knowledge or truth is compromised, for the point may simply be that we have rejected something contradictory. Once it is claimed that we cannot speak of a true perspective, however, it looks as if the thing in itself is more important than the initial argument might have suggested. I shall be arguing that Nietzsche's line of thought *is* captured by this interpretation, but that it is seriously flawed. Schacht (1983) agrees that, for Nietzsche, our perspectives have a distorting effect.
7 P. 86.
8 P. 84.
9 Nietzsche's arguments here are well summed up and discussed by Maudemarie Clark (1990, pp.78–85). Clark's book as a whole provides for a compelling and comprehensive account of Nietzsche's conception of truth, and is understandably more comprehensive than anything which is offered in the present chapter.
10 Pp. 82–3.
11 P. 86.
12 In the following chapter I shall be looking more closely at the question of whether Kant himself is committed to this 'distortive' conception of concepts.
13 Pp. 84–5.
14 P. 84.
15 P. 84–5.
16 P. 83.
17 The idea that the concept/reality relation maps onto that of the general and particular re-emerges in Kant. Furthermore, it is an idea for which Locke has some sympathy,

claiming as he does that '(g)eneral *and Universal*, belong not the real existence of Things; but *are the Inventions and Creatures of the* Understanding, made by it for its own use ... universality belongs not to things themselves, which are all of them particular in their Existence' (III.III.11). Locke's claim here need not imply that there is something our concepts fail to capture. When taken alongside his occasional commitment to the idea that things in themselves are inaccessible to us, however, it carries this implication quite explicitly.

18 P. 82.
19 Compare Locke's claim that the certainty of things existing in nature is as great as our frame can attain to, and as much as our condition needs. Compare also the distinction he makes in Book II chapter VIII between the primary and secondary properties of things.
20 1981, Ch. 3.
21 1993, p. 606.
22 This metaphor is used by David Wiggins (1986, p. 171, and 2001, p. 152).

3 Concepts and reality: Kant

1 B167n.
2 B303.
3 A51/B75.
4 A19/B33.
5 A20/B34.
6 A51/B75.
7 A19/B33.
8 Ibid.
9 A41/B58.
10 A49/B66.
11 A27/B43.
12 Kant must allow, of course, that one can think about absent empirical objects and objects with which one has never been in sensory contact.
13 A51/B75.
14 A19/B33.
15 A320/B377.
16 A52/B76.
17 A52/B76.
18 B150. See Quassim Cassam (2000) for a discussion and criticism of this aspect of Kant's thought.
19 Bxxviii.
20 B309.
21 Bxxvii. I shall return below to the question of how we are to understand the nature of this distinction.
22 A287/B343.
23 Bxxvii.
24 A369.
25 Ibid.
26 Ibid.
27 A369. Provided that we focus on the sceptical strand in Locke's position, he comes out as an empirical idealist in Kant's sense. Berkeley is a 'dogmatic idealist,' for we are told that the *dogmatic idealist* is one who denies the existence of matter. Kant claims further that the *sceptical idealist* is one who doubts the existence of matter, holding it to be incapable of proof (A377). Again, Locke can be said to fall into this category provided that we attend to the sceptical reading of his position.
28 A371. Berkeley would refer to himself as an empirical realist in this sense.
29 A327/B383.

30 A328/B385.
31 A329/B386.
32 B308.
33 B308.
34 Ibid.
35 1983, p. 13.
36 Bxxvi.
37 A252–3.
38 Kant (1997, p. 289).
39 Cf. A235–260/B294–B315.
40 A255/B311.
41 B307.
42 This terminology is to be found in Bird (1962).
43 A38/B55.
44 B306.
45 A249.
46 Bxxvii.
47 See Ameriks (1982) for a helpful discussion of the dispute concerning these two inter-pretations. Given the ambiguities in Kant's conception of a thing in itself – ambiguities I discuss below – it is unclear how we are to interpret the precise import of these inter-pretations. Allison takes a proponent of the 'two-world' interpretation to be committed to phenomenalism with respect to the things we conceptualize, and argues that Strawson (1966) provides an illustration of such a position. McDowell (1994, p. 43, n. 18) argues that this interpretation of Strawson's reading is absurd. Allison himself defends a 'one-world' interpretation – his idea being that, for Kant, there is one realm of entities with two aspects. Other variants upon the 'one-world' interpretation are to be found in Langton (1998) and Robinson (1994).
48 McDowell makes this point in his Woodbridge lectures (1998, p. 469, note 23).
49 See A278/B333.
50 The conclusions of the present section were influenced by some very helpful discus-sions I had with Harvey Brown.
51 See Langton (1998, pp. 182–185).
52 The principle concerning back action is controversial in two senses. First, not all agree that it is essential to the notion of a body, and second, there is disagreement as to whether something like the absolute space-time of special relativity is an example of such a body that acts but is not acted upon. Again, I thank Harvey Brown for bringing this point to my attention.
53 From Leibniz's point of view then, there is no scope for making the contrast which is implied by Locke's line of thought when he says of substance that we have no idea of what it is but only an obscure and confused idea of what it does. See, for example, *New Essays on Human Understanding*, Book II, Ch. xxiii where Theophilus, speaking on behalf of Leibniz, responds as follows to the Lockean claim that we have no clear idea of substance in general: 'My own view is that this opinion about what we don't know springs for a demand for a way of knowing which the object does not admit of.'
54 See A168/B210. Rae Langton (1998, Ch. 8) illustrates the way in which Michael Faraday's field theory was influenced by Kant's philosophy. As she puts it, 'Faraday thinks that in physics there is no need for any such substantial core, no need for prop-erties other than powers, and if one is a physicist, that is all that matters' (p. 181). As I have said, this way of thinking is already built into classical Newtonian mechanics.
55 See Langton, (1998 pp. 182–85).
56 McDowell advances this interpretation in his Woodbridge lectures (p. 469).
57 A371.
58 A490–491/B518–519.
59 A492/B520.

60 B522/A494.
61 A697/B725.
62 This something is 'that which underlies the outer appearances'.
63 A359.
64 The contrast between work of construal and construction is made by David Wiggins (1986, p. 179).
65 A359.
66 B179/A140.
67 B187/A147.
68 A66/B91.
69 A126.
70 A127–128.
71 B163.
72 B164.
73 A92/B125.
74 The conclusions I draw in the following section have been greatly influenced and clarified by conversations with Quassim Cassam.
75 1974, s. 1.
76 Ibid, s. 2.
77 Ibid, s. 3.
78 Ibid, s. 6.
79 Ibid.
80 1992, p. 349.
81 S.8.
82 A19/B33.
83 Ibid.
84 A52/B76.
85 A41/B58.
86 A29.
87 A28/B44.
88 A19/B33.
89 John McDowell argues in his Woodbridge lectures (pp. 452–55) that Kant is working for the most part with this second sense of the notion of an intuition. He claims also that Kant was not committed to a dualistic conception of the relation between appearance and thing. This is intended to be a correction of the two-worlds picture he presupposes in *Mind and World*.
90 A23/B38.
91 A26/B42.
92 A27/B43.
93 A43/B60.
94 B68.
95 A44/B62.
96 It is no good replying on Kant's behalf that his point is simply that the objective status of the things we experience and the spatio-temporality they exhibit is undermined by the findings of science. For, as I have said, Kant holds that scientific investigation is pitched also at the level of appearance. Of course, one could try to make the point by reference to a non-dualistic conception of the appearance/reality relation. It would not follow, however, that the things we conceptualize are appearances, that, *qua* things, they are constructed by us, and that their natures are unknowable. To be sure, we can agree that the scientist works at a level which is more basic than that which is operative when we conceptualize macroscopic things. Conceding this much, however, does not take us to the conclusion that our ordinary ontology has been discredited, nor that it is of no explanatory use. (Not all explanations are pitched at the deepest level of scientific theory.) Wiggins makes the point as follows: 'The older ontology may yet be

contenable with the more theoretical conception. Contrasting the actual discrediting of entities of some kind, palpable or impalpable, with the discovering of new entities at the atomic or sub-atomic level, let us not conceive the latter as determining the level to which everything else must be reduced, even if this is the level at which macroscopic events are promised certain sorts of explanation' (2001, p. 156).
97 My thinking here has been influenced by Galen Strawson (2002, section 6).
98 Compare the distinction I made between sensory and non-sensory dispositions earlier in the chapter.
99 Langton (1998. pp. 209–10) interprets Kant's claim here in these theological terms.

4 Concepts and reality: Hegel

1 Ralph Walker (1989, p. 94).
2 See Richard Rorty (1982, p. 16).
3 There has been much discussion of Hegel's critique of Kant in the recent literature. See, for example, Ameriks (1992), Forster (1998), Hance (1995), Maker (1994), McDowell (1994), Pippin (1989), Westphal (1989). For a sympathetic discussion of McDowell's Hegelian critique see Bernstein (2002). For a Kantian response, see Friedman (1996).
4 1991, s. 44.
5 1977, p. 77.
6 B125.
7 1991, s. 42, addition 3.
8 1991, s. 41.
9 1995, vol. 2, p. 187.
10 1995, vol. 3, p. 303.
11 1991, s. 42.
12 1995, vol. 3, p. 443.
13 Ibid., p. 441.
14 Ibid., p. 440.
15 Ibid.
16 See McDowell (1994, p. 41).
17 As long as we assume this dualistic reading of Kant, it is quite misleading to say, as Ralph Walker does, that Kant needs the existence of things in themselves to provide the source of the given element in experience, where the implication is that this allows Kant to avoid subjective idealism (1989, p. 64). On a non-dualistic reading, by contrast, this claim is both acceptable and true.
18 1991, s. 41; 1995, vol. 3, p. 428.
19 'The Absolute' can be understood as a placeholder for the thing in itself.
20 1977, s. 73.
21 1977, s. 74.
22 1979, p. 86.
23 My discussion of these issues is indebted to the work of Michael Forster (1998), in particular, Chapter 3.
24 See, for example, Sextus Empiricus, (1976, Book 2, Ch. 7).
25 Ayer's 1956, pp. 75–81 provides a good illustration of the kind of position under attack. The assumption here is that we have direct knowledge of propositions about sense-experience and only indirect knowledge of those concerning physical objects. It is concluded therefore that the transition involves an illegitimate inference.
26 Quoted in Michael Forster (1998, p. 150).
27 Hegel refers to this movement as *Aufhebung*. I refer to it as 'see-saw dismounting' in Chapter 6.
28 S. 90. All references will be to the *Phenomenology of Spirit* unless otherwise stated.
29 Ibid.

30 Jacobi and Schleiermacher are obvious examples.
31 The fact that Sense-certainty is an allegedly *immediate* form of knowledge, and, as such, is the most minimal conception of knowledge possible – a kind of naïve realism – is another reason why Hegel begins with it.
32 s. 91.
33 s. 90.
34 s. 91.
35 See, for example, Moore's and Russell's eventual dissatisfaction with any form of idealism, a dissatisfaction which culminates in the conclusion that the fundamental epistemic relation has to involve direct acquaintance with an object. Peter Hylton (1993) gives a fascinating account of the considerations which motivated Moore and Russell in this context.
36 s. 91.
37 s. 94.
38 Hegel is not claiming that the subject of such an experience must have explicit knowledge of the way in which reference is established to the object in question. All that he is claiming is that some such account must be available. Second, he is not suggesting that determinate experience requires linguistic expression. Rather, he will claim that it is *because* the experience in question turns out to be indeterminate that it cannot be successfully articulated. See Robert Pippin (1989, pp. 119–20).
39 s. 98–99. Hegel considers various responses that could be made by the Sense-certainty theorist in response to this difficulty. These responses, however, presuppose a similar understanding of the resources available to one who seeks to secure such an act of reference, and it doesn't take Hegel long to expose their failings.
40 I am not implying that Hegel is criticizing Perception as if from some external vantage point. Rather, he is going to claim that it fails by its own standards.
41 s. 112–113.
42 s. 113.
43 Ibid.
44 s. 114.
45 Ibid.
46 Ibid.
47 s. 132.
48 s. 136.
49 s. 146.
50 s. 157.
51 See Gadamer (1976, p. 40).
52 s. 157.
53 Hegel uses the expression "inverted world" (verkehrte Welt) in *Critical Journal of Philosophy* in the context of criticizing philosophers who postulate an unknowable ground of appearances.
54 s. 158.
55 The reference here is to s. 132, where Hegel characterizes the position under attack by claiming that 'consciousness is not yet *for itself* the Concept, and consequently does not recognize itself in the reflected object'. The term 'Concept' is a translation of the German word *Begriff*. Miller translates this term as 'Notion', but where I have used quotations from his translation I have substituted 'Notion' for 'Concept', doing so on the ground that this mode of expression is less misleading.
56 1969, p. 591.
57 This is how Barry Stroud (1984, opening section) characterizes idealism.
58 1977, p. 91.
59 1991, s. 44.
60 Hegel's attack upon a dualistic conception of God finds expression at various points in his work. See, for example, his history of philosophy, where he tells us that the essence

of God 'is accomplished *in the world*', and not in a heavenly kingdom that is 'beyond' (3.21). And, in a manner which is reminiscent of his criticisms of Kant's thing in itself, he claims that 'if the concept of God is viewed as that of abstract 'most real Being' then God becomes for us a mere 'out there', and of that there can be no further talk of knowing, for where there is no qualification no knowledge is possible. As he puts it, 'pure lightness is pure darkness'. Hegel spends much time discussing religion in terms which are not exclusively Christian – for example, in his *Lectures on the Philosophy of Religion*, vol. 1, pp. 89–258 and *Phenomenology of Spirit*, s. 672–83. The relevance of his positive conception of God to Christianity is made explicit in *Phenomenology of Spirit*, s. 748–87, and *Lectures on the Philosophy of Religion,* vol. 3. For a good overview and some useful references to the vast secondary literature, see Solomon, (1983, Ch. 10). The most insightful and concise discussion of his position I have come across is by Frederick C. Copleston (1969).

61 1984.
62 2000, p. 95.

5 Truth

1 A similar version of the correspondence theory can be read into some of Locke's remarks. For example, he tells us that '(t)is evident, the Mind knows not Things immediately, but only by the intervention of the *Ideas* it has of them. *Our Knowledge* therefore is *real*, only so far as there is a conformity between our *Ideas* and the reality of Things. But what shall here be the criterion? How shall the Mind, when it perceives nothing but its own *Ideas*, know that they agree with Things themselves?' (IV. IV. 3). It is with these remarks in mind that we can best appreciate the force of Berkeley's objection that the supposition that things are distinct from ideas takes away all real truth and brings with it a universal scepticism.

2 It is an interpretation which is presupposed also in some more contemporary criticisms of the theory. See, for example, Brandom (1994, Ch. 5, s. 4); Mcdowell (1994, Chs 1–2); Hornsby (1997).

3 1962, p. 110.
4 Ibid., p. 118.
5 Ibid.
6 Ibid.
7 Ibid., p. 109.
8 Ibid., p. 113.
9 1928, Book 1, s. 8, 11.
10 1952, p. 59.
11 1928, Book 1, s. 11.
12 Compare Wittgenstein at *Tractatus* 3.1432 when he says: 'Instead of, "The complex sign 'aRb' says that *a* stands to *b* in the relation of *R*", we ought to put, "*That* '*a*' stands to '*b*' in a certain relation says that *aRb*."'
13 Russell's multiple relation theory of judgement is summed up in his *Problems of Philosophy*, Ch. 12.
14 1956, p. 333.
15 1930, p. 143.
16 Ibid., p. 144.
17 Ibid., pp. 145–6.
18 Ibid., pp. 149–50.
19 Ibid., p. 148.
20 Ibid., p. 156.
21 Ibid., p. 149.
22 Ibid., p. 151.
23 Ibid., p. 152.

24 Ibid., p. 156.
25 Ibid., p. 160.
26 Ibid., p. 152.
27 Ibid., Ch. XIV, p. 141.
28 Ibid., Ch. XV, p. 151.
29 It suffices here to give just a general sketch of Bradley's solution to the problem of how we gain knowledge of truth, and how this solution relates to his previous insistence that truth, reality, and *knowledge* be identified. Bradley concedes that experience of the 'Absolute' is beyond our comprehension (Ibid, p. 169), and, consequently, that the attainment of absolute truth in the sense dictated by his identity theory eludes our epistemological grasp. He claims also that reality is a systematic and coherent whole, and that truth must therefore 'exhibit the mark of internal harmony'. (1930, p. 322). It is in this sense that Bradley is committed to claiming that a judgement is true when its content embraces this systematic and coherent whole. He believes, however, that our judgements 'can never reach as far as perfect truth'. Hence, 'they must be content merely to enjoy more or less of *Validity*'. He continues: 'I do not simply mean by this term that, for working purposes, our judgments are admissible and will pass. I mean that less or more they possess the character and type of absolute truth and reality ... We may put it otherwise by saying that truths are true, according as it would take less or more to convert them to reality.' (1930, p. 321). Thus, Bradley can allow that judgements can be ranked according to the degree of coherence they contain. In this sense they admit of partial truth, and we can gain knowledge of these truths by determining their degree of coherence. However, no set of judgements can be perfectly coherent – can be absolutely true – since judgement is inimical to truth in this sense.
30 See, for example, Robert Brandom (1994, pp. 327–33); John McDowell (1994, Chs 1–2); Jennifer Hornsby (1997, 1999).
31 The philosophers in question do not tackle the problem of whether we can be said to think truly about God – a case which, one might argue, reintroduces the very metaphysical framework they are seeking to avoid. The best response for one who is tempted by a dualistic conception of God is to say that we cannot form determinate thoughts about God, and cannot therefore think truly about Him, but that this limitation does nothing to call into question our capacity to think truly about things and to do so in the manner demanded by this version of the identity theory. Someone of Hegel's persuasion, by contrast, would be happy to allow that we are capable of forming determinate thoughts about God and of thinking truly about him in the manner this theory demands.
32 Strawson (1998, pp. 403–4) reaches this conclusion. He argues that once we concede that facts are truths, then we avoid the difficulties which have been thought to arise in connection with disjunctive, negative, and hypothetical facts, for the simple reason that there are truths of the form 'p or q', 'not-p', 'if p, then q'. See also Searle (1995, pp. 213–14), who tells us that '(w)e think that since "fact" is a noun and since nouns name objects, then facts must be complicated kinds of objects; we think that correspondence must imply some kind of isomorphism, and then we are puzzled about negative facts, hypothetical facts, etc. But once we understand the logic of the words involved, we see that facts are not complicated objects, and that there is no necessary isomorphism between the syntactical structure of true statements and the structure of facts. Furthermore, we see that there is no problem about negatives, hypotheticals, etc. The true statement that the cat is not on the mat corresponds to the fact that the cat is not on the mat. What else? And what goes for negative statements goes for all the rest. ... For every true statement there is a corresponding fact because that is how these words are defined.' I shall return to the question of whether it is warranted to use the notion of correspondence in the context of articulating these claims.
33 I am recommending then that we abandon what can be referred to as a 'highest common factor' conception of the difference between truth and falsity, that is to say, one which

assumes that the relevant truth-conferring property cannot be captured at the level of a thought's content, and that, at this level, there is nothing to distinguish truth from falsity.

34 1901, p. 717.

35 P.F. Strawson (1998, p. 402) is happy to accept a correspondence theory of this kind, claiming that '(o)nce a correspondence account is made modest enough, then everyone, including myself, does and must accept it'.

36 See, for example, Strawson (1964).

37 In a discussion of the identity theory of truth, Thomas Baldwin (1991, pp. 35–6) claims that the identity theory is similar to the redundancy theory in that they both accept that snow is white is true if and only if it is a fact that snow is white. The difference, he claims, is that the identity theory involves an assumption which the redundancy theory does not. According to this assumption, which, he tells us, is inherited from the correspondence theory, the truth of a judgement consists in a *relationship* between it and reality. The implication of his remarks is that this assumption is problematic.

38 See P.F. Strawson (1992, Ch. 2) for a discussion of these issues as they apply to the problem of how we are to understand the nature of conceptual analysis. I shall return in the conclusion to the question of how we might relate Strawson's line of thought to my own more positive suggestions.

39 See, for example, Stern (1993, pp.645–49).

40 See Baldwin (1991, pp. 35–52).

41 1991, s. 213.

42 We can compare the way in which Kant rejects the claim that truth 'consists in the agreement of cognition with the object' on the ground that 'since the object is outside me and cognition in me, I can judge only whether my cognition of the object agrees with my cognition of the object.'

43 251f.

44 s. 75.

45 Forster (1998, p. 235) discusses this point.

46 1928, p. x.

47 1991, p. 40.

48 1991, p. 287. Cited in Stern (1993, p. 646).

49 1991, s. 24, addition 2.

50 Ibid., s. 22, addition 2.

51 s. 22.

52 s. 40.

53 s. 20.

54 See, for example, Hegel's *Lectures on Fine Art*, where, in the context of discussing the relation between freedom and necessity, he tells us that: '(A)bsolute truth proves that neither freedom, by itself, as subjective, sundered from necessity, is absolutely a true thing nor, by parity of reasoning, is truthfulness to be ascribed to necessity isolated and taken by itself. The ordinary consciousness, on the other hand, cannot extricate itself from this opposition and either remains despairingly in contradiction or else casts it aside and helps itself in some other way. But philosophy enters into the heart of the self-contradictory characteristics, knows them in their essential nature, i.e. as in their one-sidedness not absolute but self-dissolving, and it sets them in the harmony and unity which is truth. To grasp this Concept of truth is the task of philosophy' (pp. 99–100).

6 Philosophy and dialectic

1 p. 23.

2 1994, pp. 445–517.

3 1996.

4 Ibid.

5 1994, p. 9.

6 Ibid. pp. 70–1.
7 Ibid. p. 73.
8 Ibid. pp. 77–8.
9 McDowell himself concedes this point: '(t)he need for reconciliation that I envisage arises at a particular period in the history of ideas, one in which our thought tends, intelligibly, to be dominated by a naturalism that constricts the idea of nature.'
10 See 1998, s. 150.
11 1994, p. 89.
12 Ibid. p. 91.
13 Explanatory metaphysics is best understood as a placeholder for the kind of strategy pursued by one in the grip of the syndrome. It is not intended to cover the approach which becomes available once the syndrome has been put to rest.
14 Ibid., pp. xxiii–xxiv.
15 Ibid.
16 1991, p.187. Hegel then goes on to say that 'contradiction is not all there is to it' – a claim which should sound warning bells to those commentators who prefer, for better effect, to take such remarks out of context.
17 1994.
18 Ibid. p. 128.
19 See 1995, vol. 2, p. 329. The scepticism here is that of the ancients – a method which, I noted in Chapter 4, involves setting in opposition equally good arguments on both sides of the issue to produce an equal balance of justification for them.
20 See, for example, Plato's *Sophist* 259 c–e. This comparison is made by Berthold-Bond (1989).
21 1969, p. 131.
22 Ibid.
23 Ibid.
24 See, for example, the closing pages of his *Lectures* (1995, vol. 3).
25 Again, the closing pages of his *Lectures* provide good evidence for this theme.
26 Robert Solomon (1983) reaches this conclusion.
27 1994, p. 113.
28 1975, pp. 99–100.
29 s. 78.
30 s. 89.

Conclusion

1 See, for example, the work of John Robinson (1963, 1967) who takes as his influence German theologians such as Paul Tillich (1953/1957) and Dietrich Bonhoeffer, 1967.
2 1967, p. 22.
3 I discuss some of these questions in an unpublished paper 'Honest to God?'.
4 See, for example, McDowell (1983, pp. 1–16; 1985, pp. 110–29; 1996, pp. 149–79), Wiggins (1976, pp. 331–78; 1990–1, pp. 61–85; 1993, pp. 301–14, 329–36), Griffin (1996, Chs III and IV). I discuss some of the issues raised by their proposals in 'On the dismounting of Seesaws' (2001).
5 See, for example, Colin McGinn (1984, reprinted in *Knowledge and Philosophy*, 1999, p. 24); P.F.Strawson (1992, Ch. 2).
6 In this context, a concern with concepts is a concern with the things the concepts are of.
7 1937, p. 173.
8 1960, p. 68.
9 Again, I am leaving on one side the question of how we are to comprehend the scope of this alternative model of analysis.
10 Hegel (1977, p.3).
11 Hegel (1977, p.18).

Bibliography

Adorno, Theodore, 1993. 'Aspects of Hegel's Philosophy' in *Hegel: 3 Studies,* trans. S. Nicholson, Massachusetts.

Allison, Henry, 1983. *Kant's Transcendental Idealism: An Interpretation and Defence,* Yale.

Ameriks, Karl, 1982. 'Recent Work on Kant's Theoretical Philosophy', *American Philosophical Quarterly,*19, no.1, January, pp. 1–24.

—— 1992. 'Recent Work on Hegel: The Rehabilitation of an Epistemologist?', *Philosophy and Phenomenological Research*, 52, no. 1, March, pp. 177–202.

Austin, J.L., 1967. 'Truth,' in *Philosophical Logic,* ed. P.F. Strawson, Oxford.

Ayer, A.J., 1937. 'Does Philosophy Analyse Common Sense?', *Proceedings of the Aristotelian Society,* supp. vol. xvi.

—— 1956. *The Problem of Knowledge*, London.

—— 1960. *Language, Truth, and Logic,* London.

Ayers, Michael, 1991. 'Substance: Prolegomena to a Realist Theory of Identity,' *Journal of Philosophy,* vol. LXXXVIII.

—— 1993. *Locke: Epistemology and Metaphysics,* London.

Baldwin, Thomas, 1991. 'The Identity Theory of Truth', *Mind,* vol. C.

Berkeley, G, 1998. *A Treatise Concerning the Principles of Human Knowledge,* ed. Jonathan Dancy, Oxford.

—— 1979. *Three Dialogues Between Hylas and Philonous,* ed. Robert Merrihew Adams, Hackett.

—— 1993. 'Philosophical Commentaries', in *George Berkeley: Philosophical* Works, ed. Michael Ayers, London.

Bernstein, J. Richard, 2002. 'McDowell's domesticated Hegelianism', in *Reading McDowell on Mind and World,* ed. Nicholas H. Smith, London.

Berthold-Bond, Daniel, 1989. *Hegel's Grand Synthesis: A Study of Being, Thought, and History,* New York.

Bird, Graham, 1962. *Kant's Theory of Knowledge,* London.

Bonhoeffer, Dietrich, 1967. *Letters and Papers from Prison,* London.

Bradley, F.H., 1897. *Appearance and Reality,* Oxford (Reprinted 1930).

—— 1928. *Principles of Logic*, Oxford.

—— 1962. *Essays on Truth and Reality,* Oxford.

Brandom, Robert, 1994. *Making it Explicit,* Harvard.

Candlish, Stuart, 1989. 'The Truth about F.H. Bradley', *Mind,* 98.

Cassam, Quassim, 2000. 'Mind, Knowledge, and Reality: Themes from Kant', in *Current Issues in the Philosophy of Mind,* ed. Anthony O'Hear.

Clark, Maudemarie, 1990. *Nietzsche on Truth and Philosophy,* Cambridge.

166   *Bibliography*

Copleston, F.C, 1969. 'Hegel and the Rationalisation of Mysticism', in *Talk of God, Royal Institute of Philosophy Lectures, vol 2, 1967–68,* London, pp. 118–32.

Danto, Arthur C., 1965. *Nietzsche as Philosopher,* Columbia.

Dummett, Michael, 1967. 'Truth', in *Philosophical Logic,* ed. P.F. Strawson, Oxford.

—— 1991. 'Thought and Perception,' in *Frege and Other Philosophers,* Oxford.

Edwards, Paul, ed., 1972. *Encyclopaedia of Philosophy,* vol. 3, London.

Ellis, Fiona, 2001. 'On the Dismounting of Seesaws', *Philosophy,* 76.

—— 'Honest to God?', unpublished.

Forster, Michael, 1993. 'Hegel's dialectical method', in *The Cambridge Companion to Hegel,* ed. Frederick C. Beiser, Cambridge.

—— 1998. *Hegel's Idea of a Phenomenology of Spirit,* Chicago.

Frege, Gottlob, 1952. 'On Sense and Meaning', in *Translations from the Philosophical Writings of Gottlob Frege,* trans. P. Geach and M. Black, Oxford.

—— 1967 'The Thought,' in *Philosophical Logic,* ed. P. Strawson, Oxford.

Friedman, Michael, 1996. 'Exorcising the Philosophical Tradition', *Philosophical Review* 105, pp. 427–67.

Gadamer, H.G, 1976. *Hegel's Dialectic,* trans. P. C. Smith, Yale.

Gerrard, Steve, 1996. 'A Philosophy of Mathematics between two camps', in *Cambridge Companion to Wittgenstein,* ed. H. Sluga and D. Stern, Cambridge.

Griffin, James, 1996. *Value Judgement,* Oxford.

Guyer, Paul, 1993. 'Thought and Being: Hegel's critique of Kant's theoretical philosophy', in *Cambridge Companion to Hegel,* ed. F. Beiser, Cambridge, pp. 171–210.

Hance, Allen, 1995. 'Pragmatism as Naturalized Hegelianism: Overcoming Transcendental Philosophy?', in *Rorty and Pragmatism,* ed., Herman J. Saatkamp, Jr., Nashville.

Harrison, Ross, 1982. 'Transcendental Arguments and Idealism', in *Idealism Past and Present,* ed. Godfrey Vesey, pp. 211–25.

Hegel, G.W.F., 1969. *Science of Logic,* trans. A. Miller, New York.

—— 1975. *Lectures on Fine Art,* trans. T. Knox, Oxford.

—— 1977. *Phenomenology of Spirit,* trans. A. Miller, Oxford.

—— 1977. *Faith and Knowledge,* ed., Walter Cerf and H.R. Harris, New York.

—— 1985. 'The Relation of Skepticism to Philosophy', trans. H.S. Harris, in *Between Kant and Hegel: Texts in the Development of Post-Kantian Idealism,* trans. G. di Giovanni and H.S. Harris, Albany, pp. 311–62.

—— 1985. 'Introduction: On the Essence of Philosophical Criticism Generally, and its Relationship to the Present State of Philosophy', in *Critical Journal of Philosophy,* trans. G. di Giovanni and H.S. Harris, Albany, pp. 272–91.

—— 1988. *Lectures on the Philosophy of Religion,* ed. Peter C. Hodgson, trans. Robert F. Brown and J.M. Stewart, California.

—— 1991. *The Encyclopaedia Logic,* trans. T.F. Gereats, W.A. Suchting and H.S. Harris, Indianapolis.

—— 1995. *Lectures on the History of Philosophy,* 3 vols, trans. E.S. Haldane and F.H. Simpson, Nebraska.

Heller, E. 1984. *In The Age of Prose,* London.

Hornsby, J., 1997. 'Truth: the Identity Theory', *Proceedings of the Aristotelian Society,* 97, pp. 1–24.

—— 1999. 'The Facts in question: a Response to Dodd and to Candlish', *Proceedings of the Aristotelian Society,* 99, pp. 1–6.

Horstmann, Rolf-Peter, 1999. 'What is Hegel's Legacy and What Should We Do With It?', *European Journal of Philosophy,* 7: 2, pp. 275–292.

Hume, David, 1978. *A Treatise of Human Nature,* ed., L.A. Selby-Bigge, Oxford.

Hylton, P., 1993. 'Hegel and Analytic Philosophy', in *Cambridge Companion to Hegel,* ed. F. Beiser, Cambridge, pp. 445–87.

Kant, Immanuel, 1929. *Critique of Pure Reason,* trans. N. Kemp-Smith, London.

—— 1968. 'Inaugural Dissertation', in *Kant: Selected Pre-Critical Writings,* ed. G.B.Kerferd and D.E. Walford, Manchester.

—— 1973. 'On a Discovery according to which any New Critique of Pure Reason has been made Superfluous by an Earlier one', in *The Kant-Eberhard Controversy*, trans. Henry Allison, Baltimore, MD.

—— 1974. *Logic,* trans. Robert S. Hartman and Wolfgang Schwarz, New York.

—— 1992. *Lectures on Logic* (Cambridge Edition of the works of Immanuel Kant in translation), ed., J. Michael Young, Cambridge.

—— 1977. *Prolegomenon to any Future Metaphysics,* trans. Paul Carus, extensively revised by James W. Ellington, Indiana.

King, P., 1829. *The Life of John Locke,* London.

Langton, Rae, 1998. *Kant's Humility: Our Ignorance of Things in Themselves,* Oxford.

Lear, Jonathan, 1984. 'The Disappearing "We"', *Proceedings of the Aristotelian Society,* supp. vol. 58.

Leibniz, G.W., 1982. *New Essays on Human Understanding,* trans. P. Remnant and J. Bennett, Cambridge.

Locke, John, 1894. 'First Letter to Stillingfeet', in A. Campbell's edition of the *Essay,* Oxford.

—— 1975. *An Essay Concerning Human Understanding,* Oxford.

Maker William, 1994. *Philosophy without Foundations,* New York.

Mandelbaum, Maurice, 1964. 'Locke's Realism', in *Philosophy, Science, and Sense Perception,* Baltimore, pp. 1–60.

McDowell, John, 1983. 'Aesthetic Value, Objectivity, and the Fabric of the World', in *Pleasure, Preference, and Value,* ed. Eva Schaper, Cambridge, pp. 1–16.

—— 1985. 'Values and Secondary Qualities', in *Morality and Objectivity,* ed. Ted Honderich, London, pp. 110–29.

—— 1994. *Mind and World,* Harvard.

—— 1996. 'Two Sorts of Naturalism', in *Virtues and Reasons: Philippa Foot and Moral Theory,* ed. Rosalind Hursthouse, Gavin Lawrence, and Warren Quinn, Oxford, pp. 149–79.

—— 1998. 'Having the World in View: Sellars, Kant, and Intentionality', *Woodbridge Lectures, Journal of Philosophy*, vol. XCV, no. 9.

McGinn, Colin, 1984. 'The Concept of Knowledge', *Midwest Studies in Philosophy,* ix, Minneapolis. Reprinted in *Knowledge and Reality,* pp. 7–35.

Moore, G.E., 1901. 'Truth', in *Dictionary of Philosophy and Psychology,* ed. J.M. Baldwin, New York.

Nehemas, Alexander, 1985. *Nietzsche: Life as Literature,* Harvard.

Nietzsche, Friedrich, 1979. 'On Truth and Lies in a Non-moral Sense', in *Philosophy and Truth,* trans. D. Breazeale, New Jersey.

—— 1954. *Twilight of the Idols,* The *Portable Nietzsche,* trans. W. Kaufmann, New York.

—— 1968. *The Will to Power,* trans. W. Kaufmann and R.J. Hollingdale, New York.

Pippin, B. Robert, 1989. *Hegel's Idealism,* Cambridge.

Putnam, Hilary, 1981. *Reason, Truth, and History,* Cambridge.

—— 1994. 'Sense, Nonsense, and the Senses: An Inquiry into the Powers of the Human Mind', *Journal of Philosophy,* 91, pp. 445–517.

Robinson, Hoke, 1994. 'Two Perspectives on Kant's Appearances and Things in Themselves', *Journal of the History of Philosophy,* July, vol. XXXII, no. 3, pp.411–41.

Robinson, John, 1963. *Honest to God,* London.

—— 1967. *Exploration into God,* London.

Rockmore, Tom, 1997. *Cognition: An Introduction to Hegel's 'Phenomenology of Spirit,'* California.

Rorty, Richard, 1982. *Consequences of Pragmatism,* Minnesota.

Russell, Bertrand, 1956. 'Logical Atomism', in *Logic and Knowledge,* ed., Marsh, London.

—— 1967. *Problems of Philosophy,* Oxford.

Schacht, Richard, 1983. *Nietzsche,* London.

Schopenhauer, Arthur, 1969. *The World as Will and Representation,* trans. E.F.J. Payne, vols 1 and 2 (1819, 1844), New York.

Searle, John, 1995. *The Construction of Social Reality,* London.

—— 1998. 'Truth: A Reconsideration of Strawson's Views', in *The Philosophy of P.F. Strawson,* ed. Lewis Edwin Hahn, Illinois.

Sextus Empiricus, 1976. *Outlines of Pyrrhonism,* trans. R.G. Bury, London.

Smith, A.D, 1990–1. 'Of Primary and Secondary Qualities', *Philosophical Review.*

Solomon, Robert, 1983. *In the Spirit of Hegel,* Oxford.

Stern, Robert, 1993. 'Did Hegel Hold an Identity Theory of Truth', *Mind,* vol. 102, 408, October.

—— 2002. *Hegel and the Phenomenology of Spirit,* London.

Strawson, Galen, 2002. 'Knowledge of the Real World', in *Philosophical Issues*, 12.

Strawson, P.F., 1964. 'Truth,' 1950, in G. Pitcher, ed., *Truth.* Englewood Cliffs, NJ.

—— 1966. *The Bounds of Sense,* London.

—— 1992. *Analysis and Metaphysics,* Oxford.

—— 1998. 'Reply to John R. Searle', in *The Philosophy of P.F. Strawson,* ed. Lewis Edwin Hahn, Illinois, pp. 402–4.

Stroud, Barry, 2000. 'The Allure of Idealism,' *Proceedings of the Aristotelian Society*, supp. vol. 58, 1984, reprinted in *Understanding Human Knowledge,* Oxford.

Tillich, Paul, 1953, 1957. *Systematic Theology,* vols 1 and 2, London.

Walker, Ralph, 1989. *The Coherence Theory of Truth,* London.

Walsh, W.H., 1982. 'Kant as seen by Hegel', in *Idealism Past and Present,* ed. Vesey, G, Cambridge, pp. 93–111.

Westphal, Kenneth, 1989. *Hegel's Epistemological Realism: A Study of the Aim and Method of Hegel's Phenomenology of Spirit,* Dordrecht.

Wiggins, David, 1976. 'Truth, Invention, and the Meaning of Life', *Proceedings of the British Academy,* 62, pp. 331–78.

—— 1986. 'On Singling out an Object Determinately', *Subject, Thought, and Context,* eds. Philip Pettit and John McDowell, Oxford.

—— 1990–1. 'Moral Cognitivism, Moral Relativism, and Motivating Moral Beliefs', *Proceedings of the Aristotelian Society,* 91, pp. 61–85.

—— 1993. 'Cognitivism, Naturalism, and Normativity: A Reply to Peter Railton', in *Reality, Representation and Projection,* ed. J. Haldane and C. Wright, Oxford.

—— 1995. 'Substance' in *Philosophy: A Guide through the Subject,* ed. A.C. Grayling, Oxford.

—— 2001. *Sameness and Substance Renewed,* Cambridge.

Wittgenstein, L, 1958. *Philosophical Investigations,* trans. G.E.M. Anscombe, Oxford.

Wollheim, Richard, 1959. *F.H. Bradley,* Harmondsworth.

Index

a priori conditions of the possibility of experience 54
Absolute 81–2
absolute idealism 95–9
absolute knowledge 142–3, 145
absolute truth 142
abstraction 62–3, 68–9, 77
accidents 17
anthropomorphic truth 44, 46–7
appearance(s) 55–6, 58–9, 64–5, 67, 72, 75, 79; and thing 58–60, 72; knowledge of 56; law of 67
apprehension without comprehension 85
assumptions: identifying 130–7
Ayer, A.J. 149–50

Baldwin, Thomas 119
Berkeley, G. 1 2, 4, 6, 20, 34–6, 38–9, 41, 43, 45–7, 51–2, 56, 65, 74, 77, 94, 99–100, 130–1, 134–5, 145–8; and the syndrome 28–33; conception of matter 25; conception of substance 9–13, 22–8; objections concerning substance 17–22; rejection of materialism 31
Bradley, F.H. 7, 117, 123, 145; alternative to the correspondence theory 104; *Appearance and Reality* 106; criticisms of correspondence theory 111; identity theory 7, 110; metaphysical position 105–6, 109; nature of judgement 107; on thought and reality 105–10; on truth 103–5, 110–11, 120; On Truth and Copying 103; *Principles of Logic* 105–6, 119; reconciliation with Hegel 121–4; Relation and Quality 106
Brandom, Robert 7
'broken up One' 90–1

categories 65–70; use of term 67
cognition 81–3, 96; and things 100; as intrument or medium 83; superior form of 97
coherentism 126, 134
community conception of thing 89
comparison 68–9
concepts 78–81; and intuition 42, 53, 96, 127; and reality 6, 49–52, 84, 95, 102, 145; Hegel 77–101; Kant 53–76; as conceptions 50; as subjective forms 53; as universals 92; connective treatment 150; nature of 67–8; use of term 49–50
conceptual thought 95, 125
conceptualization 68–9; activity of 65–6
consciousness 79, 95, 118, 136, 142; activity 91; forms of 84–5; object-directed 85
construction 68–9
contradictions as dialectic 57
copy theory 103
corporeal substances 17
correctness 120–1
correspondence 118–19
correspondence theory of truth 103–4, 111, 115, 120

dialectic 139–41; and philosophy 125–44; contradictions as 57
dialectical method 145
disagreements in philosophy 146
dismounting of the seesaw 127–8, 139–40, 142
dispositional properties: of things 61; sensory and non-sensory 62
dispositions 61
distortion 142
divine intellect 74
dogmatism 122, 124

dualism 143; of appearance and ground 116; of substance and quality 131; of worlds 136
dualistic conception of God 147–9
dualistic framework 48–9, 116, 120, 130
dualistic model 102

Ego 78
empirical employment 53, 67
empirical intuition 54
empirical knowledge 53–5
empirical objects 55–6
error: fear of 82–3; history of 145
existence 78
experience 70–3, 79, 81; indeterminate 92; matter of 79; non-conceptual 92; notion of 54
explanatory metaphysics 138
extended substances 10
external objects 63
external world scepticism 53

faculty of intuition 54
fear of error 82–3
force and understanding 91–5
formal truth 121
Frege, Gottlob 103
Fregean framework 49

German Philosophy 85
Gerrard, Steve 126, 128, 138
God: activity of 94; and thing in itself 97; and world relation 25, 27, 99–100, 149; as infinite perceiver 23; as unknowable substratum of the world 98; cognitive activity of 97; concept of 151; dualistic conception of 147–9; Hegel's conception of 99; idea of 24; ideas of imagination 26; inaccessibility to thought 52; metaphysical role 75, 99; mind of 23, 28, 30, 97; notion of 25; question of 97, 99; responsibility of 74; role of 147; self-unfolding 97; thing in itself as placeholder for 47; traditional conception of 28
God's eye point of view 51; upon reality 47; upon things 109
governing spirit 26
grammatical explanations 132
groupings of qualities 31

Hegel, G.W.F. 4–6, 33, 51–2, 112, 151; absolute idealism 77; conception of God 99; conception of intellectual intuition 97; conception of truth 7; concepts and reality 77–101; criticisms of dualistic picture 93; criticisms of Kant 81, 96; criticisms of Perception 88–9; dialectical method 8, 139–44; *Faith and Knowledge* 6, 78, 96; interest in concepts 92; *Lectures on the History of Philosophy* 6, 80, 83, 118; methodological approach 146; notion of force 93; on inverted worlds 94, 115; on truth 117–21; *Phenomenology of Spirit* 6, 81, 84–5, 118–19, 121–3, 140, 142; *Philosophy of Fine Art* 142; reconciliation with Bradley 121–4; rejection of dualism between cognition and things 100; *The Encyclopaedia Logic* 6, 77, 98, 122; 'The Relation of Skepticism to Philosophy' 83; vs. Wittgenstein 143
Hume, David 1

idealism 95; absolute 95–9; alternative forms of 77; and realism 3; subjective form of 77, 80–1; vindication of 147, *see also* trancendental idealism
ideas 107; and substance 2
identificatory exercise 91
identity theory of truth 110–14, 120
ideological explanations 132
immaterial substance 2, 24
immaterialism 30
intellectual intuition 57, 73–5, 97
intuitions 70–2, 78–81; and concepts 42, 53, 96, 127; conception of 54; empirical 54; faculty of 54; intellectual 57, 73–5, 97; pure 54; special mode of 57
inverted worlds: Hegel on 94, 115

judgement 107–8

Kant, Immanuel 3–6, 38–9, 41–2, 52, 77–9, 81–2, 84, 86, 98, 109, 130–1, 135, 145, 147; aesthetic theory 96; conception of cognition 96; concepts and intuitions 80; concepts and reality 53–76; *Critique of Pure Reason* 5, 63, 69, 80; *Inaugural Dissertation* 69; interest in the question of God 97; *Logic* 68; metaphysical framework 107; non-phenomenalist aspirations 62; On a Discovery 145; transcendental idealism 100; 'Vienna Logic' 69; vs. other philosophers 75

knowable phenomena 60
knowing: form and material of 80
knowledge: absolute 142–3, 145; and truth 43; empirical 53–5; of things 66; problem of 1; richest kind 86; use of term 80

language: and thought 44–5; limitation of 44
Lear: Jonathan 100
Leibniz, G.W. 61
Locke, John 1–2, 4, 6, 11–12, 17–24, 27, 38–9, 41, 45, 47–8, 51–2, 61–2, 65, 77, 79, 93–4, 100–1, 130–1, 133–4, 145, 147–8; *An Essay Concerning Human Understanding* 9; and the syndrome 28–33; *Astract of the Essay* 12; attack on idea of substance 15; concept of substance 9–13, 78; nominal essence 14; real essence 14, 16; scepticism about substance 12–13

McDowell, John 7, 126–8, 132–6, 139–40, 143, 149; *Mind and World* 8, 125, 138, 140, 142
material substance 9, 17, 23–4, 29–30, 38, 43, 46, 48, 61
material things: concept of 150
materialism 147–8; arguments against 20
materialist outlook 135
matter of appearance 54
matter of experience 41
metaphor: meaning of the term 40; notion of 42
metaphysical constraint 113
metaphysical framework 125
mind-independent things 94–6, 102, 138, 145
modern scepticism 83
monism 105
Moore, G.E. 113
myth of the Given 126

naturalism: concept of 136
negative aspects 127
neo-Hegelian approach 146
Newtonian mechanics 61
Nietzsche, Friedrich 3–7, 53–4, 56, 66, 77, 100, 112, 114, 130–1, 145; and the syndrome 45–9; concepts and reality 34–52; criticisms of correspondence theory 111; 'History of an Error' 3; insights 34; notion of the thing in itself 43; on truth 102–3; 'On Truth and Lies

in a Nonmoral Sense' 3, 34; paradigm of 'pure' truth 110; perspectivism 35–9; truth and metaphor 39–43; *Twilight of the Idols* 3
nominal essence 13–16
non-circularity requirement 116
non-conceptual acquaintance 87
non-conceptual apprehension 85–6
non-conceptual material 96
non-dualistic alternative 137–9
non-phenomenalist position 62
non-sensory properties 60
noumenon: in negative sense 57, 59; in positive sense 57; unknowable 60

object-directed thought 126
objectivity 78
objects: direct acquaintance with 86; empirical 55–6; external 63; notion of 55; of experience 65; of non-sensible intuition 57; use of term 121, *see also* subject and object
ontological dualism 135, 138
'outside us': use of expression 56

paradigm epistemic relation 86
perception 81, 88–91; and substance 2; characterization of 89; indifferent qualities 92; theory of 89–91
perceptual metaphors 42
perspectivism 35–9
phenomenalism 61–2
Phenomenology of Spirit 86, 88, 92, 94–5
philosophical inquiry 127
philosophical knowledge 82
philosophical problems: models of 129–30; resolution of 130; treatments 127
philosophical thinking: structure of 130
philosophical truths 123
philosophy: and dialectic 125–44; disagreements in 146
Plato 94
Platonism 134–6; and reductionism 135
pluralism 105
positive approach 139
positive aspects 127
positive position 138
Prolegomenon 58
pure: truth 45, 102, 110–11, 114
pure concepts of reason 57
pure intuition 54
pure truth 102, 110–11
Putnam, Hilary 126

quality(ies) 2, 29, 31

rampant Platonism 135
real essence 13–16
realism: and idealism 3; transcendental 56
reality: and concepts *see* concepts;
    conception of 48–9, 97, 109; God's eye
    point of view upon 47
reason: nature of 57; pure concepts of 57
receptivity: capacity for 70
recoil phenomenon 126, 128, 138
reductionism 133, 149
reductive analysis 150
reflection 68–9
religious language 148
representation 63, 65, 67–8, 70–1, 74, 78
Robinson, John 148
Roman columbarium 41–2
Russell, Bertrand: multiple relation theory
    of judgement 105

scepticism 77, 83; modern approaches to
    83; problem of 53
Schematism 66
Schopenhauer, Arthur 5
scientific reductionism 135
scientism 133, 135
scientist: concerns of 60–1
seesaw dismounting 127–8, 139–40, 142
self-criticism 143
sensation 54
Sense-certainty 85–7; as truest knowledge
    86; characterization 85; difficulties of
    91; downfall of 88–9; guiding
    assumptions 92; indeterminate 'thises'
    of 92; theory of 87, 91
sense-experience 125–6
sensibility 54–5, 80–1; pure forms of 54–5
sensory dispositional properties 60
sensuous universalities 90
sensuousness 81
single property 90
single putative quality 90
solid substances 10
space 71–2; and time 55; of reasons 132
spatio-temporal awareness 55
spatio-temporal form 71
stability 78
stammering translations 38, 48, 51
status of grammatical and ideological
    explanations 131–2
Stern, Robert 119
Stillingfeet, Edward 10–11, 17
Strawson, P.F. 150
Stroud, Barry 100
subject and object 36–8, 54, 86–7

subjective idealism 77, 80–1
subjectivity 79
substance: and accidents 17; and
    perception 2; and quality 2; as
    supporter of qualities 29; being of 10,
    13–14; Berkeley on 22–8; conception
    of 9–13, 148; corporeal 17; extended
    10; idea of 10, 12, 14–15; immaterial
    2, 24; Lockean conception of 78;
    material 9, 17, 23–4, 29–30, 38, 43,
    46, 48, 61; solid 10; thinking 10
substratum 11, 65
suicide 145
super-sensible world 94–5
support metaphor 29, 131
syndrome 126, 136, 142, 145, 147–8, 151;
    concepts involved 1; evasion 2;
    identification 34; initial illustration 1;
    Locke and Berkeley on 28–33;
    schematization 128–30; use of term 1

temporality 66–7
theology: transcendental 64
therapeutic approach to philosophy 139
thing(s): and appearances 58–60, 72; and
    cognition 100; as 'broken up One'
    89–90; as conceptualized 47–8, 92–3;
    below-the-surface activity 93;
    community conception 89; concept of
    91, 150; dispositional properties of
    60–1; God's eye point of view upon
    109; material 150; nature of 61;
    properties of 62; true nature of 108
thing(s) in itself (themselves) 47–8, 50–1,
    55–63, 77–8, 80–2, 93–4, 98–9, 102–3,
    125, 150; and God 97; and thing
    perceived 97; as placeholder for God
    47; conception of 78; notion of 43, 78;
    rejection of 77
thinking: objectivity of 79
thinking substances 10
this-here-now 87
thought 106–8; and language 44–5; and
    sense-experience 126; categories of
    78–9; conception of 97, 125; suicide
    145
thought-determinations: truth of 120–1
Three Dialogues 19
time and space 55
Transcendental Aesthetic 54–5
transcendental employment 53, 67
transcendental idealism 56, 63, 75, 100;
    overview 54–7; without the thing in
    itself 77

transcendental realism 56
transcendental theology 64
true thought and fact 114, 117, 119
truth 102–24; absolute 142; alternative
    conception of 44–7, 104; and metaphor
    39; anthropomorphic 44, 46–7; Bradley
    on 103–5, 110–11, 120; conception of
    45, 145; correspondence theory 103–4,
    111, 115, 120; explanatory account
    115; formal 121; Hegel on 117–21;
    identity theory 110–14, 120; meaning
    of 120; Nietzche on 102–3; of thought
    115–16; of thought-determinations
    120–1; pure 45, 102, 110–11, 114;
    theory of 120
two-world interpretation 64
two-world view 63

unconditioned universal 91
understanding 54–5, 67, 80–1, 91–5
universal common medium 90
Universal Scepticism 18, 20, 22, 100
universals: concepts as 92; unconditioned
    91; use of term 92
unknowable noumena 60

Williams, Bernard 73
Wittgenstein, L. 8, 78, 126, 138–9, 142;
    vs. Hegel 143